THE PRINCIPLE OF DUTY

DAVID SELBOURNE

THE PRINCIPLE
OF DUTY

An Essay on the
Foundations of the Civic Order

faber and faber

This edition first published in 2009
by Faber and Faber Ltd
Bloomsbury House, 74–77 Great Russell Street
London WC1B 3DA

Printed by CPI Antony Rowe, Eastbourne

A CIP record for this book is available from the British Library

ISBN 978-0-571-25505-4

À ELIEZER AMIEL,
*Vice-Président du Consistoire
Central Israelite de Belgique,
Officier de l'Ordre de Leopold
et Officier de l'Ordre de la Couronne*

CONTENTS

V: CONCLUSION

I can hardly help wondering all the while
whether human affairs are worth serious
effort. And yet it is our unhappy lot
to take them seriously.

The 'Athenian Stranger' in Plato,
Laws, VII, 803.

Post tenebras, spero lucem.

Don Quixote

Humane society, cohabitation, or being,
must above all things be maintained as
the earthly soveraigne good of mankind,
let what or who will perish or be confounded;
for mankind must be preserved upon the earth.

Richard Overton, July 1647

PREFACE

It has been a curious experience to learn, at a distance from Britain, of the responses since 1994 to *The Principle of Duty*. The land of Hobbes and Locke, of Bentham and Mill, is after all one in which political philosophy – as an art, as a practice of the imagination, as an expression (yes) of civic duty – has almost disappeared. But then in so many spheres of the nation's 'academic' life the intellectually moribund rule, their aspirations the stuff of footnotes rather than matters of commitment or belief; and thus, with their ethical purposes shrunk, the substance of their work is reduced to the mere syntax of thought.

In my book, now reissued in a revised edition, I sought something quite different: to address the oldest traditions and propositions of political philosophy as well as the most modern of our anxieties, so that, by means of a restatement of civic principles rooted in the Judeo-Christian and Greco-Roman worlds, we might begin to rediscover the conditions for living together in our tormented age.

In response there was considerable critical acclaim from some, while others – often the sophists of academia – looked askance, as if at an act of presumption on my part, or as if I were an intruder in the rank undergrowth which most of them inhabit. Politicians were clearly divided: my civic objections to market-driven notions (especially those which lead to the dispersal of public goods by 'privatisation') provoked much of the 'right', while my invocation of civic duty alienated some on the 'left'. Nevertheless, the terms which I employ in *The Principle of Duty* – such as the 'civic bond', the 'civic order', 'dutiless rights', 'civic disaggregation', 'social-ism', the 'universal plebeian' and others – have entered public debate.

That in Britain there should have been a marked increase in reference to, and interest in, civic themes and civic values, civic purposes and civic problems, is for me a vindication; there has been a similar response in France following the publication of this book as *Le Principe de Devoir* (Paris, 1997). Moreover, a central distinction in my text, that between a society of citizens and a society of strangers – the latter being one in which, *inter alia*, each asserts his or her 'dutiless rights' against the civic order – was readily taken up by others. The language of rights and more rights, and the blind assertion of the politics of self-realisation through unimpeded freedom of action, had been met by a countervailing force: the language of obligation, owed by us as citizens to the civic order from which we derive our rights, and upon which we depend for our safety.

But there is more at stake. A liberal, one who wishes to see liberal values survive in our Weimar-like culture – a culture of violent pleasures and aggressive plebeian disillusion – must be ready to protect the civic order which provides and guarantees our freedoms. Furthermore, no civic society has ever rested, or could rest, upon 'rights' alone. And if the liberal-minded do not learn, in time, of the nature of the needs and vulnerabilities of the civic order to which they belong, rough political forces indeed may come to remind them in ways from which all will suffer.

There have also been entertaining accusations by 'the right' that I was covertly 'on the left' – even a crypto-'collectivist' – and less entertaining accusations by 'the left' that I stood 'on the right', even the 'far right'. Then I was described (in the search by critics for a label to affix to this text) as a 'communitarian', a term for which I hold no brief: 'communitarianism' appears to me to be, or to have been, more an American folk movement than a serious political doctrine. No; it is a civic politics, a politics of the civic order – not a vacuous 'spirit of community' – which I espouse. Its premises, rooted in Britain in more than three centuries of political practice, are that the civic order belongs to us as citizens; that we gain our rights from it, as citizens, whoever we are and whether of 'right' or 'left'; and that it requires of us the performance of our citizen obligations if the gradual dissolution of the civic order is to be reversed.

The attitudinising 'libertarian', living in the freest political societies ever known, foolishly thinks that he or she is already 'unfree', a 'subject', and that almost any overarching principle, be it political or ethical, is 'authoritarian'. But civic renewal or civic repair cannot rest upon the very notions – and even the extension of those notions – which have themselves helped to disable and disqualify the civic sense, the sense of common citizenship and common obligation. Nor can a civic politics, any more than an ethical system, stand upon an unwillingness (in the name of 'inclusion' or 'social cohesion') to make distinctions between good citizens and bad, between the benign and the violent, between the dutiful and the dutiless in regard to others. Such distinctions lie at the heart of the very meaning of the social order; to refuse them is the way to the civic graveyard. We cannot be duty-free.

At the same time, a leading theme of my book, frequently repeated, is that, just as the citizen owes obligations to himself or herself, to his or her fellows, and to the civic order to which he or she belongs, so the civic order owes obligations, political, economic, social, educational and cultural in the widest sense, to the citizen. The 'left', forgetful in Britain of its ethical history, has come to dislike the first part of the equation; the 'right', equally forgetful of its tradition, has come to dislike the second. But without such mutuality no civic order can stand; and ours is on its knees for such reason.

In writing *The Principle of Duty*, I was myself free – and I believe I have shown myself to be free – of the dead hand of 'academia' and of the need to play that 'academic' game which has led to the misleading, or duping, of so many students as to the true ends of their work. Above all, no contribution can be made to the illumination of the nature of our civic and other woes when moral and political philosophy are dominated by, or even confined to, technical questions of method or of the meaning of words – to say nothing of homicidal rivalries – rather than by matters of ethical principle and civic substance. Some of those who addressed themselves to my book merely proved my point. I was told by learned sophists (at the Universities of Oxford, Cambridge, London and Sheffield) that *The Principle of Duty* was, variously, 'quite dreadful', was 'foundationless', was 'not supported by any large philosophical framework' or 'undergirding ethical theory', was composed of 'vague intellectual meanderings', moved 'from one abstraction to another', was 'vacuous', and so on.

But others, many others, have decided otherwise, and I am grateful to them. Without a civic social philosophy, the 'left' and the 'right', whatever their latest incarnations, are nothing.

David Selbourne
Urbino, 1997

ONE

The Function and Duty
of the Political Philosopher

This work is not only about duty but written from a sense of it: duty to the self, duty to one's fellows. Among other things, I take up and enlarge arguments first adumbrated in Chapter Eleven ('Citizens and Strangers') of *The Spirit of the Age* (London, 1993).

'The giant metropolis', I wrote there, 'in which violent impulse comes increasingly to dictate the responses of half-educated strangers towards each other, cannot be the model of civic society'; 'randomly surviving social instinct, mutual fear, bureaucratic rule and stoical public spirit' are not sufficient to 'compose the civic order'; and 'mere payment to the state of taxes-for-services is not a citizen relation' (ibid., p. 346). In such conditions, I argued, 'one law of common estrangement comes gradually to link all individuals . . . Individual rights, even when termed "civic rights", are shared in a phantom social order by all individuals, but between whom no citizen bond has been established. This parody of civic society . . . now increasingly stands for society itself. Socialism's failure, moreover, has (for some) ratified the parody as the only possible model of the social order' (ibid., p. 344).

But, I suggested, the failure of socialism, with its false collectivities and uprooting of civic tradition, had also helped to clear the way for an understanding of the need to 'redefine and . . . enforce civic obligation, so that a true citizenship might begin to be restored to myriads of strangers' (ibid., p. 345).

This is the theme of the present work. I have to do here not with the invention but with the enhancement of ideas of obligation; with ideas which are not so much unknown or misunderstood as forgotten. In its many variants, obligation is, after all, a long-established moral and political notion, even if today it is in eclipse.

Moreover, in the circumstances in which we find ourselves, as I set them out in *The Spirit of the Age*, I take it to be a particular moral obligation of the political philosopher – especially of the political philosopher whose intellectual provenance is that of 'the left' – to promote the principle of duty on behalf of his fellow-citizens, and as a means to recompose the civic order. He may be encouraged to the task by the fact that despite the scale of civic disaggregation amidst which he lives, the civic bond – a term which, with others, I shortly explain – resists being attenuated to the point of breakdown. How so? Not least because of the efforts to sustain it of an enlightened minority of citizens. It is this minority whose numbers must be strengthened. Their enlightenment derives from an ethically active perception of the civic order; the 'principle of duty' is its expression.

There is, of course, a sense in which all this is known and has often been repeated, however fitfully, in our culture. The notion of citizen 'rights and duties' is routinely referred to in texts of political ideas; 'rights and duties' are paired almost by reflex. It is equally routine to find that, lip-service to duty once paid, generally at the outset of discussion, it is rights which are the dominating subject of discourse. Duties, never or rarely particularised, are soon forgotten, or alluded to in token or passing fashion as if their content and implications were taken for granted. If there are as many varieties of civic dutilessness as of obligation, then such failure to fulfil intellectual obligation is one.

Gerrard Winstanley in his *Law of Freedom in a Platform* (1652, Harmondsworth, 1973, p. 363), written at the dawn of the modern 'academic' era, presciently complained of the scholar who 'only contemplates and talks of what he reads and hears, and doth not employ his talent in some bodily action for the increase of fruitfulness, freedom and peace in the earth'. An 'unprofitable son', he called him. 'The idle, lazy contemplation the scholars would call knowledge', Winstanley continued (ibid., p. 364), 'is no knowledge but a show of knowledge, like a parrot who speaks words but he knows not what he saith. This same show of knowledge rests in reading or contemplating or hearing others speak, and speaks so too [sc. the scholar repeats what he hears], but will not set his hand to work'; a description, as good as any, of much modern university life in the humane studies.

But to what work should we set our hands? Today, at a time of increasing civic breakdown, there is no shortage of practical moral tasks to which the intellect is summoned. Yet in so many sterile and insouciant scholastic worlds, from which help might be expected to come in the moral resuscitation and refashioning of the civic order, often only effete erudition is to be found. On one side, there is a vain and overweening search for a new 'grand theory', or metaphysic, by which to make good the Marxist failure; on another, empirical technical study of microcosms ever smaller; on another, 'idle, lazy contemplation' and ethical silence.

I have written this essay on duty as a citizen among citizens, or a Jewish citizen-stranger, and not as a voice of authority, 'academic' or any other; nor, least of all, vicariously in the shoes of political power, but believing (with the Stoics) that the most important concern of philosophy is with individual conduct which bears upon our fellows. In asserting a 'principle of duty' by which both citizen and civic order are bound, I also do two things: I fulfil my personal moral duty as an intellectual, and explain the need for a like duty to be assumed by others. At the same time, I seek to fulfil the more particular task – or 'historic mission', as the poet Heine put it – of the *ewiger Jude* to 'spread the seed of social transformation'. In Heine's memoir of his friend Ludwig Börne (whose given name was Louis Baruch), the poet wrote of the Jews that 'as they once led the world into new paths of progress, the world may, perhaps, expect them to open up others yet unknown' (*Collected Works*, ed. K. Briegleb, Munich, 1968–76, vol. 4, p. 118). The 'principle of duty' is one such path to progress, a moral progress whose precondition is the health of the civic order.

That such a principle of duty is not new, and is much older than the 'politics of rights' which has displaced it in the modern era, does not preclude the claim that it is a path to progress. Indeed, as I show in my argument, the performance of duty (to self, fellows, and the civic order) is the morally superior, as well as the historically prior, constituent of human association, particularly when it is set against the claims of right. The principle of duty, as well as being rooted in Greco-Roman thought, is also more Judaic than Christian. 'What little recognition the idea of obligation to the public obtains in modern morality', wrote John Stuart Mill in *On Liberty* (London, 1859), 'is derived from Greek and Roman sources, not from Christian' (p. 90).

Mill went further, and further than I would go myself, in objecting to the 'essentially selfish character' (ibid.) of Christian morality. It was, he argued, the consequence of Christianity's 'disconnecting each man's feelings of duty from the interests of his fellow-creatures, except so far as a self-interested inducement' – the inducement of personal salvation – 'is offered to him for consulting them'. He even described Christian doctrine, in its guise as a system of public ethics, as not merely a 'narrow theory' (ibid., p. 92) but as a 'grave practical evil, detracting greatly from the moral training and instruction which so many well-meaning persons [sc. Victorian social reformers] are now at length exerting themselves to promote' (ibid.).

This is severe, or too severe. But more just, especially in the eyes of a Jew, is Mill's belief that 'other ethics than any which can be evolved from exclusively Christian sources must exist side by side with Christian ethics to produce the moral regeneration of mankind' (ibid.).

At a time when many traditional or classical assumptions about individual ethical responsibility to the self and to one's fellow citizens have collapsed or been forgotten, the moral regeneration of mankind must seem to most a remoter prospect than ever. In much of the West, to go no further, the indices of family breakdown, of urban violence (including in organised form), of idle consumption – with its correlate, the increasingly rapid turnover of cultural fashions – of sanctioned deprivation, of declining educational and skill standards, of material waste, of stress illness, of environmental degradation, and of the gradual exhausting of the means of public provision would make the most heroic of moral reformers baulk.

The flux of the social order, with its movements of peoples, headlong travel, rapid technological change, increasing uninhabitability of mass conurbations, and high levels of unemployment make in turn for increasingly random forms of human association. It is a randomness not aided by our age's attempts to privilege the 'market' as the leading, or even the sole, principle of civic order itself. To find the moral or social organising principle, or principle of civic belonging, for myriads of individuals under such conditions would have daunted a Solomon or a Solon. And to compound every civic problem is the ubiquitous transfer of individual moral responsibility to 'them', 'the state' or others, while 'they', the state or others, have never been so mistrusted, nor mistrusted with greater justice.

That the language of civic morality should seem to have become the language of a lost age is both the consequence and further cause of civic disaggregation, and of the extensive dissolution of citizen feeling. The principle of duty, in its aspect as the obligation of the individual to himself and to fellow-members of the civic order, now sounds strange to many ears, and no longer possesses real moral status. The idea of the enforcement of such obligation suggests the very spirit of reaction, not of progress.

Most contemporary political moralists – John Rawls, for example – give as short shrift as any ordinary citizen to the principle of duty. In his *Theory of Justice* (Oxford, 1972), a work largely determined by the search for principles of civic order, his notions of justice are dominated by definitions of 'social justice' as a matter of 'equal' rights not of equal duties; the 'equality of respect' due to each individual citizen similarly rests upon, and is expressed by, his (or her) 'equal' civil rights rather than his (or her)* fulfilment of 'equal' civic duties. But, then, even a work such as T. H. Green's *Lectures on the Principles of Political Obligation* (London, 1885–8) is mainly concerned with rights not duties.

There is in this a now familiar form of ethical myopia. It is a product of – and further contribution to – the intellectual

* Henceforward, I shall take this explication to be redundant.

limitations of a mere politics of rights. Indeed, in corrupted liberal orders dominated by claims to dutiless right, demand-satisfaction and self-realisation through unimpeded freedom of action, a politics of rights amounts, in conditions of civic disaggregation and disorder, to little more than a politics of individual claims *against* the civic order and of duties owed by the latter *to* the individual. Missing consistently is a third term: the duties of the individual to himself and to fellow-members of the civic order to which he belongs. An ulterior development of the modern politics of claims-to-dutiless-rights, in the form of claims to public provision and welfare, it is not really a politics of rights at all but an economics of benefits, a different matter. Moreover, such benefits spring not from some extra-terrestrial cornucopia but from the resources of fellow-citizens of the civic order, and are contingent upon the latter's capacity to provide them.

Here, an already-noted blindness to the principle of duty is complemented by indifference to the ethical (and natural) limits of a politics of claims-to-rights, generally accompanied by refusal to contemplate any 'sacrifice' of 'individual freedom': the elements of a profound moral darkness. As Thomas Hobbes argued in *Leviathan* (Part Two, Chap. XVIII), 'all men are by nature provided of notable multiplying glasses, that is their passions and self-love, through which every little payment [sc. of sacrifice and of duty] appeareth a great grievance; but are destitute of those prospective glasses, namely moral and civil science, to see afar off the miseries that hang over them, and [which] cannot without such payments be avoided'.

Today, as before, the 'misery' which 'hangs over us' is not merely a 'lowering of civic vitality', as T. H. Green (*Lectures on the Principles of Political Obligation*, sect. G, para. 119) called it, but the loss of the very sense of the civic order itself. What its moral purposes are has already largely ceased to be a subject of debate. For some, perhaps for many, the existence of a functioning civic order – a subject which I discuss in Chapter Four – is a lost hope. The very word 'citizen' has been falling gradually into disuse, or is factitiously revived only for the purpose of attempting to enlarge the scope of a politics of dutiless rights.

Instead, I take it to be my obligation, so deep is the present moral crisis of the liberal civic order in particular, once more to explain, justify, and defend, both logically and intuitively, the *civic bond*, the very expression of human organisation for mutual security and well-being. As Seneca, in other times, reminded his contemporaries that they ought above all to be concerned with the sense of duty and the rest of the 'company of virtues' required of a citizen in any civic order, so our contemporary political and moral philosophers ought long ago to have begun to occupy themselves again with such out-of-fashion notions.

Why have they not, considering the scale of the liberal civic order's universal crisis? The force of academic taboo is one explanation, with its 'professional' preferences for disengaged or amoral speculation; the power of the (non-Judaic) cultural orthodoxy of moral relativism is another; 'left' unease with philosophical concern for ethics, or with discussion of values, is a third. For every philosophic thought or written page upon the nature of the tie which binds citizen to citizen, there have been a hundred, or a thousand, upon 'the state'. Nevertheless, that which citizens owe by way of duty both to one another and to the civic order which they together compose is ethically and logically prior to the relation between themselves and 'the state'.

Moreover, the nature of our relations with our fellows in the civic order is (at least potentially) more accessible to our moral and practical understandings than the nature of our relations with the formal institutions of the civic order, of which 'the state' is one. In addition, these times of civic stasis and disarray are times when practical necessity itself commands us to attend less to questions of the 'nature of the state' than to the nature and well-being of the civic order itself.

There is not only necessity for, but hope of, it. Whether as the guarantor of 'individual rights', or as the 'instrument for the realisation of individual ends', as the Italian political philosopher Norberto Bobbio has described it (*The Future of Democracy*, Oxford, 1987, p. 105), the state – one instrument of the civic order among others – has become the object of increasing citizen criticism and disappointment, as well as of transferred responsibility and

expectation. Ostensibly functioning in his interest and simultaneously serving as the focus of his wants and desires, the state's
oppressions and inefficiencies, some real and others imagined, are
both an expression and a product of a wider civic failure.

Such oppressions and inefficiencies are, in part, the consequence
of irrational citizen expectation itself, expectation which is in turn
the outcome and further cause of the emphasis upon a politics of
rights. So hegemonic has this politics become in the liberal civic
order that it has gradually deprived the citizen of the sense of what
a civic order is, or could be. It is a politics which has caused
arguments as to duty to be marginalised, or laughed to scorn; it has
even served to cancel memory of past moral traditions. Political and
moral philosophers who have made a doctrine of individual
responsibility and obligation, whether to the self or to others, an
important part of their thought have had that part ignored; in the
case of Mill, for instance, in favour of more agreeable doctrines of
individual freedom.

It is not surprising, then, that the principle of duty plays a small
role, when it plays a role at all, in contemporary political theory; as
small a role as the concept of responsibility-for-the-future in moral
theory, as Hans Jonas complained (*Il Principio Responsabilità* (1979),
tr. P. Rinaudo, Turin, 1990, p. xxviii). Modern liberal ethics,
political and moral, are too preoccupied with the ideal of individual
self-realisation through freedom of action under state protection to
enunciate a general theory of citizen obligation; in 1977, Jonas
(ibid., p. xxx) thought it 'too early' for such a theory.

In the political philosophy of the ancients, to make the matter of
present reconsideration more awkward, there is a broad presumption – as of something taken for granted or outside discussion – of
citizen obligation, but often no more. Even when civic duties are
the subject of discussion in the Greco-Roman texts, the particular
content of such duties and their mode of enforcement are not
systematically treated. And in the great works of political philosophy of the sixteenth to the eighteenth centuries, duty, as a doctrine
of 'political obligation', primarily has the sense of a passive duty of
obedience to the state or the ruler, whether from motives of fear or
as the outcome of a presumed 'consent', or both together. It only

fitfully carries the sense of a citizen's active responsibility towards the civic community to which he belongs.

Indeed, the sense of duty-as-obedience, or even as a form of obeisance, has come (with disastrous effect) to dominate every other possible meaning of the word 'duty' in our culture, the sense of individual ethical responsibility included. It constitutes a further obstacle to the resumption of concern for the civic virtues, and, in particular, for the principle of duty as set out in this essay.

Notwithstanding such difficulties, the scale of modern civic failure and of lost civic directions – in education and training, in urban planning, in the securing of family well-being, in penal policy, in population control, in environmental protection, and in other respects also – is in itself persuasive of the urgency of a new moral politics of civic obligation, in the practical interest of the better management of the civic order. There is not much further time for ethical error and civic failure on their present scale; but better that Hegel's owl of Minerva should fly at dusk than not take wing at all.

Moreover, at the deepest levels of the Judeo-Christian tradition, for all Mill's strictures against Christian ethics, disdain for the egotistical individualism which informs so much of the modern 'politics of rights', as I have called it, remains strong. It is strong, too, as I show, in the very apostles – such as John Locke – of the liberation of man's powers from old forms of fealty and blind subordination. In Locke, carefully reread and with our own thin assumptions about his meaning set aside, we can see that for him the existence of the civic bond was logically as well as ethically prior to the assertion of individual right; we can see, also, that from some of the unintended consequences of his emancipatory thought he would have himself recoiled. Even today's 'left' Jacobins, such as they now are, know in their heart of hearts that the Rights of Man are a two-edged sword.

If they do not concede it, it is because they share the prevailing sense of moral confusion – powerfully reinforced for them by old socialism's failure – about how individual self-realisation may be made compatible with civic order; about how Aristotle's εὐδαιμονία (*eudaimonia*), or well-being, can be secured in a wilderness of social despairs; about how 'progress' can be achieved without the enforcement of self-denial. Yet in this time of old socialism's collapse, and with the nostrums of the 'free market' also seen to constitute an impoverished ethical programme, there is a dawning sense that a return to certain first principles of morality and government – those principles which have been lost from sight in the modern liberal order – is required.

The crass judgment remains common, however, that the ethical and political wisdom of ages is irrelevant to the present generation of human beings. There are those, too, who coddle themselves with the vain belief that they are in some sort *sui generis*, exempt for the first time in recorded history from the ordinary moral and practical laws which govern the well-being of every civic order. But, along with such blindness, there is also a potentially redeeming unease which is not confined to the 'reactionary' or to the old. It tells those who feel it that many of the classical or traditional rules for the management of civic society, for the securing of the happiness of the individual, and for the maintenance of a moral order – rules philosophised over, implemented or taken for granted from antiquity to the beginning of the twentieth century – have been flouted to public loss and disadvantage; have even put mankind in peril.

If it is true that a civic moral philosophy adapted to our times, and even the principles of a new 'social-ism' (a concept I explain and discuss in this essay), now need to be articulated, and if it is also true that civic morality must be taught, none of this can be achieved in the existing world of academic philosophy. Its general want of 'originating mind', to use Goethe's phrase, and its preferences for the sophistical and arcane, for that which is neither practical nor ethical, are too debilitating, its passivity in the face of the world's growing ills a settled and narcotic habit.

In the words of Hobbes (*Leviathan*, Chap. XXIX), the construction of a 'firm edifice' of civic organisation requires a 'very able architect'; he felt scorn for the 'unskilfulness' of those who were 'ignorant of the true rules of politics'. Today, those who have set themselves up, the world over, to teach such skills – the rules of civic architecture – to others are in no better case. They are not

Plato's descendants; today's academe is overwhelmed not merely by sophists but by political thinkers who have not given civic morality a thought. 'As one individual may be morally incapable [ἀκρατής (akrates), without moral self-command, without moral power]', Aristotle warned (*Politics*, V. ix, 1310a), 'so may a whole state'. The modern 'university' has much for which to answer.

Indeed, we may – and now should – ask the following question: given the scale of the moral and social crises which beset us, can we turn (in a brute world) for guidance, ethical or practical, to an Isaiah Berlin, a Dworkin, a Nozick, or a Rawls? Of course not. Would you hear of civic obligation from a scholar who, with exquisite care and ethical unconcern, could declare that '*questions about* what it is that citizens may claim as of right in a democracy are also *questions about* what it is fair to expect of them' (my emphasis)? For thus is civic duty kept at arm's length by 'questions' without practical, or even comprehensible, answers: the questions not of a Plato but of a sophist, playing for ethical time.

Take Nozick, for example. For him, the 'moral right' of the individual includes the absolute control of the individual over himself and his possessions, a right not only to buy and sell but to abuse and destroy, provided only that such right does not interfere with the right of others to do likewise. It is, to put no finer point upon it, a hooligan's charter; no one has the right to do whatever he wishes, even with his own, if the common good of the civic order is harmed. Moreover, it is only within and through the civic order, and by means of the guarantees and protection which it provides, that such a wilful citizen can be said to have title at all to his possessions.

But to assert such an ethical civic principle, a taboo – the taboo erected by credulity in the face of 'scholarship' – must be overturned, in favour of an older, sceptical tradition which polemicists of our times have forgotten, or which they are too unlettered (and therefore too fearful) to maintain.

Such tradition is that of facing down, and even publicly decrying and assailing, the varieties of useless knowledge and obfuscation with which the 'professional' pantaloon – a classical figure of fun – has always belaboured the credulous of his age. In this tradition, the Stoic Epictetus (*Discourses*, IV, i, 13) describes the self-arrogated claim to be called a 'philosopher' as an 'insolent' act. 'Such a one is a philosopher,' Epictetus is told. 'Why, because he has a cloak and long hair?' Epictetus replies (ibid., IV, viii, 1); as we might say a gown and a distracted air. 'What then,' Epictetus sardonically inquires, 'do mountebanks wear?'

In his *Enchiridion* (XLVI), Epictetus continues the assault of scepticism upon empty intellectual pretension. 'Sheep,' he declares, 'do not throw up the grass to show the shepherds how much they have eaten. But inwardly digesting their food, they outwardly produce both wool and milk,' or practical wisdom and moral truth; to be a 'philosopher' at all is to be 'prepared against events' (*Discourses*, III, x, 2).

In challenging the failure of intellectuals to address themselves to the moral responsibilities of their privilege and calling, there has never been an age so disarmed or tongue-tied as this. In brave contrast, Gerrard Winstanley, whom I have already cited, castigated in his *Fire in the Bush* (1650, Harmondsworth, 1973, pp. 246–7), the 'blackness of darkness' in the 'school-learning' of 'university learned ones', who had 'drawn a veil over the truth', just as have our contemporary moral and political philosophers, with their empty syllogisms, nihilism of the intellect and delight in the destruction of creative thought. Three and a half centuries ago, too, they had 'put out the eyes of man's knowledge' and were 'all tongue and no hand'. Their scholarship, declared the simple voice – a simpleton to sophisticates – was 'not knowledge'; and he who made the error of 'por[ing] and puzzl[ing] himself in it' would 'lose that wisdom he [already] had' (*Law of Freedom in a Platform*, PP. 349–53).

That I should now come forward with my 'principle of duty' is in part owed to a refusal of the habits of mind by which I have been hitherto surrounded. An ethically active perception of the world – the most urgent of all intellectual requirements – demands a rejection of what have become conventional techniques of political analysis and inquiry. 'It is always a sign that a time is unproductive', declared Goethe (*Conversations with Eckermann*, 1836–48, tr. J. Oxenford, London, 1883, p. 506), 'when it goes so much into technical minutiae'; as does ours into the destructive analysis of language and creativity themselves. 'It is also a sign,' Goethe added, 'that an individual is unproductive when he occupies himself in like manner.'

Empirical data-mongering in political studies has also served to stifle ethical reflexes and the construction (or reconstruction) of the civic moral philosophies which the times demand. We are deluged by what the historian Jacob Burckhardt called *schutt und quisquilienforschung* (*Briefe*, ed. F. Kapjahn, Leipzig, n.d., p. 328), or the busy piling up of more and more unwanted facts. Nor is it any coincidence that the intellectual hyper-specialisation of responses to the circumstances of human existence and behaviour has been accompanied by moral confusion in the face of that which cannot be reduced to quantities and statistical tables. To address a 'principle of duty' to such a world is to speak a foreign moral language. Modern scientific thought, in its almost exclusive concern for that which can be brought within – or reduced to – the categories of 'mere fact', makes it difficult for ethical rules to be considered rational at all. Whatever is 'not-fact' – intuition, the prompting of conscience, the principle of duty – is constantly at risk of being perceived, in the optic of 'science', as mere whimsy or out-and-out unmeaning.

If this form of disparagement of ethical aspiration is the particular product of the 'modern scientific age', objection to the absence of ethical or practical significance in political thought is not. 'The attainment of wisdom is perfectly possible without the liberal studies: although moral values are things which have to be learned, they are not learned through these studies', thought Seneca (*Letters*, LXXXVIII) as early as the first century ad. 'Look at the amount of useless and superfluous matter to be found in the philosophers', he exclaimed; 'they know more about devoting care and attention to their speech than about attention to their lives' (ibid.).

Equally pertinent to the present time was his related criticism (ibid., CVIII) of 'the transformation of philosophy, the study of wisdom, into philology, the study of words'. Complaint about erudition without moral content or other redeeming purpose is clearly the most ancient of themes. For Seneca, 'subtlety carried too far' (ibid., LXXXVIII) was, worst of all, an 'enemy to truth' itself. Today, such 'subtlety' or over-refinement of professional intellectualism, with its esoteric theorising, 'piling up of unwanted facts' and attendant poverties of practical wisdom and moral instruction – when both have never been more needed – is also more obvious than ever. But the Senecas have disappeared, leaving our amoral wordsmiths to their devices, subsidised by the civic order but uncensured. 'What do you want? Books?' Epictetus inquires in his *Discourses* (IV, iv, 1). 'To what end? Are not books a form of preparation for living? And is not living composed of different things?'

Plato might argue (*Republic*, V, 473a) that 'it is never possible to give complete expression to ideas in practice. It is in the nature of things that action should come less near the truth than words'. But there are words and words. 'I know one,' wrote Montaigne in his essay 'On Pedantry' (*Essays*, 1580–95, tr. C. Cotton, London, 1892, vol. 1, p. 134), 'who when I question him what he knows, he presently calls for a book to show me; he dares not venture to tell me so much as that he has piles in his posteriors till first he has consulted his dictionary [as to] what piles and posteriors are.' Judging by the litany of knowing complaint through the ages, humane or liberal studies have often had little refining influence upon their scholars and students, or practical significance for the societies in which such studies were conducted.

Now, when there was never a higher premium upon civic wisdom, practical and ethical, we too suffer – with ever larger and direr consequences – from what Montaigne called the 'ridiculous knowledge' of the educated 'that floats on the superficies of the brain . . . perpetually perplexing and entangling them in their own nonsense . . . They are wonderfully well acquainted with Galen, but not at all with the disease of the patient' (ibid., pp. 136–7); their knowledge nothing but an 'eternal babble of the tongue' (ibid., p. 142). And so it is today, across wide swathes of the political and social 'sciences'. 'Spare your breath to cool your porridge', a 'country wench' advises in *Don Quixote*, more roughly than Montaigne but to the same end.

Yet, as Hobbes declares (*Leviathan*, Chap. XX), 'the skill of making and maintaining commonwealths consisteth in certain rules, as doth arithmetic and geometry; not, as tennis-play, on practice only'. The drawing up of ethical rules – of which the principle of duty is the most fundamental – requires books and words also. To rescue civic truths part-lost to, or concealed from, our understandings demands exposition and explanation. But such exposition cannot be made merely from the 'fine-spun cobwebs of the brain', as Hazlitt put it. Nor can we afford to create, so urgent and practical is the task, yet another 'world of forms', to use Vico's phrase, constructed in the head and ruled (with artificial coherence) by an imaginary ideal of duty.

However, even this might be preferable to that species of intellectual activity which is productive of no consequence at all, good, bad, or indifferent; that which makes 'no perceptible difference by its presence or absence', in Aristotle's words; that 'knowledge' which is good for nothing upon the earth. But it is also unsurprising that the political imagination should fail, or that the 'academic expert' should be reduced to vacuity or incoherence, in face of today's extent of social and civic disorder.

For it increasingly outruns the natural range of our feelings, perceptions and knowledge. It is ever harder for our ideas and language to keep pace with the objects and events – the 'Holocaust' of the Jews being one such – which challenge us to understand them. Once, sophistry could be blamed, as Aristotle (*Ethics*, X, 1181a) blamed it, for having 'no knowledge at all of the nature and purposes of statesmanship'. Now, such criticism, just as it may be, can be more easily met with the excuse that no art of government, nor political theory, could make practical or ethical sense of our times.

But there is also less excuse than ever for the amoral espousal – generally in the name of 'democracy' and 'liberty' – of a politics of dutiless right, of doctrines of 'unfettered' freedom, and of discourses upon the 'good life' or 'social justice' which make no mention of citizen obligation. Alongside a Hobbes, a Rawls is merely trivial; a Dahrendorf, likewise, beside a Hegel; a Nozick absurd, next to a Plato. Indeed, most contemporary political thought is inadequate less because it is wicked, useless, wrong, or without

meaning than because it is *trivial*. Market theories of political
exchange which reduce the citizen to a 'consumer' or 'customer'
are not so much amoral – although they are that too – as trivial: a
reductio ad absurdum. Similarly, a theory of democracy according to
which such democracy is perceived to be merely a matter of the
balanced representation of interest groups, or a question of one
voting method or another, or of the efficient management of
participation, or of systemic inputs and outputs, is not so much
wrong as (again) trivial. Game theory, at least, declares itself to be
what it is: trivial.

In the teeth of civic turmoil and disaggregation, the trivialising
of political thought – a process often sought to be masked by arcane
elaboration of terms and other devices – is ethically odious.
Knowledge which is neither of practical use nor of moral value is
one thing; trivia which serves, and even seeks, to undermine or
cancel ethical commitment is another. It is Seneca, once more, who
speaks directly to this ancient flaw of formal philosophical speculation. Some philosophers, he declares (*Letters*, LXXXVIII), 'provide me with knowledge which is not going to be of any use to me'.
But others – the worse, because destructive – 'snatch away from
me any hopes of acquiring knowledge at all. One side offers me no
guiding light to direct my vision towards the truth, while the other
just gouges my eyes out.'

In this respect, nothing changes at all: our eyes are successfully
gouged out as ever in the Groves of Academe. Theorists of the
world's travails, dressed in motley, conduct us always deeper into
their own ethical darkness, protected both by their *esprit de corps*
and the timidity of their critics, fearing to declare their suspicions
that the Emperor is naked. 'To be constantly asking "What is the
use of it?" is unbecoming to those of broad vision, and unworthy of
free men,' protests Aristotle (*Politics*, VIII, iii, 1338a). But the
moral priorities have changed. In our circumstances, it is not basely
utilitarian but an ethical obligation to pose the question which
Aristotle disdains.

In proposing the principle of duty as a guiding principle of the
civic order, I have chosen to follow Kant's 'universal practical
philosophy'. 'The object of practical philosophy', he declares, 'is

conduct . . . Ethics must have a practical object; that is, practice' (*Lectures on Ethics*, 1775–80, tr. L. Infield, New York, 1963, pp. 1, 3). I follow, too, my grandfather, the rabbinical philosopher, M. A. Amiel: 'Archimedes wished to weigh the Macrocosm, the world, whereas we Children of Israel, the people of the Prophets, desire to weigh the Microcosm, the "small world" of Man' (*Unto My People*, London, 1931, p. 45). That 'small world', for me, is composed, discomposed, and requires to be re-composed in the civic order.

Finally, it is the Cicero of the *Offices* who points the way to a restatement of the principle of duty. 'The getting of knowledge is a duty of much less concern and moment than the preserving [of] this society and union amongst men', he declares (I, xi, iv). It is a task which stands at the heart of philosophy's purpose as well as of the new 'social-ism' of the future. As to the name of 'philosopher' itself, 'who ever dared to assume it', Cicero demands to know (ibid., I, ii), 'without laying down some instructions about duty?'

TWO

Preliminary Aspects
of the Argument

1. The individual human being, whether or not he wishes it, is part of a web of moral relations. These moral relations help to form, and express themselves within, (*inter alia*) the *family*, the *community*, and the *civic order*, of the last of which the principal types are the nation and the city. I take it as axiomatic that the self-realisation and well-being of each individual are dependent in great part upon the existence of such moral relations and that each individual has an interest, both ethical and practical, in their content and quality.

2. The term *family* does not require to be defined, justified, or explained. It is mankind's home and first refuge, school of the principle of duty, in which is to be found the moral archetype of every other form of responsibility: that of the individual to his fellows.

3. By *community*, I mean a voluntary association of human beings, most commonly settled and maintaining itself in a given place, and held together or cohering (to differing degrees) by virtue of some or all of such habitual social ties as those of extended familial relationships, combined interest and purpose, and shared or related memory, language, belief, values, custom, and knowledge. There may be several, or even many, such communities within a determinate area; which may (to differing degrees) be diverse from one another in memory, language, belief, values, custom, and knowledge.

4. By *civic order*,* I mean the community or communities of a determinate area ordered under a common rule as a polity, or a united body politic, whether that of a nation or a lesser entity such as that of a city; self-governing in whole (as in a nation) or in part (as in a city); and subject, above all, to the principle of duty. Such civic order, whether that of a nation or a city, is made up of an aggregate of citizens composed, within such determinate area, into an association which embraces and is superior to all other associations within its bounds, and in the form of the nation is sovereign, a sovereignty which resides in the entire citizen-body.

Such civic order, further, is fashioned, modified, and renewed through time by its members, acting in their common interest; is possessed, however plural its composition, with institutional coherence under the rule of law, and a common ethical direction; whose members, or citizens, are vested by virtue of their membership with determinate duties and rights; in which distinctions in respect of duties, rights, privileges, and benefits are made between citizens and non-citizens, or strangers; and which, as a body, has an ethical and practical obligation to observe and enforce the principle of duty in self-protection and in protection of the interests and well-being of its members.

5. By *civic bond*, I mean the ethic, voluntarily assumed but sustained by law and shared by the individual members of the civic order – to whatever community they may belong – which, governing the relations between individuals *qua* citizens, dictates to and teaches such citizens that they compose a single civic order, whether of nation or city, to which they are affiliated and bound by the

---

* In place of the term *civic order*, I occasionally employ the terms *civic society or social order* as synonyms for it.

principle of duty, and for whose well-being they are responsible in their common interest.

6. *Civic consciousness*, or *civic sense*, are the terms I give to the awareness and understanding of this ethic, or civic bond, on the parts of individual members of the civic order, and in particular to the recognition by the citizen of his co-responsibility for the well-being of the civic order to which he belongs.

7. By the process of *civic disaggregation*, I mean the gradual waning of knowledge of, and respect for, the civic bond and the principle of duty; the gradual transformation of the citizen-members of the civic order into a randomly associated mass of individuals or citizens-turned-strangers; the gradual dissolution, or disassociation, of a civic public possessed of civic consciousness, or civic sense, that is of a sense of co-responsibility for the well-being of the civic order; the gradual loss of the civic order's institutional coherence and sovereignty, the diminution of its citizen-members' confidence in the rule of law, and the reduced readiness of the civic order to sustain the common ethical direction of such civic order; the gradual ceasing of the civic order to be an association which embraces and is superior to all others; and the gradual loss of the civic order's capacity for self-preservation, and the preservation of the well-being of its members.

8. It is a premise of my argument that the existence and well-being of the civic order, provided that it is governed by the principle of duty as I set it out in this work, is the precondition for the present safety and well-being of its individual members, as well as of the secure continuance of the diverse communities of which it may be composed. Subject to the same proviso, the well-being of the civic order is also the precondition for the safeguarding of the future interests of its members, and, properly conducted under the terms of the principle of duty, for the survival of the species.

It is also a premise of my argument that the civic order cannot be composed of a randomly associated mass, or aggregation, of individuals. The civic order requires, in addition, to rest upon more than the physical propinquity of its members and of their homes and employments. Nor is a *citizen* a mere bundle of rights which may be asserted against the civic order of which he is a member.

Where citizenship is so confined and reduced, I define it as *ostensible citizenship* only. By the same token, the civic order cannot be founded upon relations between individuals who are *moral strangers* to each other.

It is a further premise of my argument that the civic order may be organised in accord with different political models and programmes, of which the 'democratic' form (in all its variants) is one. A democratic civic ordering of the nation is one in which sovereignty resides in an ordered community of free citizens, but which is as subject to the principle of duty as is any other form of civic order. The civic order of the city, which may likewise be organised in accord with different political models and programmes, is also subject to the principle of duty.

9. The *state* is the term I give to the public arm and instrument of the civic order acting on behalf, and in the interests, of the civic order as a whole, to whose well-being it is bound by the principle of duty. It is a premise of my argument that the inordinate present power of the state in the corrupted liberal orders is in large part derived from, and a further cause of, the ethical and practical debility of such civic orders, whose own powers and responsibilities it has progressively supplanted. This debility I attribute in the first instance to the desuetude or failure of the principle of duty, as it applies to the obligations of the citizen to himself, to his fellows, and to the civic order to which he belongs.

The relative strength and power of the state and the relative weakness of the civic order are thus related: above all, the primacy of the true relations between citizen and citizen, especially important to democracies of every form, has been supplanted by the primacy of the false relations between the citizen and the state, a mere instrument of the civic order. Whatever the political form of such civic order, and whether the civic order be that of the nation or the city, it is the civic order (as I show) and not the state which is properly the fundamental and main expression of ordered relations among the members of the citizen-body.

It is a further premise of my argument that the assertion of the authority, ethical and legal, of the civic order as a body over its individual members – by means of a revived emphasis upon, and reinforcement of, the principle of duty – has been made necessary, especially in the corrupted liberal orders, by the increasing failure of citizens voluntarily to observe the principle of duty in their relations with their fellows, and therefore to sustain the civic bond. Without such assertion of civic authority in the interests of the members of the civic order themselves, the merely repressive use of already over-strong state power must increase.

10. I therefore place as an axiom at the heart of this body of ideas the notion that a constellation of moral and practical duties, some embodied in law and others the preserve of conscience alone, is owed by the individual to himself, to his fellows, and to the civic order to which he belongs. I do so in the conviction that egoistic *homo sapiens*, increasing as if inexorably in numbers, as well as in the insatiable impatience of his desires, is a present danger to himself, to others, to the civic order, and to the natural world itself; that a settled condition of *dutilessness* makes him more dangerous still; and that, upon the fulfilment of the individual citizen's duties to the civic order – whose moral health is a precondition for individual well-being, and which is the source and guard of individual rights – the civic order depends.

It is a related premise of my argument that there are no absolute rights, whether to life, liberty, property, happiness, or any other good. Even were rights to such goods to be considered absolute, there could be no practical guarantees of entitlement to, or enforcement of, such rights in any civic order whatever. They are limited and constrained in fact by the finite nature and frailty of human life, by the risks of human existence, by material scarcity, by the ultimately unpredictable actions of others, by the fallibility of all systems of public provision, and by the irreconcilability of any presumed 'absolute' rights in one citizen with the same presumed rights in another.

Moreover, the principle of duty – which is also not absolute, as I show – constitutes a permanent limitation upon such 'absolutism'.

I also reject the argument, therefore, that the individual can 'do what he likes with his own', to which I have already briefly referred. As a member of a civic order, he is constrained from such licence by the principle of duty. The individual citizen, while necessarily acting by his own lights as a possessor of free will, and in accordance with what he perceives to be his own interests *qua* private individual, has a prior ethical and practical obligation as a member of a civic order to act in accordance with the principle of duty *qua* citizen. 'Whatsoever is created on earth was merely designed, as the Stoics will have it, for the service of man; and men themselves for the service, good and assistance of one another' (Cicero, *Offices*, I, vii). It is upon such a ground that the principle of duty – as also of a new *social-ism* founded upon engagement to such duty – rests.

Thus, while the exercise of the individual's rights as the member of a civic order permits that individual to express his purposes and (hopefully) his rationality as a human being, such individual is a prior bearer of obligations to the civic order in which he exercises such rights. The fulfilment of such obligations, upon which the civic bond and the cohering of the civic order rely, is as much an expression of rational purpose as is the exercise of rights. Arguably, it is more so.

11. Morality is the soul of society's existence, of today's forms of society as of any in the past. Hence, Hobbes' citation (*Leviathan*, Chap. XX) of the prayer of King Solomon to God – 'Give to thy servant understanding, to judge thy people, and to discern between good and evil' – has the same political import for us as for Hobbes: that 'it belongeth therefore to the sovereign', the citizen-body of a democratic civic order for example, 'to be judge and to prescribe the rules of discerning good and evil'. De Tocqueville was anxious, to the same end, that the 'moral tie' between citizens living under democratic conditions be not relaxed, indeed that it be strengthened, in order to make good the dissolution of older, pre-democratic forms of obligation.

'Despotism,' he wrote (*Democracy in America*, New York, 1838, p. 288), 'may govern without faith, but liberty cannot. Religion . . . is more needed in democratic republics than any others.' It is a premise of my argument, however, that – whether De Tocqueville's prescription of religion be wise or foolish – it is too late and too importunate to prescribe faith in this fashion to the citizens of the modern civic order, especially in the latter's corrupted liberal form. Indeed, De Tocqueville himself, referring to the 'democratic

nations of Europe', declared (as early as the 1830s) that religion had
'lost its empire over the souls of men' (ibid., p. 308).

He thus left open the issue of how the 'moral tie' might be
reinforced under democratic conditions. I do not. Both the god-
fearing – whichever be the god who is feared – and the faithless
citizen are bound by the secular principle of duty, whose purpose
is the sustaining and strengthening of the civic bond, or 'moral tie'
by another name; so that, in the interests of the well-being of the
members of the civic order, and therefore of the civic order itself,
the process of civic disaggregation may be halted.

But the argument will remain, for the god-fearing, that if it is to
hold moral sway, the sense of ethical obligation to the civic order
must be founded not upon the secular persuasions of reason, law,
utility, or the inherent moral sense – as I hold – but upon the
sanctions of faith; and that without such faith the 'civic sense' must
rest upon secular sand. It is, however, an axiom of this work that
the sense of ethical obligation to the civic order, of which the
principle of duty is the organising principle, is, like its correlate the
'voice of conscience', a sense which does not require God's aid.
Man's sense of duty to himself, his fellows, and the civic order to
which he belongs can survive and prosper without being grounded
in the Platonic aspiration towards the ideal, the Jewish 'fear of
God', the Christian 'love of God', or Marx's 'class consciousness' –
alike expressions of desire that a transcendent force should lend
further dignity to man's highest purposes and fondest dreams.

Indeed, it is the defeat of Marx's moral relativism (or social
determinism) which has now begun to restore to us the very sense
of the civic order and of the principle of the citizen's duty to it. No
more do we need to pay amoral heed to his Preface (1867) to
Capital, in which he announces (without shame) that 'Individuals
are dealt with [sc. in his analysis] only in so far as they are
personifications of economic categories, embodiments of particular
class relations and class interests. My standpoint . . . can less than
any other make the individual responsible for relations whose
creature he socially remains' (Vol. 1, Moscow and London, 1954,
p. 10). With such 'individuals', who are thus the irresponsible or
dutiless objects, not the responsible subjects, of the civic order,

there could have been neither practical scope nor ethical ground for a principle of civic duty at all.

Now, the political philosopher (whose provenance is of the 'left') can return, with thought freed, to his principal ethical task: that of establishing the rules and means by which the citizen may be saved from himself, and the civic order be protected from disaggregation, in the interests of all.

12. It is a premise of my argument, as I have made clear, that such rules for the civic order are rules not merely relating to rights but to duties, and that such rules as to duties are morally prior. I further follow Kant in holding that 'we must have rules to give our actions universal validity and to mould them into a general harmony' and that 'these rules are derived from the universal ends of mankind' (*Lectures on Ethics*, p. 17).

13. It follows from the moral priority I give to civic duties over civic rights, and from the grounds on which I make this allocation of priority, that I consider a politics of dutiless right – whether as ideal form or partially-realised universal tendency – to be the politics of the civic graveyard. For such a politics would make of the citizen (whose true nature I discuss in Chapter Four) a consumer of civic benefits and allowances oblivious of the civic bond, and make over the notion of the 'good life', or Aristotle's εὐδαιμονία (*eudaimonia*), into a theatre of asocial egoism, greed and licence.

Even where, as in the corrupted liberal order, the aspiration for such a dutiless ideal is denied to be the governing ideal of the civic order, the mere lip-service paid to duty in the couplet 'rights and duties' – often no more than a catchphrase – points into a moral vacuum. It is a vacuum in which the concept of duty remains essentially notional and substanceless: that is, without practical meaning or outcome, even if considered as a (shadowy) good.

But, as Seneca again reminds us (*Letters*, XC), 'nature does not give a man virtue; the process of becoming a good man is an art'. Or, as Spinoza puts it (*Tractatus Politicus*, 1677, Chap. V, 2), 'citizens are not born, but made'.

In the moral vacuum created by a politics of dutiless right,

Seneca's art can only with difficulty be practised, and Spinoza's citizens are ever harder to make.

14. If there is such a moral vacuum *in esse* or in process of formation within the corrupted liberal order in particular, and if such moral vacuum is attributable in whole or in part to the generalisation of a politics of dutiless right, demand-satisfaction, and self-realisation through unimpeded freedom of action as the amoral and asocial norm of such civic order, the following questions may be asked. How, in ethical conditions which are shaped by 'egoism, greed, and licence' and characterised by accelerating civic disaggregation, shall a common moral understanding be reached among the individual members of the civic order that the principle of duty is ethically binding upon them? How, in such circumstances – made additionally inchoate in the great metropolises of competing desire – can the moral reformation of the civic order be found? And is it not in the face of such questions, thought to be unanswerable in the corrupted liberal orders, that the political philosopher of today has preferred to abandon the field entirely, or taken intellectual refuge in a private world of academic trivia, *schutt und quisquilienforschung*, and hair-splitting?

15. There is no doubt that the internal variety and complexity of modern communities and of the civic orders to which they belong constitute an obstacle, both ethical and practical, to a politics of duty. This and other obstacles I discuss in detail in Chapter Eight. But it is such variety and complexity, and the moral confusion and disaggregation of the civic order to which they contribute, which themselves justify the principle of duty and its enforcement.

Moreover, it is a form of pessimism of the intellectual will to refuse or to scorn such a principle *ab initio*: a pessimism which is a contributory factor in, as well as a further consequence of, the moral confusion from which it recoils, or which it considers to be beyond amendment.

It is also notable that despite the presumed difficulty of arriving at moral agreement upon the desirability of the principle of duty – supposing such moral agreement to be required and that the principle of duty did not already exist, at least in embryo, in every civic order – there do not appear to have been similar difficulties in the way of the universal consensual advance, for three centuries, of a politics of rights.

Although there is an adequate (and obvious) explanation for the different respective fortunes of the politics of rights and the politics of duties – which I discuss further in Chapter Eight – the explanation cannot reasonably be employed to displace the moral priority of the principle of duty, nor to suggest that the securing of the principle's political legitimacy and practical enforcement is an unattainable end.

If it is the case, which I dispute, that there is in the modern civic order no 'popular consensus' in support of the principle of duty, there is certainly no popular consensus in favour of the disaggregation of the civic order, nor popular approval of the manifold causes and consequences of such disaggregation. It is upon this that the political moralist must set to work. Indeed, the forms of public disapproval of such causes and consequences are sufficiently widespread, and share sufficiently common moral premises and conclusions – even in the corrupted liberal orders – that there must at least be a modest presumption in favour of the moral acceptance of the principle of duty, of its particulars as they apply both to the duties of the citizen and of the civic order, and of the rationale for its enforcement.

'Uniform ideas born among whole peoples ignorant of one another must have a common basis of truth', declares Vico (*La Scienza Nuova* (1744), Milan, 1963, Bk. I, sect. 2, axiom 13, p. 110).

16. It is an important aspect of my argument, discussed in Chapter Five, that the interests of the civic order itself may require a significant transfer, or restoration, to its individual members of certain obligations and burdens assumed – in the corrupted liberal orders among others – by the state, by government, and other public institutions, and that the enforcement of the principle of duty is a means to securing this end.

Among the chief purposes of such a transfer, or restoration, to the members of the civic order of obligations, including obligations to self, which I argue to be properly theirs on both ethical and practical grounds, are the maintenance and strengthening of the civic bond, the diminution of dependency upon state provision, the enhancement of citizenship, and the reduction of the powers of the state. These purposes are also met by the enforcement of the principle of duty in general.

In particular, I take the sustaining of the civic bond to be ethically paramount, not only under the compulsion of practical conclusions to be drawn from the phenomena of civic disaggregation, but from the premise – already touched upon – that the health of the civic bond is a prerequisite for the well-being of individual members of the civic order. It is thus a fundamental obligation not only of the individual citizen (and the political philosopher) to sustain and strengthen the civic bond, and thus to strengthen the civic identity or sense of belonging to the civic order of the entire citizen-body, but it is the duty of the civic order as a whole, and of its instruments the state and the law, to sustain the civic bond in like fashion.

I add here that, until the tradition was lost in modern times in the corrupted liberal orders, political philosophy gave a privileged place to the 'civic arts' and to the knowledge of how individual members of the civic order might best live together, and how attain within the civic order the self-fulfilment they justly seek. Such knowledge, including knowledge of how to 'maintain conditions of life in which morality shall be possible' (T. H. Green, *Lectures on the Principles of Political Obligation*, sect. A, para. 18), must be recovered and relearned. The principle of duty, as I set it out, is a form of such knowledge, both for the citizen and the political philosopher, whose principal ethical concern it must once more become.

17. In a *well-functioning* civic order, which I discuss in detail in Chapter Four, and in particular in a civic order which is not yet under the hegemony of the 'universal plebeian' – a figure I discuss further in Chapter Five – the social coexistence, in a condition of peace, goodwill, and mutual assistance, of the individuals and communities belonging to such civic order may be maintained with relatively little recourse to sanction.

That is, the authority of a sovereign civic order, expressed through its instrument the state and other civic institutions, requires the less exertion the greater the degree to which the moral and social obligations owed by individual members to themselves, their fellows, and the civic order, and by the civic order to its citizens, are voluntarily discharged. Conversely, the less the extent of commitment to, and understanding of, the civic bond – that is, the less the extent of civic consciousness, or civic sense, as I have defined it – the greater the need for the coercive or authoritarian enforcement of the principle of duty.

It follows that, in the interests both of the unforced 'good life' and of a rational exercise of personal freedom, knowledge of and respect for the civic bond are overwhelming ethical and practical political necessities.

18. In a *badly-functioning* civic order, egotistical individualism, delusions about the proper nature and extent of personal freedom, and a politics of dutiless right between them lead to a habituation with, and contempt for, the ineffectiveness of sovereign power in the civic order, coupled with the transfer of responsibility (and blame) for individual fortune (and misfortune) to 'them', others, or 'the state'.

An associated phenomenon of the badly-functioning civic order is the masking of fundamental political truths from the individual members of such civic order: principally, the truth that the collectivity of individual members of the civic order is itself the sovereign body of the civic order, and that individual citizens are co-responsible for the well-being or otherwise of the civic order to which they belong.

19. The secret of the defects and failures of the modern civic order in its leading democratic form – the form of 'liberal democracy' or democracy which places the freedom of the individual at the centre of its moral concerns – is not, in essence, to be found in the limits placed upon the exercise of authority over the individual on the part of the state, the government and the law. It is to be found, rather, in the marginal role allocated to the principle of duty in the relationships between citizen and citizen, and citizen and civic order.

The assertion of John Stuart Mill, typical of the conventions of liberal democratic thought, that it is 'indispensable to a good condition of human affairs' to 'find the limit' to the 'legitimate interference of collective opinion with individual independence' (*On Liberty*, pp. 13–14) in fact gives philosophical and ethical priority to a presumption in favour of a politics of rights over the principle of duty. This is so even if the notion that duties are owed to oneself and to one's fellows by individual members of the civic order finds a (limited) space in Mill and in liberal democratic thought in general. Individual 'independence' is the former's first ethical term; the alternative of 'interference' is its unattractive-sounding second.

It is from this matrix of the liberal ideal that there stems the further notion of the 'rights of the individual' as, *prima facie*, rights *against* society rather than as rights exercised by individual members of the civic order, or by associations of such members, *within* the civic order to which they belong.

There also flow from these seminal positions of liberal democratic thought the narrow preoccupations of moral, legal, and political philosophy (at least in liberal democratic civic orders) with the legitimation, defence, codification, and regulation of individual rights, interests, wills, and wants. It is the purpose of my work not to overturn these preoccupations, but to broaden their scope so that they may encompass a renewed emphasis on the principle of duty: both in the form of the duties owed by individuals, acting their citizens' parts, and in the form of the duties owed by the civic order to its individual members.

It is a premise of my objection to this matrix of liberal democratic thought that there are *unchanging necessities of the civic order* which give ethical priority to the principle of duty, and demand the prior fulfilment of certain practical civic obligations both on the part of the civic order (and its instrument, the state) and on the part of individual members of the civic order, if the well-being of such civic order is to be maintained.

20. Among the principal unchanging necessities of the civic order is, as I have indicated, the assumption of responsibility – preferably spontaneous or voluntary rather than induced or coerced by sanction – by its individual members for the condition of the civic order from which they derive their citizen rights and the hopes of the 'good life'. The failure of a larger or smaller number of citizens

to assume such responsibility is an expression, *inter alia*, of the degree of the attenuation of the civic bond. But it is also an unchanging necessity that there should exist in the civic order itself, and in its instrument the state, a general duty-of-care for the well-being of the individual members of the civic order, such that no citizen shall be so affected or disabled by neglect of the duty-of-care towards him as to be prevented from acting the citizen's part, and from fulfilling his obligations to himself and to his fellows.

It is a premise of the argument that the primary end of this and other forms of state action – that is action taken on behalf of the civic order – is to enhance the well-being of the civic order as a whole, and to reinforce the civic bond. To seek this end is an ethical obligation imposed upon the civic order, and upon its instrument the state, by the principle of duty; an obligation which has no less moral weight than, and which is the counterpart of, the obligation of the individual citizen to himself, his fellows, and the civic order to which he belongs.

This moral politics, governed by the principle of duty, of conjoined obligation on the part of the state as the instrument of the civic order on the one hand, and of the individual *qua* citizen on the other, is the ethical basis on which the civic order rests.

21. It follows that I reject, as amoral, the most characteristic form of ethical relations between the state and the citizen in the corrupted liberal orders, under which the state, failing to fulfil a large part of its obligations to the citizen, and the citizen, failing in large measure to observe the principle of duty, together give legitimacy to the moral primacy of a politics of rights, generally understood as mere claims to the satisfaction of wants. In such circumstances, the state fails in its duty to enhance the civic bond, and the citizen fails in his duty to play the citizen's part; and both contribute to the acceleration of the process of civic disaggregation.

Moreover, it is an outcome (and further cause) of the displacement of the true moral relations between the civic order and its members that the a-civic, or asocial, 'universal plebeian' – to be discussed further in Chapter Five – has been permitted, by default, gradually to become the archetypal citizen, or *ostensible citizen*, of the corrupted liberal democratic order. The 'universal plebeian' is, *inter alia*, the citizen in whose eyes citizenship has been ethically reduced to the possession of a passport, the right (diminishingly exercised) of suffrage, and the entitlement to a cluster of insecure benefits furnished by public provision. Just as the mere payment of taxes-for-services is not sufficient to ground a citizen relation, so the dutiless receipt of benefit is not a true badge of civic identity or belonging.

22. The plight of the 'universal plebeian' as no more than an *ostensible citizen*, and the debility of the civic bond in civic orders whose membership is increasingly composed of 'universal plebeians', are together expressions of the process of civic disaggregation. They are also phenomena of the mass civic order – whether that order be of the nation, the region, or the city, and liberal democratic or not – whose members are rendered anonymous to one another by (among other things) the scale of the civic order itself and by the failure of the principle of duty.

In addition, the collapse of the old socialist utopias and the overthrow of the schemata of the 'left' – including the organising principle of 'class' – have, on the one hand, swelled the ranks of the 'universal plebeian' with millions of former 'proletarians' and, on the other, disorientated 'left' judgment about how corrupted civic orders, liberal and former socialist alike, might be reconstituted and citizenship be once more invested with meaning.

Dismissed from the scene of political speculation upon the nature and well-being of the civic order, are those whom the prescient Flaubert in *Sentimental Education* (1869) called 'the whole cartload of socialist writers', who had sought to 'reduce mankind to the level of the barrack-room, send it to the brothel for its amusements and tie it to the counter or bench'. Nevertheless, in the world of failed old socialism, the civic damage – damage both to the civic bond and the civic order itself – has been done, while in the non-socialist polities of the West an ethically impoverished politics of dutiless right, demand-satisfaction and self-realisation through unimpeded freedom of action has wrought morally-related mass damage to the civic order.

Damage has also been done to minds: above all, to the capacity of 'left' intellectuals to think civically after decades of cerebral thraldom to political ideas which – to adopt the words of Edmund Burke in his *Thoughts on the Cause of the Present Discontents* (1770, London, 1902, pp. 81–2) – had 'a plausible air and appeared equal to the first principles', principles which 'served equally the highest capacities and the lowest', and were 'at least as useful to the worst men as the best'; and which helped, in consequence, to create an ethical wilderness in the communist social order.

Of such outcome many had long ago had premonition. Thus, Giuseppe Mazzini in his *The Duties of Man* (1860, tr. Thomas Jones, London, 1907, pp. 107–8), writing of communism more than fifty years before the Bolshevik revolution, warned 'working men, my Brothers' that 'time spent over these illusions would . . . be time wasted'. 'Humanity', he declared, could not be created 'by means of decrees', nor 'according to the plan of some particular mind, contradicting the universally adopted bases of civil existence'; men would 'always rebel against any such attempt'.

In the aftermath of the fall of such illusions, civic thought – of which the principle of duty is the keystone – must proceed, if it is to proceed at all, without obeisance to the dogmas of either 'left' or 'right', albeit that those dogmas remain worthy of notice and even, in some cases, of respect. My argument owes nothing to class analysis and rejects the old socialist goal of an egalitarian Utopia; a new civic social-ism, as I urge in Chapter Twelve, must be of a different order. To this new social-ism the old left – and right – is called.

It is in ethical civic thought and the practice of a new social-ism that the old left's moral and intellectual resurrection will be found; that is, in the understanding of the nature of the civic bond, in fulfilment of its own obligations to sustain it, and in the rehabilitation of the civic order. But for those still steeped in the old socialist principles of a politics which damaged civic orders the world over, the taking of a difficult but progressive step towards recognition of the principle of duty will require gradual acknowledgment *in pectore* of the largely negative role which the socialist chimera has played in the history of liberal and democratic ideas.

This history is a history of the notion that a member of the civic order possesses determinate duties and rights by virtue of his membership of such civic order; a history which can be traced from the times of the articulation of the civic ideal in classical antiquity, through the revival of classical learning and civic thought in medieval Europe (and beyond), and until the violent culmination of the progress of democratic aspiration in the American and French revolutions, and their nineteenth-century *sequelae*. It was at this historical juncture that first socialist, and later communist, orthodoxies sought to impose an unattainable egalitarianism (in the name of 'socialist democracy') upon the civic order; fatally gave preference to class-belonging over citizenship as the associative principle of the civic order; and turned the proud *citoyen* into a mere *comrade*. Now, with the fall of old socialism, it is the citizen who can and must be rescued.

23. It was not only the orthodoxies and impositions of 'socialist democracy' which did harm to the idea of the citizen, the civic bond, and the civic order alike. Certain nineteenth-century liberal orthodoxies on the proper relations between the state and citizen were as rigid, and ultimately as damaging in their effects on the civic order, as those of the 'left'. They have also proved more resilient, and their cultural reach has been longer.

Posited, as we have seen in Mill, upon the ethical principle that 'the state' – or instrument of the civic order – should interfere as little as possible in the life, especially the private life, of the individual citizen, while protecting and guaranteeing the latter's rights and freedoms, the orthodoxy of liberal democracy has served in the outcome to depose the principle of duty from the place it had hitherto occupied in the long history of the civic idea. Even if an unintended consequence of liberal democracy's espousal of the cause of individual freedom, the politics of dutiless right is nonetheless the deformed progeny of the liberal ideal. The orthodoxies of socialist and liberal democracy, however opposed in other respects, have between them and in different ways dealt great blows since the mid-nineteenth century to the principle of duty.

Delusions as to the meaning and just scope of individual liberty, which I discuss further in Chapter Three, may be considered the most damaging of the consequences of the latter orthodoxy for its effects upon the process of civic disaggregation. They were wiser in seventeenth-century Lucca, in Hobbes' account of it (*Leviathan*, Chap. XXI): 'There is written on the turrets of the city of Lucca in great characters, to this day, the word LIBERTAS; yet no man can thence infer that a particular man has more . . . immunity from the service of the commonwealth there, than in Constantinople.'

In the civic deserts made of the modern nation and the metropolis, with the civic bond attenuated and a politics of dutiless right the ethical norm, the ideal liberal principle that that which is not specifically forbidden it is lawful for the citizen to do has proved a principle of too high civic cost: to the asocial individual, or *ostensible citizen* of the civic order, the silence of the law in an ethical wasteland betokens only official impotence, or even moral unconcern, for whatever anti-civic acts of omission or commission such individual may choose in 'freedom' to commit. Indeed, the principle of 'non-interference', one of the lynchpins of the liberal ethic, is a principle best suited – or perhaps only suited – to conditions of established civic order where the civic bond is strong, and where the individual citizen is autonomously conscious not only of his rights but of his duties.

Ethical insensibility to the misuse and abuse of individual freedom – an insensibility increasingly commonplace amid the wreckage wrought by civic disaggregation – has traditionally been 'rationalised' and countered, as Jonas (*Il Principio Responsabilità*, p. 219) has pointed out, with the simple or simple-minded liberal arguments that 'freedom is better than lack of freedom'; that the variety of individual responses to the possibilities of individual freedom is preferable to the 'homogeneity of the collective'; and that the 'toleration of diversity' is morally superior to Obligatory conformism'.

Such false liberal counterpositions may, in the mouths of some, have grown more confident since communism's fall and old socialism's discomfiture. But, for others, the ethical and practical shortsightedness of such seeming insouciance as to consequences is becoming more apparent. (It is this growing awareness which gives both urgency and legitimacy to the renewed espousal of the principle of duty.) The moral thinness, in our civic circumstances, of the proposition that 'freedom is better than lack of freedom' excludes the possibility, as if a *priori*, that the principle and politics of duty might be necessary to the preservation of the 'liberal state' – that is, the civic order organised in liberal democratic form – itself; necessary, too, to the quelling of future demands for, say, a severely repressive moral order in which the 'toleration of diversity' will no longer be tolerated.

The understanding that these and other civic issues transcend old differences between 'right' and 'left' must inevitably grow in the corrupted liberal orders as the extent of civic disaggregation increases. The relearning of the history of political ideas, and the freeing of this history from domination by the incubus of old socialist orthodoxies of interpretation, will be a longer matter. But such intellectual progress is vital to the prospects for a new civic social-ism which is neither of 'right' nor 'left'. We have also to learn that the goals of the English, American and French revolutions – to secure the Rights of Man as a free citizen in a free civic order – were vulgarised (and plebeianised) by the nineteenth-century pleasure principle of 'the greatest happiness of the greatest number': a principle which rained down further blows, those of an amoral hedonism, upon the principle of duty, and therefore upon the civic bond and the integrity of the civic order itself.

No doubt the socialist chimera, the utilitarian calculus and the liberal Utopia were all aspects together of the 'modernising' of the political and economic world of the high Victorian era, an era of heady secularism and technical innovation, of new degrees of social mobility and ethical iconoclasm. But, at the same time, moral claims as to the equal worth of individuals – upon which the claims both of old socialism and modern doctrines of individual freedom rest – easily became amoral claims to dutiless right, demand-satisfaction and self-realisation through unimpeded freedom of action.

Under the terms of such a politics, the free and equal individual calculator of his own interests, who is presumed to know where his own interests lie, asserts the right to act without much reference, and sometimes without reference at all, to the interests of the civic order as a whole. Indeed, for the largely dutiless individual, mere self-interest typically becomes the criterion not only of calculation but of association with, or disassociation from, both *community* and *civic order*. It is here that the liberal ideal is corrupted; here that neither the ζωὸν πολιτικόν (*zoon politikon*), or social being, of Aristotle nor the *homo economicus* of Adam Smith can flourish; here, that the source of our anxiety about the fate of the free civic order is to be found.

I do not argue that the value placed upon individual freedom should not be so placed, nor that it is ethically wrong *per se*. I argue instead that false notions as to its meaning, and false claims as to its scope, have been both cause and further consequence of the attenuation of the civic bond, and have assumed a role in the corrupted liberal order which is morally prior, and even antithetical, to the principle of duty. Nor do I argue that the individual's judging of the final worth of things for himself is wrong. I argue instead that it is not the ultimate criterion of value; that if it is a mark of freedom it is also the ground upon which a sense of moral direction may be dissipated and lost, and the principle of duty be denied and forgotten. This admitted, we may the more clearly judge the dire ethical and practical strength of a politics of rights reduced to nothing more than a politics of individual interest – that estranging individual interest whose free exercise in the corrupted liberal orders permits us to see that, while duties without rights make men slaves, rights without duties make men strangers to one another.

In our relearning of the history of political ideas and our revival of the principle of duty, we may come to understand that in seventeenth-and eighteenth-century debates about civic society, 'natural rights', and individual liberty it was the issue of freedom from outmoded forms of hierarchical obligation, or obeisance, which stood at their heart. The principle of duty, although not absent from such debates – as for example, in Locke – was cast into the shadows by different preoccupation.

But in late twentieth-century conditions of the disaggregation of those free civic orders which the seventeenth-and eighteenth-century revolutions helped to establish, it is clear that without the fulfilment of individual obligation to the free civic order itself, the free civic order (and individual freedom with it) must come to be lost. If personal liberty is to retain its high ethical status, and the habitual use of force to maintain the civic order is to be disavowed, then the civic order must rest upon acceptance – preferably voluntary, but coerced by sanction if not – of the principle of duty; a principle which must be brought from the shadows into the political and moral light.

Nor does this represent any serious peril to the moral doctrines which underlie the politics of rights, albeit debased as this politics has become in the corrupted liberal orders. On the contrary, observance of the principle of duty, by strengthening the civic bond, sustains the *fans et origo* of right itself. The politics of rights, together with the moral doctrines on which such politics rest, are more exposed in the corrupted liberal orders to harm wrought to them by abuse and misuse of the rights themselves, than by constraint upon them from enforcement of the principle of duty.

Moreover, in the long-standing liberal-democratic cultures, however debased, claims of right, however abused, have deep roots. From the Roman *jus naturale* and *jus gentium* to Locke's 'rights in the state of nature', from the Rights of Man asserted by the French Revolution to the welfare 'rights' of the plebeian democracies of the modern period, the argument from rights – whether 'God-given', 'birthrights', 'natural rights', or rights guaranteed by law and constitution – is also an argument about the integrity, and not merely the interests, of the individual as a human being.

But the same human being has duties also – to self, to fellows, and to the civic order – which are fully the moral equivalent of the rights he possesses or claims. If claims of right are held to be authorised by 'natural law' or the 'principles of natural justice', many of the obligations enjoined by the principle of duty may – equally persuasively or unpersuasively – be attributed with the like moral force. There are duties which are as 'natural' as any right; and, to those of religious faith, as 'God-given'. Moreover, duties may be found to be prescribed, as rights are inscribed, in constitution and law, including in the English common law – as I show in Chapters Ten and Eleven – even if to a lesser extent and less frequently invoked than in the case of rights, and under provisions which have too often been permitted to become dead letters.

24. The principle of duty is neither alien nor unknown to the

modern liberal tradition, for all its corruption by a politics of
dutiless right. Thus, 'there are many positive acts for the benefit of
others which he [sc. 'Anyone'] may rightfully be compelled to
perform', declares Mill in *On Liberty* (p. 24), a liberal principle less
familiar (now) than that recommending non-interference with
individual 'independence' and 'private conduct' where such conduct concerns, or is said to concern, only the individual in question.
These 'positive acts for the benefit of others' include, for Mill, not
only the bearing of a 'fair share in the common defence' but also,
more remarkably, 'in any other joint work necessary to the interest
of the society of which he enjoys the protection'. The citizen,
declares the philosopher of modern English liberalism, can even be
'compelled to perform certain acts of individual beneficence, such
as saving a fellow creature's life, or interposing to protect the
defenceless against ill-usage, things which wherever it is obviously
a man's duty to do, he may rightfully be made responsible to society
for not doing' (ibid.).

Such formulation of a principle of duty, at the outset of *On
Liberty*, is wider and less specific than any I would myself propose
or accept. It is not as wide as the Hobbesian ascription to the civic
order of the general function of directing citizens' actions towards
the common good, or as authoritarian as the proposition that the
function of the law is to keep citizens 'in awe' (*Leviathan*, Chap.
XVII). But it is wide and authoritarian indeed, in particular to
sensibilities shaped by the long rule of dutiless right.

It demonstrates, however, that the principle of duty is an aspect
or feature of the classical liberal tradition, but an aspect lost from
view in the overwhelming of every other ethic by the later history
of the politics of rights, which is the 'deformed progeny' of the
liberal ideal itself. Indeed, contemporary Victorian critics of liberal
principles feared the very corruption of such principles that has
come to pass, in which an ethically demeaning relationship is
established between the *ostensible*, or dutiless, citizen and the civic
order to which he merely formally belongs; in which the *ostensible
citizen*, turned 'universal plebeian', plays the benefit system for
what he can extract from it, as in Britain; or in which, as in Italy,
vote-buying is the correlate of the right of universal suffrage; or in

which the free citizen is 'reduced to the status of a protected subject', as the Italian philosopher Norberto Bobbio has put it (*The Future of Democracy*, p. 111).

A 'protected subject' is not what Mill's liberalism, with its stress upon notions of 'independence' and 'non-interference', had in mind; and even less did it have in mind the 'universal plebeian'. Its citizen ideal, rather, was the active member of a free civic order, exercising his civic rights and fulfilling his civic duties – and conscious of the ethical relation between them – but otherwise at liberty to conduct his life and pursue his aspirations in his own fashion, provided that such conduct did not interfere with the rights of others likewise engaged.

A politics of dutiless rights, further diminished to a politics of dutiless wants and demands, is a far cry from, even if a predictable outcome of, Mill's starting positions. But the fact that many such wants and demands, especially 'welfare' demands, are easy to justify morally, or are unjustifiable extensions of justified demands which are already being met (to a greater or lesser degree), gives the politics which embraces them an equally easy ethical precedence over the principle of duty. Indeed, where the making, the attempted satisfaction, and the actual satisfaction of demands constitute the core of the citizen relation with the civic order and its instrument the state, habituation to such a relation, more Pavlovian than political, renders it increasingly difficult for any other civic ethic to flourish.

It is also one of the causes, and further consequences, of 'political apathy', that condition in which the active citizen according to the liberal ideal is turned not merely into a 'protected subject' but a passive protected subject. It is not a coincidence that a politics of the gradual extension of dutiless civic rights, the politics pursued for a century and more in the Western liberal democratic orders, has gone hand in hand with the deepening of apathetic disengagement from the affairs of the civic order. Dutilessness, disengagement, and moral indifference are ethically related. They are also related in practice. Moreover, the condition of dutilessness leads to the moral undervaluing – an aspect of 'apathy' – of the rights themselves; they become mere consumer items, to be taken up or not, in the political supermarket of demand-satisfaction.

Yet duty, as Kant frequently reminds us and as Mill also knew, but as we have largely forgotten, is not antithetical to freedom. 'The degree of [man's] freedom grows with the degree of his morality', the former declares (*Lectures on Ethics*, p. 29); 'the more he gives way to moral grounds of impulsion, the freer he is'. 'In duty,' similarly thought Hegel, 'the individual finds his liberation' (*Philosophy of Right*, Third Part, para. 149). Indeed, not only is the principle of duty compatible with the individual freedoms of the liberal ideal, but essential both to the well-being of the liberal democratic civic order as a whole and to the satisfaction of the true civic interests of its members. This is not least because of the growing (but blind) preference of states and their administrators and politicians, acting ostensibly as the instruments of their respective civic orders, for a passive citizen-body: that is, a citizen-body whose members consume their benefits, rather than asserting their rights as citizens or actively fulfilling as citizens their moral and other duties to their fellows. In this a-civic parody of the civic order, both the active assertion of rights and the active fulfilment of duties come to be seen as forms of 'interference' in the civic order itself.

It is in such circumstances – in which Mill's liberal principle of non-interference has been turned on its head – that the relation between dutilessness and the loss of sovereign power by the civic order can also be most clearly seen. To neglect or deny the principle of duty is to weaken the civic bond; to weaken the civic bond is to weaken the civic order; a weakened civic order may the more easily have its sovereign powers and responsibilities usurped by its own instruments and administrators. Thus, acts of assertion of right and acts of fulfilment of obligation on the part of individual citizens may alike come to be perceived, by mere administrators of the state, as derogations from or threats to the civic order itself; a judgment which represents a usurpation of the civic order's sovereign responsibility for the well-being of its members.

Such loss of sovereign authority in the civic order is a consequence, clearly seen in the corrupted liberal orders, of the rule of dutiless right, the reduction and humiliation of the citizen by his subjugation to a politics of claims, demands, and satisfactions, and the accelerating process of civic disaggregation. As Hobbes warns (*Leviathan*, Chap. IX), there cannot be two sovereign powers in one society: either the civic order, or its instrument the state, must be supreme.

It is my argument that observance of the principle of duty is a prerequisite not only for maintaining the strength of the civic bond but for preserving the sovereignty of the civic order; and that a liberal democratic civic order in particular is sustained by the performance of the citizen's obligations to it.

25. The contrary belief, ironic in conditions of accelerating civic disaggregation, that the well-being of the individual citizen can be enhanced and 'civic virtue' increased by the extension of the scope of dutiless right, I therefore reject. Moreover, I hold that citizens in active possession only of entitlements-to-benefit as badges of their civic belonging – that is, citizens who have been reduced to the status of protected subjects – already stand on the very periphery of the civic order.

The principle of duty, which (as I later show in Chapters Nine and Ten) dictates the fulfilment by the civic order of certain fundamental moral obligations to the citizen, as well as the performance by him of equally fundamental duties to himself, his fellows, and the civic order, is required to restore citizenship to such 'subjects', and in so doing to restore sovereignty to the civic order.

26. If such restored citizenship and restored sovereignty are essential to the proper functioning of the liberal democratic form of civic order in particular, they are also the precondition of the new civic 'social-ism' whose nature I make it one of my tasks to define. Just as the liberal ideal of the active citizen in a free civic order was transmuted by time, circumstance, and human folly into a politics of egotistical individualism and dutiless right, so the old socialist ideal of an egalitarian 'social justice' – whether to be achieved by redistribution of wealth and by (dutiless) public provision in a still democratic order, or by expropriation and dictatorship in a party-barracks – helped form the 'universal plebeian' in one case and made a prison of the civic order in the other.

In the first case, an attenuated socialist outcome was sought within the institutional framework and legal norms of the liberal democratic system, at a time when the Victorian liberal ideal was itself being gradually overwhelmed by a politics of dutiless right, a politics to which socialist aspiration made its own large contribution. During this socialist period, the principle of duty as it applies to the citizen's obligations to the civic order was falsely associated by the 'left' with class obeisance, and was thus allowed less moral purchase than ever. Moreover, despite the survival of an old socialist moral politics in which concepts of duty to self and to one's fellows had been central, the politics of demand-satisfaction also became the dominant politics of democratic socialist movements.

In the second case, that of a draconian state socialism which overthrew the norms of the liberal democratic system, the principle of duty became an ethically destructive principle of subjection to the diktat of a few, and not the means of expressing and defending the ethic of the civic bond.

But the principle of duty, as I set it out, is both a prerequisite for the maintenance of the sovereignty of the civic order in its liberal democratic form, and the governing principle of a new civic social-ism whose premise is the co-responsibility of the individual for the well-being of the civic order to which he belongs.

27. I use the term *social-ism*, rather than socialism, the better to establish that, historically, 'social-ism' – a politics, or an '-ism', of the social – was perceived by early nineteenth-century 'social-ists' to be the ethical antithesis to 'individual-ism'.

It was an antithesis which rested upon the assertion by 'social-ists' of the ethical and practical importance of the 'social question' of the day, the moral condition of the 'lower orders', in contrast to the casual unconcern shown for their fellows by many privileged members of the civic order. Old socialism was in origin the politics of the 'social question', finding an 'answer' to which was seen by 'social-ists' – but not by 'individual-ists' – as a civic obligation, or expression of the principle of duty to the civic order in practical form. A new civic social-ism can be no different.

Even before the appearance on the scene of the nineteenth-century 'social-ist', the perception that the civic order was a 'commonwealth', and not a mere source of rights and benefits, was a commonplace one, as was the notion that the individual citizen's relation with such 'commonwealth' was governed by the principle of duty. A modern civic 'social-ism', similarly governed by the principle of duty to the civic order and directed towards the 'social question' of the day – the disaggregation of the civic order itself – will therefore rest upon the securest of historical and ethical foundations.

28. Nevertheless, the term 'principle of duty', especially as it applies to the duties of the individual citizen to himself and to the civic order to which he belongs, has in the ears of old socialists – defeated as they may have been in their own vain endeavours – the sound only of 'reaction'. This is in large part the outcome of continuous failure, decade on decade, to keep pace with and adjust to the changing nature of the primary 'social question' of the day. Indeed, whether under pressure of ideas of class or of the supposedly transcendental movements of history, or from the priority given to the unattainable goal of equality, or in consequence of the short-term pursuit of the politics of wants and demands, old socialism at its fall had barely any conception of the civic order at all.

That the principle of duty is, in the civic circumstances now found in the corrupted liberal orders, a principle of radical and progressive reform, is thus hard for the 'left' to grasp. Even harder for an old socialist to acknowledge is the notion, a last premise of my argument as a whole, that it is not primarily the civic order which must be reformed in the interests of the individual members of it, but the individual's relation with the civic order which primarily requires to be transformed, as by observance of the principle of duty in the interests of the civic order as a whole.

Old socialists, and the 'left' in general, have not been willing to show regard for the interests of the civic order as a whole – that is, in its integrity – except where the civic order has been regarded as socialist. In capitalist societies, it has been perceived as a mere congeries of classes and interests, many of them mutually opposed, and some of which it has been considered the 'left's' obligation to favour, and others to penalise, or otherwise rein back. This partial view of the civic order (and of the civic bond) has not only represented a disabling weakness of 'left' thought but has contributed to the process of civic disaggregation.

29. For all that, the assertion and observance of the principle of duty is the necessary foundation of a new social-ist morality, as well as of the only possible progressive morality in civic orders subject to disintegrating social and other pressures. Moreover, it is the common interest of mankind, transcending the narrow loyalties of 'left' and 'right', that the civic order (as I describe it in Chapter Four) should survive and that its members – when the civic order is that of the nation – should constitute the sovereign body of such civic order. 'A commonwealth without sovereign power,' Hobbes reminds us (*Leviathan*, Chap. XXI), 'is but a word without substance, and cannot stand.'

Today, the civic order as a citizen-body can barely lay claim, in the corrupted liberal orders, to be sovereign, its ethical status and practical authority usurped from 'above' by supranational bureaucracies and state apparatuses, and from 'below' by the undermining of the civic bond and by the increasing dominance of the values of the a-civic and anti-social 'universal plebeian'. History teaches us that weak forms of the liberal democratic civic order, unable to resist such pressures because unable (and even unwilling) to assert their sovereignty against them, may fall prey to authoritarian, cruel, and socially destructive attempts to restore the civic bond; in their most destructive form in the name not of all, but only of some, of its citizen-members.

'How,' Seneca asked (*Letters*, XLI), 'can people be called back when the crowd is urging them on?' By the principle of duty, which alike commands the fulfilment of the civic order's duties to its citizens and its citizens' duties to the civic order. Through the assertion, exercise, and enforcement of the principle of duty, citizenship and moral being may be restored to the 'universal plebeian' and citizen-turned-stranger, and sovereignty to the civic order; 'right' and 'left' may be drawn to a common purpose in the strengthening and defence of the civic bond; and by establishing the ethical basis of a new civic social-ism, they may between them help to redeem the corrupted liberal order, in particular, from the spreading social consequences of civic disaggregation.

THREE

The Losing Gamble
of Liberty

Benefits and risks of the gamble of liberty –
uncertainties of liberal thinkers – individuality and society –
responsibility and choice – the assumption of reason analysed
and discussed – natural rights – dutiless rights – history of claims-to-right
– market freedoms – desert and merit – 'social rights' and social provision
– reason and reasonableness – reason and unreason.

30. The potential principal benefits of the 'gamble of liberty' are
the enhancement of the 'independence', individuality, and sense of
ethical responsibility of the person. The principal risks of the
'gamble of liberty' are of its corruption into egotistical individualism
and of the habitual recourse to what Hobbes called 'private strength'
against the public good, the good of the civic order.

The gamble has been, on balance, a losing one. To its protagonists, the liberal ideal appears as open, flexible, unauthoritarian,
and morally good. But it may also be perceived as composing a
rigid dogma, resting upon *a priori* assumptions as to the equality,
and especially as to the equal rationality of men, upon which in
turn are erected closed, inflexible, and authoritarian concepts of the
nature of individual freedom, the scope and content of individual
rights, and the secondary importance (where it is considered
important at all) of the principle of duty.

In the corrupted liberal order, the last has generally come to be
considered a principle of moral and political reaction, despite the

presence of the principle of duty in the founding texts of the liberal ethic.

31. The ethics of classical liberalism as they apply to individual 'independence' and potentiality have always been justified, as they were by Mill (*On Liberty*, Chap. 3, passim), on the grounds that they are conducive to the personal and social development, enlightenment and improvement of the individual, and that without the degree of personal liberty which they have in mind life would become a 'stagnant pool' (ibid., p. 115).

A closer examination of what Mill intended by his conception of 'individuality' discloses that his formulation of the liberal ethic is often less sure (and much less egalitarian) than the subsequent corruption of liberal ideas – into a justification of egotistical and dutiless individualism for all – has made it out to be. 'When the opinions of masses of merely average men,' Mill can write (ibid., p. 120), wrestling with the risks of liberal doctrine, 'are everywhere become or becoming the dominant power, the counterpoise and corrective to that tendency would be the more and more pronounced individuality of those who stand on the higher eminences of thought.' 'Exceptional individuals,' Mill added, thinking doubtless of himself, 'instead of being deterred, should be encouraged in acting differently from the mass' (ibid.).

Similarly, he complains (ibid., pp. 117–8) that 'at present individuals are lost in the crowd'; counterposes 'originality' and 'genius' to the 'commonplace' and the 'tendencies and instincts of masses'; and declares that 'mediocrity' is the 'ascendant power among mankind'. However, Mill has no sooner expressed, than sought to cancel, his doubts: 'it is not only persons of decided mental superiority who have a just claim to carry on their lives in their own way . . . Human beings are not like sheep' (ibid., p. 121).

The doubt about liberal first principles which such tergiversation – commonplace in Mill – expresses is no longer expressed by liberal thinkers, either in these snobbish high Victorian terms or at all. Indeed, the assumption of the equal rationality of free men, and of the justice of the corpus of liberal ethics and institutions which have been erected upon it, is outside discussion in the corrupted liberal orders: the 'assumption of equal rationality', and other cognate assumptions, have the unchallengeable moral status of holy writ.

I do not myself object ethically to certain liberal assumptions; rather, I share them. But I note here that they are generally considered in corrupted liberal democratic societies to be *a priori*, and that this status helps to explain the equally *a priori* marginalisation of the principle of duty.

32. Not much more secure (on closer examination) as a liberal first principle is the asseveration of Adam Smith in *The Wealth of Nations* (1776, Bk. II, Chap. 3) that there is at work in the civic order the 'uniform, constant and uninterrupted effort of every man to better his condition', and that this effort, 'protected by law and allowed by liberty to exert itself in the manner that is most advantageous', maintains the progress of the civic order 'towards opulence and improvement'. Against the beneficent 'natural inclinations of man', Smith argues (ibid., Bk. III, Chap. 1), stands the 'injustice of human laws' which disturb the 'independency' of the ideal citizen of Smith's Utopia of free entrepreneurial rights.

Yet, as with Mill's uncertainties, there is more ambiguity in Smith than meets the eye at first sight, and which similarly complicates the drawing of simple conclusions about his meaning. 'All for ourselves', he for example declares (ibid., Bk. III, Chap. 4), 'and nothing for other people, seems, in every age of the world, to have been the vile maxim of the masters of mankind.' Again (ibid., Bk. IV, Chap. 3), 'merchants and manufacturers' – with their 'interested sophistry' and 'avidity' – 'neither are, nor ought to be, the rulers of mankind'.

Once more, it is the dogmatism of the latter-day politics of dutiless right in the corrupted liberal orders which has imposed itself, ethically and in practice, upon contemporary judgment as to the nature of the liberal ideal. Such dogmatism has concealed from us not only the doubts of liberal thinkers about the two-sidedness of the principles they espoused, but shorn from our awareness of their thought whatever acknowledgment they themselves made of the principle of duty.

If 'all for ourselves and nothing for other people' was a 'vile maxim' to an Adam Smith, the supposed apologist for the licensed egoism of *homo economicus*, then the principle of duty, as it applies to our duties to our fellows, is surely inscribed as an implicit civic assumption even in his form of liberal doctrine.

33. The earliest modern philosophers of individual liberty, chief of them John Locke, could not and did not dissever their notions of individual right from correlative notions of duty, as I show later. But by formulating their principles of right as they did, and in the context of a struggle for the establishment of civic orders freed from the shackles of blind obedience to kingly power, they launched us upon the losing gamble of liberty, whose ulterior consequence has been the headlong process of civic disaggregation.

Thus, 'every free man naturally hath', or 'hath a right to', what Locke dangerously calls (*Two Treatises of Civil Government*, 1690, Bk. II, para. 74) the 'executive power of the Law of Nature'. That is, he has a 'natural right' to act upon the dictates of reason, as he interprets it, by his own free will, to use his talents and possessions as he wishes, and to pursue his self-chosen purposes and ends by virtue of his condition as a free human being – or by virtue of his existential condition, as later times would call it. Locke's argument, as was to be the case with Adam Smith's, rests upon the ethical premise that each individual member of the civic order is the unaided best judge of his own interests: precisely the same premise, readily turned to a-civic and anti-social ends, of the dutiless egoist bent to purposes wholly selfish.

Mill, following suit and carrying the gamble of liberty forward, pronounces similarly (doubts notwithstanding) in *On Liberty* (p. 27) that 'the only freedom which deserves the name is that of pursuing our own good in our own way'. Mill's rider – 'so long as we do not attempt to deprive others of theirs [sc. their good], or impede their efforts to obtain it' – is ethically of the first importance, in particular in relation to the civic principle of duty. Yet its importance has been characteristically subordinated to, or suppressed by, the later moral triumph, in the corrupted liberal orders, of the politics of dutiless right; which hollow victory was itself an unintended consequence of Mill's liberal principles, among others.

That Mill's social, or civic, purpose in espousing the cause of individual potentiality should have been so largely lost in a welter of claims to egotistical self-realisation through unimpeded freedom of action may be laid at the door of incautious formulations as to the extent, and content, of individual right; formulations which, turned into expectations, now dog the fortunes of every liberal democratic order.

'The liberty of the individual must be thus far limited', wrote Mill (*On Liberty*, p. 101), that 'he must not make himself a nuisance to other people. But if he refrains from molesting others in what concerns them and merely [sic] acts according to his own inclination and judgment in things which concern himself . . . he should be allowed, without molestation, to carry his opinions into practice at his own cost. It is desirable, in short, that in things which do not primarily concern others individuality should assert itself.'

That such a point of division is a matter of ethical artifice – but made necessary, in practice, by the formulation of right in Mill's terms – is plainer still in his attempt to distinguish between the sphere of 'individuality' and the sphere of 'society'. 'To individuality should belong the part of life in which it is chiefly the individual that is interested,' Mill declares (ibid., p. 134), and 'to society, the part which chiefly interests society': arguably the most circular and question-begging of 'principles' ever proposed in the history of ethics.

In our conditions of civic crisis, the notion of a 'purely personal conduct' in which the civic order can, and should, have no interest continues to contribute to the accelerating process of civic disaggregation.

34. Although Mill's tergiversations led him radically to qualify his ethical 'principle' that 'our desires and impulses should be our own' (ibid., p. 107) with the rider that the individual should be 'prevented from gratifying his inclinations to the injury of others' (ibid., p. 113), the risky premise of his argument as to the moral autonomy of the individual is at the flawed, or broken, heart of the liberal ideal.

For it is to a corrupted 'individuality', not to a redeemed or even successfully functioning 'society', that the acceptance of the practical and ethical priority of Mill's premise – over its subordinate qualifications – has tended; as has, too, the acceptance of Locke's doctrine of 'natural right', stripped bare of the principle of duty. Between them, in liberal democratic civic orders which rest upon the (truncated) principles of their thought, they have, however unjustly to their intentions, furnished a moral charter for forms of egoism – including that of the basest hedonism – whose point of reference begins and ends with itself; and in which 'living for oneself' and 'living for nobody' become hard to distinguish.

35. But even without taking into account the modern falsification in the corrupted liberal orders of the principles of individual right, and the abasement of the Rights of Man to the ends of moral self-immolation in contempt of the civic bond, the ground upon which 'individuality' turns to egoism and egoism to the wilfully asocial is also the ground of 'human nature'.

'Does the essence of good consist in nothing but pleasure?' asked Epictetus abrasively (*Discourses*, II, xx, 2). 'If it be so, lie down and sleep, and lead the life of which you judge yourself worthy – that of a mere reptile. Eat and drink and satisfy your passion for women, and ease yourself, and snore. What is it to you whether others think right or wrong about these things?'

The very argument, even to its details, which I conduct here upon the meaning and limits of individual liberty is age-old; that it is so is also largely forgotten. 'What has come to prevail in democracies is the very reverse of beneficial,' wrote Aristotle (*Politics*, V. ix, 1310a) in the mid-fourth century bc. 'The reason for this lies in the failure properly to define "liberty" . . . Liberty is seen in terms of doing what one wants . . . each lives as he likes and for his "fancy of the moment", as Euripides says. This is bad.' And, remarks Aristotle further (ibid., VI, iv, 1318b), 'freedom to do exactly what one likes cannot do anything to keep in check that element of badness which exists in all of us.'

Similarly, 'if we hear it said that the definition of freedom is the ability to do what we please,' Hegel declared over two thousand years later in his *Philosophy of Right* (Introduction, para. 15), 'such an idea can only be taken to reveal an utter immaturity of thought, for it contains not even an inkling of the right ethical life.' In such past complaint, the principle of duty, whether explicitly or implicitly, generally represents the ethical antithesis to the promptings of the selfish will, or to unbounded claims to right.

'Woe to you and to your future,' thus warned Mazzini (*The Duties of Man*, p. 81), 'if the respect which you owe to what constitutes your individual life should ever degenerate into a fatal egoism'; or if liberty should be reduced to a 'mean, immoral individualism', in which 'Ego is everything'. To the 'blind seductions of egoism', he counterposed the 'path of duty' (ibid., p. 74); a classical, or traditional, ethical counterposition which in the corrupted liberal orders has been effectively lost from sight.

36. The particular form of modern 'individualism' with which I have to do here expresses both an old moral disablement – the hypertrophy of the selfish ego – and a newer aspect of the losing gamble of liberty. It is that dutiless 'individualism' which is characterised, and perhaps definable, by its lack of a sense of co-responsibility for the condition of the civic order to which the individual belongs. More than that, it is the expression of a circumstance in which the 'individual', *despite his unconcern for the civic bond*, has acquired the moral status which the 'citizen' once enjoyed, even if– often – he enjoyed it only in name.

Driving all other ethic before him under the 'tyranny of the demand for autonomy and more autonomy' (Jonas, *Il Principio Responsabilità*, p. 181), the greater this individual's 'autonomy' the less not only his sense of obligation to the *civic order*, but the less (in general) his affiliation to the *community* to which he belongs; and, conversely, the greater his real need that the principle of duty become once more a living principle of the civic order, and, where necessary, be enforced against him.

37. For personal freedom as 'autonomy', or 'independence', expressed in the form of dutiless right, of claims to demand-satisfaction, and of expectations of self-realisation through unimpeded freedom of action is insufficient to provide the individual with a sense of his own identity, whether civic or private, let alone with a sense of ethical direction.

38. Furthermore, the basest form of 'individualism', such as that of the asocial egoism which is licensed in the corrupted liberal order, ethically 'autonomous' as it may strive to be, measures itself

– and must measure itself – against others. When bent (*in extremis*) upon the destruction of the civic order, the asocial ego still acquires its sense of significance and identity in relation to, and in context with, fellow members, or ostensible members, of the civic order. It also observes its own asocial principles of loyalty and duty – even if the civic order does not – which it too may seek to enforce, including by violent and criminal means.

39. In theory, and especially in the hopes of those still faithful to the protestant ethic, personal responsibilty for the self, and co-responsibility for the well-being of one's fellows, are the moral correlates of the liberty of the individual.

But this liberty, reinterpreted under the licence of false notions of the liberal ideal as the dutiless moral autonomy of such individual, has become the mere egoism of the *moral stranger* to the civic bond and civic order, a figure I describe in further detail in Chapter Five.

Under the rule of such egoism – which is also one of the distinguishing marks of the 'universal plebeian' – the civic order becomes decreasingly able to rely upon the spontaneous exercise by the individual of personal moral responsibility in its behalf. Yet in every society the evolution and adaptation of the civic order is a matter of organic processes of growth and change as well as of rational direction, in which the civic bond is sustained by voluntary acts of moral commitment and practical participation, as well as by civic education and the sanction of law.

In the corrupted liberal orders, however, spontaneous and voluntary acts on the part of the citizen, or ostensible citizen, increasingly take on the character of a-civic or anti-social acts, necessitating countervailing responses from the civic order and its instrument the state. Such responses may be considered administrative acts of self-defence of the civic order. But the logical outcome of such trends, in which the violent egoism of the moral stranger comes to be met by the repressive or violent force of the civic order, is the destruction of the civic bond in the name of the civic bond itself.

40. The gamble or risk of liberty, as I have described it, derives in large part from the moral reliance which is placed, in the liberal ideal, upon the *rationality* of the pursuit of self-interest by the individual. The just rejection, often by revolutionary means, of (pre-democratic) forms of personal obligation, which were expressed in fidelity, devotion, and fear, and their replacement by 'moral ties' whose ground was rational choice and (according to theory) voluntary consent, was in effect to place faith in the citizen rather than to expect or demand faith *from* him.

The civic order organised in liberal democratic forms is the most dependent of all forms of civic order on the requital of such faith in the rational citizen. Conversely, it is made more vulnerable than any other form of civic order by the transformation of the rational pursuit of individual self-interest within the civic order into irrational acts carried out in bad faith against the civic order. *In extremis*, such civic order must come to be sustained neither by pre-democratic forms of fidelity and devotion nor by the democratic rule of reason, but by the repressive maintenance of the civic bond.

41. At the heart of the gamble of liberty in liberal democratic civic orders is, as I have indicated, the reduction of the 'citizen' to the 'individual' whose interests and desires are made the ground of the civic order itself, as well as the mainspring of both individual and social impulse.

Such 'individualism', equated with reason itself and assumed to have been ratified by civic consent, is also legitimated in the liberal democratic civic order by its association with the presumed moral virtue of 'free choice'. Indeed, the possession of 'freedom of choice' is often held to be the distinguishing mark above all others of the free citizen-member of a free civic order; the 'power to choose' is seen as the means *par excellence* of individual self-realisation.

But 'freedom of choice', for all its ethical virtues as an expression of free will, is also easily made synonymous in practice with the mere free assertion of individual interest, or of 'doing what one likes'; a different matter. Under the rule of egotistical individualism in the corrupted liberal order, no moral reliance can be placed by the civic order upon the individual citizen's rational use of such freedom.

42. I have also already asserted that a politics of dutiless right, insofar as it weakens the civic bond, gradually renders the

democratic civic order an ineffective sovereign power, and unable to act democratically in the interests of its members. In today's circumstances, in which the 'freedom of choice', with other individual freedoms, is additionally interpreted as the generalised free assertion of dutiless interest and, at worst, becomes asocial arbitrariness or mere personal whim – a principle which is no principle – the sovereignty of such democratic civic order cannot be sustained without the enforcement of the principle of duty.

Freedom of choice is not a civic principle; and in the democratic civic order in particular, dependent in large part upon the voluntary assumption by the individual citizen of ethical co-responsibility for the well-being of such order, there is no right to choose to act asocially or anti-civically in the name of 'freedom of choice'.

43. The assumption of rationality in the citizen is a basic assumption upon which the civic order in its liberal democratic form rests, a rationality which it is also assumed informs his exercise of choice, among his other 'freedoms'. 'The freedom . . . of man, and liberty according to his own will,' declares Locke (*Two Treatises of Civil Government*, Bk. II, para. 63), 'is grounded on his having reason, which is able to instruct him in that law he is to govern himself by, and make him know how far he is left to the freedom of his own will.'

We are, to Locke, 'born rational' (ibid., para. 61). The 'law of nature', which dictates to us our need to unite with our fellows for 'mutual preservation', is 'plain and intelligible to all rational creatures' (ibid., para. 124); is unwritten; and 'nowhere to be found but in the minds of men' (ibid., para. 136). Moreover, men have been 'given reason' in order to 'make use of [the world] to the best advantage of life and convenience' (ibid., para. 26).

Hobbes, although more sparing or grudging in his recourse to the assumption of reason, attributes to men's rational 'foresight of their own preservation and of a more contented life thereby' their acceptance of 'that restraint upon themselves in which we see them live in commonwealths' (*Leviathan*, Chap. XVII). Hobbes further declares (ibid., Chap. XXVII) that 'every man that hath attained to the use of reason is supposed to know he ought not to do to another what he would not have done to himself.'

For his contemporary Gerrard Winstanley – no less profound a political thinker than Hobbes – the 'light in man' was the 'reasonable power, or the law of the mind', which provides an 'onward, watchful oversight of all motions to action, considering the end and effects of those actions [so] that . . . no excess . . . break forth to the prejudice of a man's self and others'. This is reason in service of the duty to self and to one's fellows, a reason which Winstanley calls the 'witness or testimony of a man's own conscience' (*Law of Freedom*, p. 375).

In the American Declaration of Independence of July 1776, made as the assumption of reason extended its democratic reach, the 'truths' which it contained, including that of men's creation as equals, were held to be 'self-evident'; that is, grounded in a universal human rationality. It was Reason, expressed in and sustained (as for Locke) by the Law of Nature, which also entitled one people or nation to equality of status and parity of esteem with another. But the crowning (and most risky) assumption of the modern liberal ideal is the attribution to the individual member of the civic order not merely of an ethical 'conscience', but of a capacity to live autonomously and dutilessly according to self-derived and untutored dictates of rational action, dictates which will serve both to restrain him from certain forms of inclination and to impel him towards others.

In conditions of the corruption of the liberal ideal, the corollary of such assumption of reason – that it is *only* the 'rational citizen' who is willing to live according to the law of reason, and only the 'rational citizen' who is capable of rationally exercising his rights and freedoms – has been cancelled or forgotten, even if both Hobbes and Locke make room for the corollary in their thought. Indeed in a final inversion, it is this very corollary which, in the corrupted liberal order, it is now thought irrational to entertain.

44. The assumption of reason has not been considered an *absolute* or *unconditional* assumption in this fashion until modern times, times in which unreason – as in the unreason of the 'Holocaust' – has manifested itself in the civic order on an unprecedented scale.

45. In ancient and more recent pre-modern thought, the assumption of reason, although commonly advanced in the discourse of

political and moral philosophers (and of the tragedians of the
classical Greek drama) as the criterion of distinction between man
and the less-than-human, is not only never absolute or unconditional, but not permitted to go unquestioned or unchallenged.
Reason itself has hitherto prevented such taboo.

In the ancient world, the very definitions of 'reason' and the
attempted explanations of its nature and provenance – for instance,
in Epictetus, as the 'gift of the gods' – contain their own cautious
sense of its special donation, limitation, frailty, and risk. Reason
was discovered in the Garden of Eden, but at great human cost;
Prometheus brought reason and human cultivation to the race of
men but only by dangerously stealing the gods' secret of fire; *hubris*
is the insolence of reason. Plato's assumption of reason is of a
reason ultimately attainable only by the philosophical guardians of
the ideal state. In the real state, reason is contingent and imperfect.
'Reason,' declares Aristotle (*Politics*, VII, xiii, 1332a), hedging it
with qualification, 'causes men to do many things contrary to habit
and to nature, whenever they are convinced that this is the better
course'; not 'all things', but 'many things' only, and only when they
are so 'convinced'. Otherwise, 'habit and nature' command their
choices.

In general, as for Cicero (*Offices*, I, iv), reason is a human
endowment which distinguishes men from beasts, providing them
with a 'power to carry their thoughts to the consequences of things
[and] to discover causes'. But it is a latent power only. Man remains
a 'creature endowed with reason' (ibid.), that is, a denizen of the
naturally-created world, who, by using his reason, distinguishes
himself from the rest of animal creation; but not otherwise.

We are no longer sensitive to the echoes of such qualification and
caution, which are to be found even in the seemingly least qualified
sentences of Locke. 'The rule of reason,' he declares (*Two Treatises
of Civil Government*, Bk. II, para. 8), is 'that measure God has set
to the actions of men for their mutual security'; reason is that
which 'God hath given to be the rule betwixt man and man' (ibid.,
para. 172); or, more plainly, 'God gave the world . . . to the use of
the industrious and rational' (ibid., para. 34) – but not, so the

taboo-corollary follows, to others, the not-measured, the not-industrious, the not-rational.

Nor is the clear warning of the supreme rationalist, Spinoza, known or acceptable to the liberal ideal. 'Men are led more by blind desire than by reason', he tells us (*Tractatus Politicus*, Chap. II, 5); 'and so their natural power . . . must not be defined in terms of reason, but must be held to cover every possible appetite by which they are determined to act.'

Nevertheless, it is upon an unconditional and dogmatic version of the assumption of reason, an assumption that is not now permitted to be challenged or questioned, that the corrupted liberal ideal has erected its politics of dutiless right.

46. Aided by such unqualified assumption of reason, unprecedented in the history of political ideas, a path or passage has been traced in the name of the (corrupted) liberal ideal from the noble principle of the freedom and dignity of the individual to the base politics of dutiless right.

This politics of dutiless right rests on the ethical premise that human beings, by virtue of being human and therefore rational, possess rights not merely to have and to do certain things, but to have and to do them in pursuit of self-determined interests, free from the presumption of the right of the civic order, acting in its own interests and in fulfilment of its own duties, to interfere with the determination by the individual as to where his interests lie.

It is a further ethical premise of the politics of dutiless right, and one sustained by the assumption of reason, that it is the task of the civic order, and of its instruments the state, the government and the laws, to secure, give effect to and even extend such rights; and to reconcile such conflicts as arise between different, and competing, members of the civic order in consequence of the free exercise of dutiless rights to which they are all equally entitled.

47. In the name of the corrupted liberal ideal, *distinctions of value* are generally no longer made between the fundamental human and civic rights of a democratic order – rights to physical integrity of the person, to universal suffrage, to freedom of opinion and expression, to freedom of movement and association, and to a fair trial – and the contingent privileges, benefits, and licences which

may be attached, at any time, to membership of a particular civic order.

Also lost, or discarded, is memory of the historic tradition of explanation in liberal democratic orders of the nature, provenance, and limits of the rights of the individual citizen. I refer in particular to explanation which derives such rights from a (fictitious) civic or social contract, under which the principles of duty and of right are attempted to be given equal legitimacy in morality and reason.

48. Instead, the theory of 'natural rights', without benefit of context, explanation, qualification, or civic education, stands alone as the implicit philosophical and moral ground of the uninstructed belief that individuals possess absolute rights which are not only anterior to their presumed entry upon membership of the civic order – as Locke also believed – but which have no direct, or even indirect, connection with such membership.

It is similarly believed that 'all powers that be are restraints upon [the individual's] natural freedom which he may rightly defy as far as he safely can,' as T. H. Green put it (*Lectures on the Principles of Political Obligation*, sect. C, para. 5D); that the individual's possession of rights requires no correlative fulfilment of duty to the self, to one's fellows, or to the civic order; but that, nonetheless, the possessors of rights are entitled to expect that their rights will in all circumstances be upheld by the civic order to which such dutiless individuals belong.

49. Now lost from view, also, is the once commonplace knowledge that such individuals' rights – which can never be absolute but are contingent upon circumstance, including that of the frailty of human affairs – remain moral abstractions, or mere statements of principle, unless rooted in and adapted to the interests of the real and existent civic order.

Lost, too, is the knowledge that rights and duties in practice belong to the individual as a member of the civic order, that is as a *social being*, and are secured to him, expected of him, or imposed upon him, by virtue of his membership of such civic order. (This remains so even in the modern era of supranationalism and other derogations from the sovereignty of the civic order.) Hence, despite egoism's claims to, and demands for, rights which are unconditional and absolute – sustained in the political process by parties for whom the politics of dutiless right is a *raison d'être* – such rights are not absolute; not least because they are in fact subject to the principle of duty, however neglected or suppressed.

The principle of duty is addressed not to an abstract or ideally rational figure, free-floating above the realm of the contingent, but to the member of a determinate civic order. It decrees, as I show in more detail in Chapter Ten, that the individual not only cannot do, but cannot be permitted to do, 'what he likes with his own', whether 'his own' be considered to be his physical body or self, his family, his resources and possessions, or his juridical rights.

Without knowledge of, and instruction in, such limitation the individual member of the civic order has had concealed from him – as is the case in corrupted civic orders ruled by a politics of dutiless right – the true nature of the relation between individual and civic order. Such relation rests upon the moral priority of the obligations of the former to the latter.

50. Instead, in conditions of the corruption of the liberal ideal, the individual comes to consider himself to be not a citizen but an 'independent' dutiless actor upon his own account. The alienated ego of such *ostensible citizen* not only perceives itself as the possessor of unqualified right, and 'the state' as the guarantor of such right, but comes no longer to recognise that the civic order has an objective existence at all. (The base notion that there is 'no such thing as society' is a related expression of this atrophying of the civic bond.)

Even citizenship itself – to which there is also no absolute right – may come to be ethically disparaged, or be felt to have no objective meaning. Nevertheless, in corrupted liberal orders, the rights (including to citizenship) of the individual *qua* isolate ego, or of a particular community *qua* separate community, continue to be asserted, even militantly asserted, against the civic order. Such forms of right, fondly considered by some to be those of 'empowerment', thus asserted, are themselves a badge of isolation and separation from the civic order.

Moreover, dutiless right, asserted under the conditions of the corrupted liberal order, is right which does not enhance but diminishes citizenship – citizenship as mere right is a hollow vessel – as it likewise weakens the civic bond. And when the very existence of the civic order comes, in consequence, to be opaque and even invisible to its members, the exercise of such right by the isolate individual or separate community comes to possess diminished ethical significance for its possessors themselves.

In the *terminus ad quem* of a politics of dutiless right, the individual, the community, the concept of right, the sense of citizenship, the civic bond, and the civic order itself come to be diminished together.

51. In the conditions of the corrupted liberal order where a politics of dutiless right holds sway, the mere exercise of such dutiless right by the seemingly 'empowered' individual does not thereby make such individual a citizen, but (at best) an *ostensible citizen*, or protected subject, who remains in other respects a moral stranger to the civic order.

The objection to such individual's claim to true citizen status is both ethical and practical. It is ethical in that the exercise of dutiless right does not elicit, and does not merit, the moral regard which attaches to the performance of duty to oneself and to one's fellows. The objection is practical in that the 'respect for the rights of others' which Kant regards as 'sacred' is not in practice gained, or is gained unwillingly and fitfully, by those whose sense of their own citizenship is reduced to mere claims to dutiless right and benefit.

'There is nothing more sacred in the wide world,' Kant declares (*Lectures on Ethics*, p. 193), 'than the rights of others. They are inviolable.' Right, however, is not inviolable, and is regularly shown to be not inviolable, not least in the corrupted liberal order. But such derogation from the 'rights of the individual' is, in part, a consequence of the generalised assertion of dutiless demands upon the civic order, which has served – neither unexpectedly nor paradoxically – to undermine the moral status and security of right itself.

52. Furthermore, the greater the extent of 'empowerment' of the individual *qua* isolate ego, and of the particular community *qua* separate community, the greater the degree both of civic disaggregation and of the diminution of the effective meaning of such

'empowerment' in the civic order. In such conditions, the ostensibly 'empowered' individual or community may be found to be crowing on a civic dunghill.

For 'power over one's life', if not accompanied by observance of the principle of duty as it applies to the individual's obligations to himself, his fellows and the civic order to which he belongs, tends in the corrupted liberal order to become a power exercised without regard to the interests of the civic order, and even a power exercised against such interests.

Likewise, where such 'power over one's life' can (seemingly or in fact) be exercised only by holding at bay other claimants to the same power in respect of their own lives, the principle of duty comes to be perceived as an obstacle or encumbrance to the 'rights of the individual', rather than as a precondition of the maintenance of the civic bond and of our ethical relations with fellow-members of the civic order.

False perceptions and expectations as to the meaning and consequence of possessing 'power over one's life' are thus frequently accompanied in the corrupted liberal order by moral unconcern, and even intolerance, towards the principle of duty. Such unconcern gains an unintended legitimacy from the formulation by Rousseau – glibly repeated today, without regard to its context in a political doctrine of authoritarian imposition upon the individual in the name of the civic order – that 'man is born free, and yet we see him everywhere in chains' (*Social Contract*, Bk. I, Chap. 1). But the individual human being is not 'born free'; he takes his place in an already existing filiation of moral and other relations, familial relations included, to which the principle of duty is addressed. 'To renounce our liberty', Rousseau further declares (ibid., Bk. I, Chap. 4) – to the misused benefit of the modern politics of dutiless right – 'is to renounce our quality of man'. The maintenance of the civic bond, however, makes its own moral and practical demands upon us, demands of which Rousseau was entirely aware. The conundrum he thus posed to himself was, to paraphrase, 'how shall a man live in the civic order, obey its rules, and yet remain as free as before?'

The answer I give is simple: he cannot. But Rousseau felt

constrained – by the libertarian premises of his argument – to pretend that the individual member of the civic order, in obeying the dictates of the 'general will' as Rousseau understood it, was merely being 'forced to be free'; and in such obedience remained 'as free as before'. This sophistry the principle of duty, as I set it out, does not permit.

To observe the principle of duty to oneself and to one's fellows in the civic order, or to have it enforced against one by sanction, is not at all to be 'as free as before', nor as free as the politics of dutiless right in the corrupted liberal order pretends that the citizen can be.

53. I now return to issues related to the provenance, and therefore to the nature, of the politics of dutiless right. The gradual historical overturning and transformation of worlds dominated by varieties of feudal and quasi-feudal forms of obligation – a process both violent and peaceful which has not yet been completed on the globe – brought the principle of citizen right to parity of moral esteem with the principle of duty, and to the practical entrenchment of the former in constitutional provision and legal enactment.

The ulterior process of setting rights above duties, of setting notions of individual right above notions of citizen right, of setting the principle of duty at naught and of rendering the civic order opaque or invisible to its own members, has followed to differing extents and at differing speeds in different civic orders.

In the growth of right, the citizen (and later the individual *qua* individual) found protection and the means of self-defence against despotism, arbitrariness, and authoritarian imposition of many and varied kinds. Defiance of injustice took moral precedence in the struggle to create and maintain a civic order, often in a wilderness of abuse of privilege and power. Oppressed communities and denied interests gained their due places in the civic sun; the struggle for rights itself served to sustain and enhance the strength of the civic bond.

At different times and in different places, in an historic process which continues, the claims and demands of individuals and groups that they had a right to assert their interests and powers in old and new fields of human activity came to seem more significant, practically and ethically, than other claims and demands that there was a duty to protect existing forms, laws, and customs in the civic orders to which the aspiring individuals and groups belonged. The history of free self-assertion of individuals and groups and the development of the modern civic order, especially in its liberal democratic form, may be said to have gone hand in hand.

Moreover, the principle of free self-assertion and the principle of duty may be readily made to appear, and sometimes are, at odds. Indeed, the history of the 'triumph' of the politics of rights over the politics of duty may even be (falsely) presented as the victory of the present and future over the past, or, as I have already suggested, of 'progress' over 'reaction'.

And so it might justly be seen, if consideration were alone to be given, say, to the historic widening of claims-to-rights in liberal democratic civic orders: from claims made by seventeenth-century property-owners to the concomitant political rights to which they believed themselves entitled by virtue of their ownership; to claims made by non-property-owners in the nineteenth century to a variety of civic rights which should owe nothing to wealth or position; to claims made by all citizens (and even non-citizens) in the twentieth century to rights of protection from the consequences of misfortune, including the consequences of unemployment, old age, homelessness, and sickness.

In this evolving history of claims-to-rights (and, in the corrupted liberal orders, of claims to dutiless rights), two broad processes have been at work which have had consequences for the principle of duty, insofar as it concerns the duty of the citizen to himself and to his fellows.

The first is the gradual historical transition from claims-to-rights made essentially as the expression of the *wills* of the claimants, to claims-to-rights made essentially in the form of demands for the meeting of the claimants' *needs*, to claims-to-rights made essentially in the forms of demands for the satisfaction *both of needs and wants*, some of them gratuitous and costly.

With the last set of claims-to-rights has come a new 'functional' question, not previously posed by members of the civic order, which is addressed, however obliquely or opaquely, to the civic order and to its institutions: 'Does it, and do they, meet my wants?' Under the terms of such a question, the legitimacy and 'acceptability' of the institutions of the civic order, and even of the civic order itself, are determined – especially in the corrupted liberal order – by whether or not the civic order 'delivers' to the citizen, or *ostensible citizen*, the satisfaction of wants which he claims from it.

The relation to the civic order which such a criterion of the latter's 'acceptability' expresses is one from which the principle of duty could not be more distant, ethically or in practice.

The second, and connected, 'broad process' which may be traced in the history of claims-to-rights is the gradual imposition upon – and acceptance by – the civic order, and by its instrument the state, of a wide range of obligations *to* the citizen. Some of these were hitherto borne, often only with difficulty or barely at all, by the citizen himself; many are now justly considered to be preconditions for the well-being of the civic order itself. To these I will return in Chapter Nine.

54. It is not only the claimant to the satisfaction of gratuitous wants to whom the politics of dutiless right has given licence in the corrupted liberal order. Modern claims to dutiless 'market freedoms' – some of which, as I have already indicated, would not have met with the approval even of Adam Smith – are as much part of the licentious politics of dutiless right as other expressions of egotistical individualism, and share the latter's ethical blindness.

They are the 'capitalist' or market counterpart to, or mirror image of, old socialism's claims, in the corrupted liberal orders, to dutiless 'rights' to work and to varieties of unmerited reward. Just as there are no absolute rights-in-general in the civic order, so there is no absolute right to a 'free market', nor can there be absolute rights *in* a 'free market', whether such rights are claimed by capital or by labour. It may, or may not, be a *desideratum* of a successful economic order to have, or to aspire to, a 'free market', but it is no one's political *right* that there be such. Whether it be economic policy or social anthropology which makes of the 'free market' a lodestar of the civic order, such 'free market' has no higher juridical status than does the 'welfare state'. Access to the benefits of the (dutiless) free market is also as contingent as is access to the benefits of the (dutiless) welfare system.

Moreover, for all that the 'ethic' of the free market has gained powerful consensual approval in the corrupted liberal order, its moral and practical limitations as the supposed ground of the civic order remain. The free market might have been thought by an Abraham Lincoln, in December 1861, to be the 'just and generous and prosperous system which opens the way to all, gives hope to all, and consequent energy and progress and improvement of condition to all' (*Speeches and Letters*, London, 1907, p. 187). But, at the same time, the 'spirit of trade', as Hazlitt described it in *Free Thoughts on Public Affairs* (1806, London, 1886, pp. 375, 378), 'can but ill supply the place of principle', not least the principle of duty; 'mere mercenary advantage', as he called it, knows little or nothing, when left to its own devices, of the civic bond, or of the citizen's co-responsibility for the well-being of the civic order.

Nevertheless, under the rule of the politics of dutiless right, 'mere mercenary advantage' has been permitted to clothe itself, as has every other similar claim to the satisfaction of wants, in civic dress – and even to present itself as the ethical and practical precondition of the 'good life'.

55. The politics of dutiless right has not only served as an organising principle of political parties of both 'right' and 'left' in the corrupted liberal order, and even of the *ostensible citizen*'s aspiration and plan-of-life, but also of movements specifically organised to pursue the interests of claimants to the satisfaction of gratuitous wants.

On the one hand, dutiless 'mercenary advantage', organised in its own interest and even seeking to command the state, pits itself against the civic order in the name of the free market; on the other, demand for dutiless benefit from the state and the civic order, similarly organised on behalf of ostensible citizens (or 'protected subjects') in their own interest, seeks to transform claims into rights by mere force of numbers: 'civic' activity in parodic form.

Indeed, in the corrupted liberal order, parties, movements, and organised groups, otherwise required to give shape and voice to the interests of the citizens in the mass-scale civic order – interests which, without them, might remain inchoate or go unheard – also serve, often, to distance the individual from ethical and practical engagement with the civic order to which he belongs. He then ceases to be a protagonist in his own right; is 'absolved' by certain forms of public provision from the performance of important aspects of his duty to himself and to others; and, ethically lost amid competing political claims to dutiless rights against the civic order, loses his sense of the civic bond, and even, as I have pointed out, his awareness of the existence of the civic order itself.

In a final contempt of the forgotten principle of duty, such ostensible citizen may feel himself to be so oppressed and over-shadowed by the powers of organised interest as to demand from the civic order yet more compensatory (but always dutiless) right and benefit – in the name of the very 'citizenship' which such dutilessness voids of ethical substance.

56. In the corrupted liberal order, the citizen's fundamental (but never absolute) rights – as of suffrage, opinion, expression, association, assembly, movement, and physical protection – are thus promiscuously mingled, in ethical status and practical significance, with rights, both real and imagined, of lesser order; with privileges, licences, and exemptions which attach to membership of civic society; with mere claims to benefit; even with pretended entitlement to the satisfaction of gratuitous wants.

In this moral confusion, of which the principle of duty is the main victim, the old socialist – once disposed to regard all claims-to-right in a 'capitalist' civic order as a surrender to 'bourgeois' illusion – can now be found in the van of those making the politics of dutiless right central to their cause. Extensions of the 'rights of citizenship' even to encompass protections of the citizen from the civic order to which he ostensibly belongs are pursued in a civic void. The 'mere desire for certain events to take place' – to have a good job, money, housing, private means of transport and so on – is confused, as Bobbio (*The Future of Democracy*, p. 77) has pointed out, with a *right* that such events should occur.

And in such confusion, to arrive at a commonly agreed and rational definition of political rights, and especially one which distinguishes rights from mere claims ('I need', 'I want'), becomes increasingly difficult in the corrupted liberal order. With such difficulty, the possibility of devising any rational political theory at all in such civic order also begins to fail.

57. The politics of dutiless right in the corrupted liberal order also rests upon notions of egalitarian entitlement to such right which *owe nothing to the individual's deserts or merits.*

It is unsurprising, therefore, that the principle of duty has obtained little (and diminishing) purchase in this ethical wilderness. For the principle of duty, unlike the politics of right, contains within itself a means by which both desert and merit may be distinguished ethically and practically from their contraries. But in the corrupted liberal order, the principle of equality of entitlement sedulously avoids, and even makes a taboo of, the criterion of individual merit.

This modern exclusion of desert and merit (in all their possible expressions) from considerations of entitlement to right, privilege, benefit, and satisfaction of want does not merely deter and disable claims as to the moral priority of the principle of duty. In the long history of civic society, the corrupted liberal order alone has risked, with dire consequences to itself and to the members of such form of civic order, the exclusion (as a matter of 'principle' itself) of desert in matters of entitlement to right.

Equal entitlement to right, privilege, benefit, and satisfaction of wants in the name of 'equity', without regard to desert, and in conditions where the principle of duty has become largely a dead letter, represents a false equality, a misplaced equity, and an ethic which cannot serve the well-being of the civic order as a whole; it even undermines, in a vicious circle, the substance of right itself. It is also incompatible with the principles of a new civic social-ism, as I set them out in Chapter Twelve.

To give equal *honour* to persons who are unequal in desert or merit also represents, but more plainly and palpably, a false equality and a misplaced equity. Yet, entitlement to civic right, as I discuss more fully in Chapter Eleven, is no less honour, even if in the desuetude of the principle of duty and the attenuation of the civic bond it is not now perceived to be so.

Equal entitlement to right, privilege, benefit, and satisfaction of wants, without regard to desert and in a corrupted liberal order, rests upon that egalitarian fallacy which Aristotle best diagnosed (*Politics*, V, i, 1301b). It afflicts those who believe, and in our times take up such belief as a political cause, that if individuals are 'equal in any respect', as they are, 'they are equal in all', which, observably, they are not.

58. The politics of dutiless right assumes its basest form, and one corrupted by the doctrines of equal entitlement without regard to desert, in the politics of demand-satisfaction.

Under its rule, the meeting by the civic order of real need – in fulfilment of the civic order's obligation to the citizen, as I further describe it in Chapter Nine – is compromised by, and confused with, a politics of consumer-preoccupation, which engages equally the citizen and the civic order. In its thrall, the citizen comes to be perceived and treated by the civic order (and its instruments, the state and government) not as a citizen but as a consumer, customer, and bundle of wants; and the citizen, perceiving himself in like fashion, loses sense of his duties, as a citizen, to himself, his fellows, and the civic order, at worst without sense of honour or shame.

In communities in which a high moral value was once ascribed to self-reliance and the principle of duty, this loss of civic sense – on the part both of the citizen and of the civic order to which he belongs – must be counted severe.

59. Such civic loss, suffered under the rule of the base politics of demand-satisfaction in the corrupted liberal order, has received a continuous legitimation, albeit false and meretricious, from the undiscriminating support generally given by the 'left' to all claims to welfare right, whether such claims have to do with real needs or gratuitous wants; most commonly being presented as the 'social rights of citizenship' or even of 'universal humanistic ethics' (cf. R. Titmuss, 'The Limits of the Welfare State', *New Left Review* 27, Sept.–Oct. 1964, pp. 28–37). Any system of ethics which dictates the meeting of real need by the civic order is indeed humane. But not even in the case of real need, let alone of gratuitous wants, does it give rise to absolute rights, whether termed 'social rights' or any other.

Indeed, the 'entitlement' of the individual citizen to public provision by the civic order, or by its instrument the state, may in many forms of such provision be an ethical good. But the latter serve, at best, as attenuations of the accidents of fortune and of the disabilities which it metes out to individuals. Even where provision against such accidents of fortune is justly the subject of obligation on the part of the civic order to the citizen, the right to such provision remains contingent. To term the expectation of such provision a 'social right' cannot affect its ultimately contingent status.

For 'social rights' are not the same as political rights, which latter are defining rights of citizenship; that is, rights of the individual member of the civic order – and, in some cases, of the associations to which he may belong – which pertain to him not only in virtue of such membership, but whose exercise by him is an expression of the sovereignty of the civic order to which he belongs and to which he contributes.

Instead, the conflation of so-called 'social rights' and political rights has further served, in many citizens, to diminish awareness of the value and distinct meaning of the latter. It has damaged the sense, an element of the *civic sense*, that the former have largely to do with the provision (and generally passive consumption) of benefits, and the latter with the active discharge of the citizen's part, including in his observance of the principle of duty; and, hence, helped further to undermine, in the corrupted liberal order, the citizen's sense of co-responsibility for the condition of the civic order to which he belongs.

60. The benefits of public provision do not, however, lead and have not led – contrary to what the prejudices of the 'right' would suggest – to the members of the corrupted liberal order being permitted to run riot on the public spoils.

But the undue extension of 'welfare provision' by the civic order and its instrument the state, together with the consequent growth and organisation of 'welfare interests' and the institutionalisation of the 'welfare life', have had a generally negative ethical and practical outcome for the civic order. The 'welfare industry' in the corrupted liberal order has the nature of a parody of productive effort, with

its own 'workers' and forms of output: those of benefit acquired by
its clients, or 'protected subjects'.

In many areas of social provision, what is provided goes beyond
the meeting of real need – while failing in others to meet such need
– to the outermost ethical limits and practical purposes of the civic
order as such. ('I think I know how to lick my own fingers,' declares
Sancho Panza in *Don Quixote*.) Equality of entitlement to *provision
without need*, the moral correlate of equality of entitlement to *right
without regard to desert or merit*, has also in some cases strained the
civic order's finite resources to the point of near breakdown, when
the existence of need could be the only rational ground for
attempting to meet such need in the first place.

Indeed, public provision has run upon a prodigious scale for
decades in many civic orders – above all, in corrupted liberal orders
where the politics of dutiless right prevails – and in almost every
social field. Yet it has not served, in general, to 'social-ise' the
members of such civic orders, nor to induce in them any greater
preparedness for the voluntary assumption of co-responsibility for
their own well-being or the well-being of the civic order to which
they belong.

For every client of the welfare system who, his burdens removed
to his justified relief, need no longer protect himself, there are
arguably two who, physically able-bodied, no longer see why they
should so protect themselves, or who would not be capable of it
should they be put to their own devices, and who thus stand at a
far remove from playing the citizen's part. That which, in the light
of old socialist ethics, was considered to be 'socially progressive' as
policy has not often been translated, *pari passu*, into social progress
in fact, whether it be measured by the indices of educational
advance, urban peace, domestic concord, or the overcoming of
diseases of neglect and excess.

Nor has the process of civic disaggregation been arrested by it;
on the contrary. The murderous daughters of Danae were sorely
punished in Hades: by being doomed to fill, and to refill, leaking
jars for ever.

61. In such circumstances, particularly in the corrupted liberal
order, the recovery and reassertion of the sovereignty of the civic

order, and the renewed observance of the principle of duty by ostensible citizens habituated to a politics of dutiless right and demand-satisfaction, is a necessary but hard task.

'When the exercise of power laid by is for the public safety to be resumed' – that is, when a power set aside by, or denied to, the civic order must be returned and exercised for the well-being of the members of such civic order – 'it hath the resemblance of an unjust act', Hobbes reminds us (*Leviathan*, Chap. XXIX); such resumption of sovereign power even 'disposeth great numbers of men, when occasion is presented, to rebel'. In addition, similarly, great numbers of citizens, or ostensible citizens, of the corrupted liberal orders, accustomed to dutiless hedonism under the conditions of the prosperity which they enjoy – theirs is a 'prosperity liberalism' – are ill-adapted, both ethically and practically, to the forms of restraint and self-restraint which the principle of duty, as I set it out in Chapters Seven, Nine, and Ten, enjoins.

But it is the rootedness of false and vain notions of individual liberty, propagated in corrupted liberal orders, which stands most redoubtably in the way of the strengthening of the civic bond and the recovery of the sovereignty of the civic order.

Chief of such notions is that individual liberty, even in the form of an egotistical individualism which utterly denies the principle of duty, is a *value-in-itself*, whatever the outcome of the use to which it is put. Under the rule of this notion, misuse of such liberty is perceived as the risk (or gamble) to be taken, and the price to be paid, for an always greater good: the possession of individual freedom *per se*.

To this there are many ethical and practical objections, including not only that the argument implies such liberty (and the rights by which it is expressed) to be absolute, but that it renders such liberty simultaneously abstract and of arbitrary content. Insofar as the argument – that individual liberty is a value-in-itself – does not appear to concern itself with ends or context, and in particular rides roughshod over the consequences for the civic order of the exercise of such liberty, it is shorn at once of much of its ethical worth and even of its meaning.

But its principal weakness is that it rests implicitly upon the *assumption of reason* (sects. 40–46). More specifically, it is upon the 'reason of the citizen' that faith in individual freedom, and in the manner of its exercise in the civic order, reposes. Those who possess such faith must presuppose that rational purposes will on balance prevail over irrational purposes in the use of such freedom; without such presupposition, the argument that individual liberty is a value-in-itself would surely not be espoused. It must further be presupposed that rational purposes can be effectively harnessed to rational means in order to achieve rational outcomes; and that the irrational use of such freedom, presumed always to be that to which only a minority of citizens will be disposed, will not be so potent in its purposes and effects as to undo, or overthrow, the rational uses to which the majority of citizens puts its same freedom.

As I have already indicated, taboo continues in the corrupted liberal order to prevent the rejection, or even the radical questioning, of the assumption of reason, and to refuse Spinoza's warning [sect. 45]. Indeed, this taboo is the very totem of the corrupted liberal order, a totem which stands unshaken in the midst of every assault upon the civic bond; on it the 'triumph' of the politics of dutiless right, and the accelerating process of civic disaggregation, make little impression. The early lack of illusion of Mill himself as to the 'modern spirit of liberty' led him to refer to it ('Guizot's Essays and Lectures on History' (1845), in *Dissertations and Discussions*, vol. 2, London, 1859, pp. 244–5) as no more than the 'self-will of the savage, moderated and limited by the demands of civilised life'. But such judgment, insofar as it might be thought to raise taboo doubts about the very assumption of reason, is one which the corrupted liberal order has rarely permitted itself to hear.

62. It is, however, in the interests of the sovereign civic order, and of its citizen-members, that neither the politics of dutiless right, nor that of the equal entitlement to right, privilege, benefit, and satisfaction of wants without regard to desert, nor the assumption of reason which underpins them both, should remain immune from moral judgment and practical rejection.

The assumption of reason is, in any case, often no more than a self-coddling vanity. He who judges *homo sapiens* to be rational declares himself to be rational also. But this vanity contains, in addition, an ethical judgment: the assumption of reason is an assumption, too, of the *reasonableness* and benignity of purpose of others. Indeed, the special inadequacy of liberal rationalist assumptions as to the rationality, and even the liberal-humane sympathies, of others lies in the programmatic discounting, as an article of faith, of the true meaning of that vast pall of suffering which human unreason has cast across the face of the earth.

In the era of the 'Holocaust', the assumption of reason is not merely abstractly Utopian but an offence against reason itself. In particular, it brings the policy-makers of the corrupted liberal order to make ethical and practical misjudgments of the motives and intentions of others which may put at risk the well-being, and even the survival, of the civic order itself. The assumption of reason has contributed to the decay, and even outright denial, of the principle of duty, as being an unnecessary imposition upon rational citizens who can be expected voluntarily to act the citizen's part; it has dignified such expectation as a virtue-in-itself; and, at the last, it has come, by the route of a series of logical and practical *non-sequiturs*, to ratify the politics of dutiless right as a rational fulfilment of liberal faith in the reason of the individual.

The rational, reasonable, benignly-intended and duty-fulfilling 'average citizen' of the corrupted liberal order is a creature of fancy. However touching the (liberal) faith upon which belief in such a naive construct rests, the citizen whom it posits is ideal, not real. Where he exists, he does not exist in numbers of sufficient magnitude in proportion to the whole to justify the optimistic assumption in liberal theory as to his ubiquity or the reach of his values. Nor does he exist in sufficient proportion to have been able inin practice to arrest the generalisation of a politics of dutiless right, or the accelerating process of civic disaggregation.

Moreover, expectation that such civic ideal, even if 'not yet' to be found in the plenitude of its existence, can be brought to gradual realisation without radical criticism and rejection of many articles of the unrealisable faith upon which it rests is itself beyond reason. The new civic social-ism of the future, whose lineaments I set out in Chapter Twelve, must be grounded in such criticism and the rejection of liberal illusion.

63. The assumption of reason, its ethical standpoint predisposing those who espouse it in the liberal democratic order to toleration of a politics of dutiless right, and hence to the undermining of the very ground on which they and it stand, cannot, especially if unqualified, furnish the premise for a body of principles by which the civic order might be safely and justly governed. At the same time, such false premise cannot be replaced by an equally false *assumption of unreason*. For the principle of duty is, *inter alia*, itself a rational principle, requiring rational actions by which it may be given meaning and effect in the civic order.

As I show in Chapter Seven, the principle of duty is also a principle which rests upon moral intuition, as well as upon rational calculation and action. Moreover, the founding fathers of the liberal tradition of political thought can no more be regarded as 'pure' rationalists themselves than they can be made responsible for all the ulterior degradations of the liberal ideal to be found in the corrupted liberal order.

The rational impulses which Locke attributed (*a priori*) to those who 'entered' the civic order in the first instance – as if such an historic 'entry' had ever taken place – had to do more (in Locke's account) with an uneasy or frightened awareness of the vulnerability of man in a 'state of nature' than with the settled condition of mind which the latter-day liberal rationalist optimistically attributes to the ideal member of the civic order.

It may be argued, once more, that the assumption of reason has invested Locke's 'natural man' with qualities he does not possess. Nevertheless, such search as Locke's for a rational explanation of human behaviour, and the hope of its predominance in the civic order, can no more be permitted to give way to that pessimism of the intellect which sees *only* irrationality in men's conduct than can the assumption of reason in its corrupted liberal form be exempted from the critique of reason itself.

64. The principal presumption upon which the ethically passive acceptance of the politics of dutiless right rests (and relies) in the corrupted liberal order is not simply that of the rationality, or

rational predisposition, of each individual member of the civic order. It is also presumed, more absurdly, that such rationality, or rational predisposition, is 'natural' or innate, self-developed and self-sustaining, and informs the conduct of the individual in the civic order.

The contrary presumption, a premise of my own argument and one upon which the civic social-ism of the future will rest, is that rational predisposition and behaviour, in particular of the individual *qua* citizen, require to be taught and learned in the family, in the community and in the civic order itself, and to be sustained by reward and sanction; and that such rationality of predisposition and behaviour is manifested in, and characterised by, observance of the principle of duty.

65. A second and related presumption underlying passive acquiescence in the politics of dutiless right, and which equally demands rejection, is similarly a product of false rationalistic expectation. It is the presumption that morally benign purposes and outcomes will generally prevail in the civic order over malign intentions and consequences without a powerful sense of the civic bond, without observance of the principle of duty, and without resort to sanction in order to enforce it.

66. Finally, the justification in the corrupted liberal order of the 'gamble of liberty' and of a politics of dutiless right, demand-satisfaction, and self-realisation through unimpeded freedom of action has required that the classical form of the assumption of reason be abbreviated and falsified in one respect above all.

This falsification has erased from memory and intellectual tradition the old arguments of moral and political philosophy as to the potential dangers which men represented for one another and for the civic order as a whole. 'The passions of men', Hobbes for example declares (*Leviathan*, Chap. XIX), 'are commonly more potent than their reason'; and 'if men had the use of reason they pretend to, their commonwealths' – or civic orders – 'might be secured, at least from perishing by internal diseases'. In his *Ethics* (X, 1180a), Aristotle, who held the view that the rational and the irrational constitute the 'two parts of the Soul', judges harshly that 'the mass of men are amenable to compulsion rather than to reason, and to punishment rather than to a sense of honour.'

Indeed, from antiquity to the early modern period, political philosophers who espoused the assumption of reason, whether as a premise or as a constituent element of their thought, did so with a vigilant sense of the risk that such assumption might be betrayed. An individual member of the civic order could, by his conduct at any time, demonstrate an unwillingness, and even an inability, to live a fully rational life; and, in the eyes of this tradition, to act anti-civically in a civic order is to set up a presumption of unreason. Moreover, not only is the possibility of unreason an ever-present threat, but the individual endowed with rational purpose and the brute beneath the skin are perceived to be first cousins, and can even be the same person. Those who are not 'rational creatures', Locke declares (*Two Treatises of Civil Government*, Bk. II, para. 163), writing within this tradition, are 'void of reason and brutish'.

Animal imagery is, in fact, a commonplace in the language of classical political and moral philosophers, in particular when a contrast requires to be drawn between reason and unreason in individual conduct. In Locke – whose entire second *Treatise of Civil Government* may be considered an essay upon reason and the rational individual on the one hand, and upon the 'way of beasts' on the other – those who commit violent crime are compared with the 'lion or . . . tiger, . . . those wild savage beasts with whom men can have no society or security' (ibid., para. 11).

The inference is clear that 'society' and 'security' are feasible only among those who are not-'wild' and not-'savage', and that only the rational, those governed by reason, are fitted for life in the civic order. In like fashion, Locke, remarking upon parents' duties to 'inform the minds' and to govern the actions of their offspring, speaks of the 'ignorant nonage' of children until 'reason shall take its place' (ibid., para. 58).

There is here no warrant for the falsified form of the assumption of reason which, in a corrupted liberal order, imputes to the individual virtues which he does not, and cannot without civic education, possess. In Locke, as in other early philosophers of the modern liberal ethic, the assumption of reason is hedged round with qualifications and cautions. In Greco-Roman and Judeo-Christian civic thought, the sense is constant of the exertion required if the fallible members of the civic order are to be raised, and kept, above the level of the merely 'brutish'. Freedom, to Kant (*Lectures on Ethics*, pp. 122–4), might be the 'inner value of the world' and the 'source of virtue which ennobles mankind', but it is also the 'root of the most dreadful vices'; 'all evil in the world springs from freedom'.

Thus, if the freedom of men were not 'kept within bounds by objective rules', asserts Kant, 'the result would be the completest savage disorder', for there could be 'no certainty that man might not use his powers to destroy himself, his fellows and the whole of nature' (ibid., p. 122). Old socialism, always ill at ease with the problem of individual freedom, and additionally deprived of a coherent philosophy of liberty by virtue of its rejection of the notion of 'human nature', preferred determinist 'explanation' of human misconduct to such Kantian realism as to the brute-within-us.

'Man,' Kant further declares (ibid., p. 249), 'must be disciplined' – and few liberals would have disagreed until the present era of the corrupted liberal order – 'because he is raw and wild. He can be brought to proper behaviour only by training. Animal nature develops of its own accord; human nature must be trained.' There must not be 'slavish compulsion', Kant adds, but 'if we allow nature unfettered sway, the result is savagery.'

From all this, the corrupted liberal order, with its falsified form of the assumption of reason, prefers to turn away, giving ethical pride of place to the politics of dutiless right, ensuring that the 'gamble of liberty' will be lost, and rendered helpless in the face of the accelerating process of civic disaggregation.

FOUR

The Civic Order
in Principle

Nature of the civic order – fables of the philosophers –
the individual and the civic order – nature of the civic bond –
disruption of knowledge of civic principles – the particular civic order –
self-defence of the civic order – the problem of scale –
the civic order and the state – the civic order as a moral order –
self-interest – civic education – old socialism and new –
the citizen and citizenship – civic consciousness or civic sense.

67. In the civic order [**sect. 4**], as in the community, the individual lives a life shared with others. But in the civic order, whether that order be of the nation or of the city, it is a life ordered to civic ends; that is, to the ends of the individual as a citizen. The citizen, whose membership of the civic order is generally unchosen and involuntary, and continues without the necessity of his consent, is *more* than a mere member of a community [**sect. 3**], or voluntary association of human beings linked by kinship, habituation, shared custom, or common interest. This is so, notwithstanding that community is historically prior to civic order as well as the first precondition of the latter's existence, and that a 'sense of community' is generally a powerful constituent of civic consciousness [**sect. 6**], and provides a strong impulse to the maintenance of the civic bond [**sect. 5**].

For the citizen is the member of an organised polity or body politic, whether of nation or city, which, however plural in its composition, is possessed of institutional coherence under the rule of law and a common ethical direction, is self-governing in whole (as in a sovereign nation) or in part (as in a city), and whose members are vested by virtue of their membership with generally unchosen and involuntary, but determinate, duties and rights.

Such civic order, whether of nation or city, exists to furnish its members with a refuge against their common vulnerability to the forces of nature, to provide them with security from the risks they may pose to one another, to promote by its actions their physical, moral, cultural, and material well-being, to safeguard the exercise of their civic rights and to enhance their mutual ethical relations by a just enforcement of the principle of duty.

This ordered community of citizens, or civic order, is by definition and necessity not a mere conglomeration or aggregation of people, but a coherently governed social body whose individual members are conscious of the civic bond, and whose actions are ethically determined by it. Where they are not, it is the duty of the civic order to enforce such ethic in the interest of all.

Nor is such civic order, when that order is the order of the nation, synonymous or co-terminous with 'the state', which is no more than an instrument of such civic order, in whose citizen-members, as a collective body, sovereignty ultimately resides. It is the civic order – not 'the state' – which is also the true locus of the 'public domain' or *res publica*, of which the city is a microcosm. Moreover, it is the ethical duty of the civic order, and of its instrument the state, to defend and enhance the sovereignty of the civic order – sovereignty being, *inter alia*, a principle of cohesion in the civic order – in the interests of the well-being of its members as a whole.

Since, as I have already pointed out [sect. 24], such sovereignty is imperilled and undermined by the process of civic disaggregation, and since observance of the principle of duty is a necessary precondition for the arresting of such process, it is an obligation of the civic order – as I discuss further in Chapter Nine – to enforce such principle in its own sovereign interest and in the individual interest of its members.

68. It is immaterial, in principle, under what particular form of rule the civic order, whether of nation or city, is governed and its

members represented in such government, provided that the civic ends delineated in the previous section are sought to be achieved. But it is only in a democratic civic order in which the political rights of the citizen [sect. 47] can be effectively exercised under the rule of law, that the sovereignty of the civic order can reside where it ultimately belongs – in the citizen-members who comprise such order – and be embodied in, and be defended by, the institutions of the civic order itself.

Nevertheless, the term 'civic order' is neither synonymous with any particular politico-economic system, nor dependent upon the existence of such particular system's institutions. Different forms of such system, of differing degrees of moral worth, may equally seek to maintain the civic order and the well-being of its members; the existence of such civic order is ethically and historically prior to the particular politico-economic system or particular institutions which may come to regulate it. So, too, observance of the principle of duty is owed, equally by 'left' and 'right', to the civic order itself and not to the politico-economic system which may at any time govern its affairs.

Conversely, the civic order owes duties to its citizen-members, as I set them out in Chapter Nine, which, under any politico-economic system whatever, it is obligated to fulfil.

69. For the main distinctions in the social and moral condition of man are not those which derive from differences in the nature of his life under one passing politico-economic system or another, but those which derive from the nature and quality of the civic order to which he belongs. His basest ethical condition is to live as a merely *ostensible citizen* of the civic order, and as a moral stranger to his fellows, in circumstances of accelerating civic disaggregation, and therefore of mounting insecurity and diminishing well-being.

In distinguishing between civic order and civic order rather than between politico-economic systems as the true ground of the differences in the social and moral conditions of men, there is immanent the distinction I have already established between 'community' and civic order, a distinction rooted in the deepest traditions (and lost ideals) of moral and political thought, and which serves to shed light on the purposes of civic order itself.

Thus, to Cicero (*Offices*, I, xvi-xvii), seeking the criterion of the civic in his own fashion, there are 'several degrees' of 'fellowship and society', or of 'natural conjunction and community', between human beings, even if all are – taken together – expressions of that humanness or natural sociability which binds mankind together; what the Greeks termed κοινωνία (*koinonia*), and Kant *humanitas*, or a 'habit of harmony with all other men' (*Lectures on Ethics*, p. 232).

Of such 'degrees', there is, said Cicero, that of belongingness to the 'same country, nation or language', which 'knits and unites men to one another'. It is a bond which is 'closer yet among those who are all of the same city. For a great many things,' he declares, 'are in common to fellow citizens, such as markets, temples, walks, ways, laws, privileges, courts of justice, freedom of votes, besides common meetings and familiarities.'

These may represent, in certain respects, a conflation of that which pertains (in my understanding) to 'community' and that which pertains to the civic order. But the distinction Cicero is seeking to establish is plain – that between 'natural conjunction and community' on the one hand, and civic association, or the association of citizens in a civic order, on the other. The impulse to the former is generic; the ground of the latter specific.

70. Indeed, each civic order, whether of nation or city, is a specific form of the civic, a social body with its own history, rules and widely-shared common customs and manners, as well as a subjective interest (or self-interest) in, and need for, its own cohesion. That the world is 'one great city', as Epictetus declares in his *Discourses* (I. xxiv, 1) is true, but true only as a civic metaphor for man's universal *humanitas*. For it is in the particular civic order to which the individual belongs that his *humanitas* is expressed (or denied), as a citizen with determinate duties and rights.

71. In addition to Cicero's 'degrees of fellowship' which culminate in the civic order, there are also differing degrees of human flux and disassociation whose tendency, unless resisted, is to carry every civic order, whether of nation or of city, towards disaggregation. Such disaggregation it is the ethical obligation of the individual citizen to resist, as I argue further in Chapters Seven and Ten,

unless such civic order is founded (as it only rarely will be) upon a principle of deliberate evil-doing to the citizens themselves.

Political philosophers have, in different ways, always sought to express their sense of this flux; that is, their sense of the tendencies to aggregation and disaggregation of communities and civic orders, and of the citizen's obligation – albeit formulated in varied fashions and embodied in varied rules – to resist the dissolution of the civic order to which he belongs. Thus, random human movement and unpurposive, or inchoately purposive, human conduct have been located by philosophers in a primordial 'state of nature', where aggregation is temporary and evanescent, where rights do not exist or are insecure, and where dutiful reciprocity and mutuality, together with the institutions which they inspire, can gain no lasting purchase.

In search of such ethical and practical goods, so the political philosophers' fables run – but pointing to the deepest of civic truths – the rational individual forms, with others, a civic society, or civic order, by which such needs for security and settled association might be met. In such civic order, by mutual compact and consent, the individual's rights, limited by association itself, are secured to him in return for the fulfilment of his duties to his fellows and to the order which he and they compose.

The civic order, further, stands or falls according to his readiness and capacity, and the readiness and capacity of the ruler he appoints, to maintain and defend it against its foes, both within and without. It is either implied, or explicitly declared, that the civic order remains a slender thing, encompassed by danger: a port in a storm which does not, and cannot, abate. A return to the primordial flux, or a resumption of the conditions of the 'state of nature', is understood (in such fables) to be the price of civic failure.

The parabola which such notions describe – that from flux to flux, or from political dust to political ashes – is a metaphorical representation of the threat and risk of civic disaggregation, a threat which (in the actual world) is constant and real. Thus, the modern civic order, particularly in its corrupted liberal form, is vulnerable to the disagreeable consequences of anti-social and anti-civic action by individual citizens, or ostensible citizens; to the undermining and even dissolution of civic and other social institutions; to the atrophy of the principle of duty; to the dispersal of voluntary association and the rejection of voluntary community service; to the loss of sense of place and to environmental harm; to the perishing of historical memory and to the decline or even refusal of educational effort and aspiration; to the surrender of the civic order itself to a politics of dutiless right, and to the neglect of the civic bond; and to other failures by the civic order to fulfil its ethical and practical obligations to its citizen-members.

Under such pressures, the civic order may pass through degrees of disaggregation, in which community is threatened, *humanitas* or natural sociability is harmed, and the degraded civic order threatens to become no more than a conglomeration of people 'whom circumstances have brought together and different circumstances will separate' (Mazzini, *The Duties of Man*, p. 57). Yet since the individual's well-being is allied to, and dependent upon, that of the civic order to which he belongs – a truth of which the individual is often aware only negatively, as when degradation of the civic order *harms* his interest, security, and well-being – resistance to such disaggregation, even if only on the part of a minority, also remains a constant prospect.

Moreover, 'men have a desire for life together', as Aristotle (*Politics*, III, vi, 1278b) declares, 'even when they have no need to seek each other's help'. On this, the principle of duty ultimately rests.

72. The true relation, an eternal relation, between the individual and the civic order to which he belongs, is both moral and practical, and partakes of but transcends the relation between individual and family, and between individual and 'community', as I have described it. 'To be no part of any body is to be nothing', wrote John Donne (*Complete Poetry and Selected Prose*, London, 1946, p. 456), 'and so I am, and so judge myself, unless I could be so incorporated into a part of the world as . . . to contribute some sustentation [sc. support] to the whole.' 'What is a man?' similarly asks Epictetus (*Discourses*, II, v, 4), and answers: 'A part of a commonwealth . . . and, next, of that to which you immediately belong, which is a miniature of the universal city.'

Such belonging, or 'incorporation', is generally involuntary, as I have already pointed out. Like it or not, know it or not, egotistical atom or not, the individual member of the civic order is a member and part of the whole; that is of a civic order which, with or without his consent, provides the conditions, rules and values (insufficient as may be) of his existence.

Moreover, 'the whole is superior to a part, and the city to the citizen', as Epictetus (*Discourses*, II, x, 1) declares. The individual, however, is *distinct* from the civic order, and cannot be permitted, nor permit himself, to be lost in a putative 'general will'. But he also composes the civic order, and while not subject to it – as I describe further in Chapter Eight – is bound to it by the principle of duty.

Indifference to the civic order, like ignorance of the law, is no excuse for the asocial. However 'private' or estranged from the civic order the citizen, or the ostensible citizen, may feel himself to be – and be in fact – such citizen is, willy-nilly, a part of the whole; if not in his own eyes, in the eyes of his fellows. And being so in the eyes of others (including in the purview of the civic order and its institutions), he is so. Consequently, whether such an individual may wish it or know it or not, he is in law and ethics co-responsible for the condition of the civic order as a whole; just as even his private-seeming actions or lack of action, behaviour and misbehaviour, help to determine the quality of life of the civic order, and make it what it is for others and therefore for himself.

It is, thus, as a member of the civic order that the individual becomes or fails to become in the eyes of others – and therefore in his own eyes – a moral person, or moral being. Likewise, it is within the civic order that he succeeds or fails in his practical efforts to pursue his goals and to realise his endeavours.

I therefore do not share that rabbinical ethic (Amiel, *Ethics and Legality in Jewish Law*, Jerusalem, 1992, pp. 51, 54–5, 71) which preaches, as a fundamental principle, the 'absolute freedom of the individual'; which declares that, 'although the public good is important', such freedom 'cannot be abrogated on behalf of society'; and which urges that 'society exists for the sake of the individual' – the Adam whose creation is said to have preceded that of the civic order. Nor is this argument made any more persuasive by the theocratic proposition that 'living like a bird in a cage, in the midst of society, a man cannot have a righteous relationship with his Creator' (ibid., p. 87).

Instead, I hold neither that the individual 'exists for' the civic order, nor that the civic order 'exists' for the individual. Neither exists for the other. Rather, the individual is (even despite himself) a member of the civic order, gaining a large measure both of his 'private' and his social identity from it, realising his ends through it, and discharging his responsibilities as a moral person to it. As I show further in Chapter Eight, to discharge such responsibilities is an act not of 'subservience to the public good' (Amiel, ibid., p. 87), nor of obedience to authority, but of the fulfilment of the principle of duty – which if not fulfilled, the civic order, acting in the interests of all its members, has both a right and a duty to enforce.

73. The civic order possesses such right and owes such duty to enforce the individual's obligations to it precisely in virtue of the fact that the latter's lack of autonomy – and, hence, vulnerability – as a single individual has drawn him into an inescapable practical and moral 'conjunction and community' with his fellows. His reliance upon them, and upon the civic order which they together compose, not only gives the civic order its *raison d'être*, but also gives it, acting on behalf of its members as a whole, the right and duty to expect a correlative responsibility from him in his relation with the civic order to which he belongs.

Moreover, such expectation, being equally addressed to all, also provides the moral foundation of that mutual responsibility among members of the same civic order which constitutes the *civic bond*; while the individual's reliance upon and duty to the civic order, on the one hand, and the civic order's obligations to him on the other, provide the moral ground of the relationship between the citizen and the civic order.

The civic order may expect such display of mutual responsibility among its members, and such fulfilment of the individual's duty to it, exactly as – and on the same ethical and practical grounds as – the individual may expect the civic order and his fellow-members to help him to meet his needs, including the need for security from harm at the hands of his fellows. Hence it is that the *civic bond* rests, in the first instance, not upon shared rights but upon reciprocal obligations; the sense of which, with other ethical losses, has been largely lost from sight in the corrupted liberal order.

The fulfilment, or requital, of such reciprocal obligations is, ethically and practically, as compelling as are the needs from which they derive, and more compelling than claims of right. Yet such principle of duty is not securely established in classical liberal political thought, despite the role (most frequently a minor role) given to concepts of duty in its works. 'God,' Locke tells us (*Two Treatises of Civil Government*, Bk. II, para. 77), 'having made man such a creature that, in His judgment, it was not good for him to be alone, put him under strong obligations of necessity, convenience and inclination, to drive him into society, as well as fitted him with understanding and language to continue and enjoy it.'

But no similar, God-given, and imperative obligations are attached by Locke to the beneficiaries of the mercy of civic refuge and protection, by which they may ethically requite the meeting of their needs, the exercise of their rights, and the fulfilment of their purposes. Where the fictional idea of an originating 'social contract' is adduced as the legitimating ground of the civic order, it is the calculation of individual interest – not the moral reciprocity of mutual obligation – which is made to determine its content.

And where, as in Locke (ibid., para. 163), mutuality enters in, it is merely in the form of a search by the members of the civic order for their 'mutual good', in which the terms for living in such civic order preoccupy the judgment of 'rational creatures'. In such preoccupation, the classical preoccupation of liberal thought, right has ethical precedence over duty; duty comes, in general, to be cast into the shadows; or is reduced, in practice, to no more than a gentlemanly expectation of decent conduct.

The source, or pedigree, of the selfish individualism licensed in the corrupted liberal order by such priority, and which takes or keeps with more eagerness than it offers or gives – whether the goods in question be political or material – is, however, older than the classical liberal tradition. 'To what end were cities and commonwealths established,' asks Cicero (*Offices*, II, xxi), 'but that everyone might be safer and securer in the enjoyment of his own? For though men are by nature sociable creatures', he tells us, 'yet it was the design of preserving what they had' – 'without any danger or fear of being deprived of it' – 'that first put them on building of cities for a refuge.'

Nevertheless, it is such arguments about the nature and ground of the impulse of association which themselves justify the principle of duty as I set it out. If, as Locke declares (*Two Treatises of Civil Government*, Bk. II, para. 13), 'civil government is the proper remedy for the inconvenience of the state of Nature', then the principle of duty as it applies to the citizen's obligations to the civic order which 'remedies' such 'inconveniences', even if imperfectly, is *prima facie* established.

The civic order may not, and arguably cannot, arrange the affairs of its members 'to the best advantage of life and convenience' (ibid., para. 26). But insofar as it constitutes, whether in the form of the nation or the city, a 'human refuge and place of cultivation', as Voltaire calls it, and is the inherited work of generations of endeavour, the citizen is, again *prima facie*, under an ethical obligation to prevent its disaggregation or dissolution by all means in his power.

Nor, as I show in more detail in Chapter Seven, does it require us to adopt, in the manner of Rousseau, oppressive and mystical arguments as to the primacy of the civic order over the individuals who compose it, so that we may explain or justify such *prima facie* obligation; nor to hold, with the philosophers of the medieval Italian *comune*, that without the civic order 'man is nothing, or less than a man'. 'Destroy this city,' the Florentine friar Remigio de' Girolami fancifully added, 'and a citizen is like a painted or a stone image' (quoted in L. Martines, *Power and Imagination: City States in Renaissance Italy*, New York, 1980, p. 128).

Nevertheless, it is also the case that the strength of the *civic bond*, that bond which governs the ethical relations between individuals *qua* citizens, is not reducible to the prompting of reason or the calculation of mutual interest alone; too thin, the proposition that 'what is common to . . . different interests . . . forms the social bond', as Rousseau himself reductively argued (*Social Contract*, Bk.

II, Chap. 1). Neither does the civic bond depend for its survival upon the support of the law, important as such support may be; nor even upon the shared assumptions of the citizens, and a common ethic. For it ultimately rests upon something deeper still: the intuitive judgment or instinct of those individuals possessed of *civic consciousness* that their well-being is an aspect of, and is determined by, the well-being of the whole. It is a civic sense which neither requires a fictional fiat to bring into existence, nor a mystical cause to explain, and which cannot be utterly destroyed even in the worst conditions of civic degradation and despair.

For in every civic order, as in every place of human community, such social instinct – which is expressed at its highest in the civic bond – is to be found. Human association cannot be sustained without it, and it is common to all mankind. Moreover, the forms of conduct which are required in order to live peaceably and trustfully in association with others (whether in the family, the community, or the civic order) are known and understood, or capable of being known and understood, by almost all; the forms of conduct which harm and destroy such association, likewise. More than an appeal to reason, interest, or a supposed 'common sense' is needed to explain the provenance and working of such social instinct, as it is needed to explain Plato's 'virtue' or Kant's moral law. But the social instinct itself, upon which the civic bond rests, is a universal commonplace, however it may be explained and however harmed and threatened.

74. The relatively simple schemata found in political philosophers' explanations of the *civic bond* and the impulses underlying it – however varied the terms and fabulous the concepts they employ – are not the less profound or true for their simplicity, nor the less persuasive for having been discounted or forgotten in the corrupted liberal order.

Thus, in his *Offices* (I, xvii), Cicero considers the family which 'inhabits together' to be, 'as it were', the 'first beginnings of a city, and ground or seed-plot of a whole commonwealth'. Further, he declares that 'most of us' – *o tempora, o mores!* – 'have our principles instilled by our parents' (ibid., I, xxxii). Or, with equal simplicity, he tells us (ibid., I, iv) that it is the 'force of reason' which 'strongly inclines men to keep up societies one amongst another'; it is one of the 'general virtues' of men that they seek to 'uphold society' and to 'keep up mutual love and good nature amongst mankind' (ibid.).

The arguments of a Kant as they apply to the moral status of the civic bond are only superficially more complex. The ethical and practical commands which the need to maintain the civic bond dictates to the individual citizen are imperatives of the moral law, and are open neither to the choice nor rejection of the citizen; nor, it may be added, are they subject to that relativism of moral values which the rule of a corrupted liberal order has imposed upon us. If Kant is followed, it is only the practical content of the principle of duty – which I discuss in Chapters Nine and Ten – and not the principle itself which may be put to question. For the latter is a morally *a priori* feature of any civic order whatever, while the civic order in turn is a precondition for a moral, or human, life. From the Kantian imperative, there is little escape.

A less strenuous moral justification for the principle of duty than Kant's, and a less forced historical legitimation for the principle of duty than that which might be furnished by the imaginary 'social contract', can be arrived at, as I do, from the facts and needs of human association itself. Yet the forms of traditional argument as to the true nature of the civic bond challenge the absence of such arguments and concerns in the corrupted liberal orders. But the challenge falls on deaf ears: the rule of dutiless right, demand-satisfaction, and self-realisation through unimpeded freedom of action implies (and even imposes) the suppression and discarding of inherited civic principles which might stand in its way. For only thus can legitimacy be given to the moral agnosticism from which the corrupted liberal order draws its strength, and in which it flounders.

The discounting of the classical principles of the civic order – as under the pressures of the radical utilitarianism of Jeremy Bentham, who led the nineteenth-century liberal assault on traditional civic concepts and terms – can now be seen to have done great harm to our knowledge of the civic order itself. The transmission of civic ideas was interrupted for more than a century by the combined influence of practical hedonism on the one hand and of class theory on the other. The old and deeply-pondered metaphors of the 'State of Nature' and the 'Social Contract' were replaced by the banality of the 'greatest happiness of the greater number'; the struggle to secure the civic 'Rights of Man' by the civic solvent of the class struggle.

Even where a residue of such civic principles remained in the nineteenth century, the form in which they were expressed became increasingly uncertain and apologetic. Thus, Mill could argue (*On Liberty*, p. 134) that 'though society is not founded on a contract and though no good purpose is answered by inventing a contract in order to deduce social obligations from it, everyone who receives the protection of society owes a return for the benefit'; and T. H. Green hopefully declared it to be a 'presumption' that 'a man in his general course of conduct will of his own motion have respect to the common good, which entitles him to rights at the hands of the community' (*Lectures on the Principles of Obligation*, sect. M, para. 208). But such declarations, disjoined from any certain or coherent theory of the foundations of the civic order, were even then losing their ethical and practical force, as new popular expectations, claims, and demands carried the liberal order further and faster towards a politics of dutiless right.

75. The *civic bond* itself and the grounds for its existence are nonetheless bound to remain, however weakened the former by the gradual breakdown of civic tradition whether in political theory or political practice. 'We are nature's guests,' declares Kant (*Lectures on Ethics*, p. 192); 'we all have an equal right to the good things which nature has provided . . . [But] God . . . has left men to do the sharing.' This is a task of mutuality, or 'two-sidedness', which only an acceptance and respect for the civic bond, regulated by the principle of duty, could fulfil.

Nor can the discarding of the idea of an originating 'social contract' in itself dispose of the sense of mutuality upon which the civic bond rests. It is the 'tie', as Locke describes it (*Two Treatises of Civil Government*, Bk. II, para. 8), 'which is to secure [men] from injury and violence'; it is the sense of 'living for more than oneself', which, for Seneca (Letters, XLVIII), 'leads to our associating with our fellow men and believes in the existence of a common law for all mankind'; it is the bond which, in Christian ethics, makes men not merely 'members one of another' but their 'brothers' keepers' also. Such mutuality is inscribed in the Greeks' word for citizen itself. The Greek πολίτης (*polites*), or member of the civic order, means both citizen and fellow-citizen: the moral essence of the civic bond is in the two-sidedness of the single word.

In the midst of civic disaggregation, and against the world created by the politics of dutiless right – the 'right' to demand-satisfaction, the 'right' to a 'free market', or other expression of dutiless right – the civic order can still be recalled to the hidden bond on which it rests. For whether or not they know or desire it, men constitute a social body of whose ethical and practical purposes they are part, and to which they therefore owe duty.

At the last, not even the most corrupted of liberal orders can extricate itself from the civic tradition which it has inherited, and harms. As long as the civic order exists, the civic bond claims the citizen's duty, just as the citizen lays claim to right. The mutuality and commonalty discovered in 'civic society' both in ancient times and at the dawn of the modern liberal era, and by political and moral philosophers of every stripe, cannot be gainsaid.

The same private and public duties upon which the maintenance of the civic bond has always depended – whether they are the duties of the citizen to himself and to his fellows, or of the citizens to the civic order as a whole – remain our common obligation. The more is this the case where the duties owed to the citizen by the civic order and by its instrument the state are honoured, or are attempted to be honoured, under the (unwritten) terms of the same civic bond. For it is only on the basis of a reciprocity of obligation, in accord with the ethic of the civic bond and the principle of duty, that 'commodious and peaceable living' is possible in the civic order; that civic disaggregation can be arrested without recourse to draconian measures; and that the life, health, and true liberty of the individual can be preserved.

76. The *civic order* – the Greeks' πόλις (*polis*), the Romans' *civitas*, Hobbes' 'commonwealth', Locke's 'civic society' – is also the civic κόσμος (*cosmos*): a word which, for the Greeks, signified both 'world' and 'order'. Thus, μικροκόσμος (*microcosmos*) is both the

world-in-miniature and order-in-miniature. But κόσμος (*cosmos*), in addition, had the extended meanings of 'ornament' and 'honour'.

The *civic order*, in which life is ordered to civic ends, ends of public safety and well-being, and secured by the principle of duty, is also a civic *world*. Remote from the mere casual aggregation of men, its right ordering by its citizens for their common good is an *ornament*, or art, worthy of *honour*; an order, and a world, which by definition coheres.

Like the family and the community, such civic order, or civic world, is the epitome of human association. But, unlike them, its coherence is the work of institutions as well as of custom and habit, of the rule of law and not merely of choice and desire, and of constitutional and other formal regulation of its rights and duties as being public, not private, matters; in Greek, a single word, πολιτεία (*politeia*), stood for the civic order, citizenship and the constitution.

The *civic order*, whether of nation or city, is no mere genus. To be real, it must be particular, a particular civic order, with a particular history and evolution, particular collective memory and tradition, and particular heritage of past civic effort – which heritage it is the task of its present citizens to protect, adapt, improve, and commit to the similar care of following generations of members of the same civic order. To do otherwise is to fail to fulfil one of the principal obligations both of the citizen and of the civic order, as I set them out in Chapters Nine and Ten.

Each civic order is the product of a process of accretion, of a process of becoming a distinctive social entity, or social body, with its own civic existence, its own citizens, its own rules, privileges, and customs, its own political life, its own public buildings, markets, charitable bodies, hospitals, educational institutions, and so on. Nearly every civic order also possesses a history of past struggles for its autonomy or unity, or in self-defence against a foe; sometimes, too, of the imposition of common duties upon the citizenry in times of danger or crisis, sometimes of conflicts among the citizens over their various rights, claims, and needs.

More particularly, each civic order, whether of nation or city, has (often less palpably) its own character, atmosphere or ethos, much of which is known to, and understood by, its own citizens only. It has its own 'moral being'; that is to say, its own institutions (and habits) of mutual assistance, peacekeeping, public provision, education, and religious observance, or their deficiency and lack. It has its own aesthetic also; that is to say, its own outward appearance – 'if you have not seen Athens, you are a blockhead', declared Lysippus (fl. 434 BC) – dimensions, styles, materials, colours, textures, and configurations of buildings and open spaces. It has its own geography or location, natural environment, flora and fauna, and climate; and its own political and juridical system, that is to say, its own institutions and practices of public discourse and information, representation of interest, law-making, adjudication of disputes, regulation of rights, and enforcement of duties.

These are the means, and the means only, of the civic order, means which take particular forms in each. The end to which such means are directed, if it is to be real, must be a particular end: the well-being of the citizens of a particular civic order. Such well-being must also take particular forms in particular places and circumstances, but in general, and in its broadest and most necessary aspect, it signifies the citizens' physical safety, dignity and self-regard, health, knowledge, and the material means to the enjoyment of life in conditions of peace.

In Renaissance Venice, we are told by Jacob Burckhardt (*The Civilization of the Renaissance in Italy*, London, 1990, p. 63), the 'supreme objects' of the civic order – in which citizenship rights were severely restricted – were the 'enjoyment of life and power, the increase of inherited advantages, the creation of the most lucrative forms of industry, and the opening of new channels for commerce'. There were Renaissance philosophers who regarded the 'production of noble thoughts' as an end of the civic order; others, the creation of the aesthetic *città ideale*, perfect in the harmony of its proportions and forms.

But to the fifteenth-century Aristotelian of the Renaissance, the rightly functioning civic order was one, above all, in which the means of ethical and practical wisdom – the art and science of politics – were directed to the well-being of the members of the civic order, so that it might become in turn the school of such wisdom.

77. Now in the corrupted liberal order, where (generally) the overwhelming majority of its inhabitants are citizens, or ostensible citizens, it is not civic wisdom which must be taught and learned, but, first, knowledge of the existence of the civic order itself; not the ethics of Kant nor the politics of the Aristotelian, but, in conditions of accelerating civic disaggregation, the most elementary of civic manners.

However, as I show later, should the civic order – whether the corrupted liberal order or any other – fail in its own elementary duties towards the citizen, and should he come to lack the fundamental reassurances which the civic order is obligated to provide, then lack of 'civic manners', loss of self-regard, and refusal of the principle of duty become as one. The imposition upon the unwilling individual citizen of the constraints of belonging to the civic order sorts ill with the civic order's own failure to fulfil its essential responsibilities to him.

Nevertheless, offence to the civic order, and the rejection of, or wilful assault upon, the civic bond, offend and assault the ethical and practical ends of the civic order themselves. Moreover, the civic order has an overriding obligation to all its members – as I argue in Chapter Nine – to preserve and defend itself, while the individual's duty to the civic order is both morally prior and the logical first term in the preservation of such civic order.

This mutuality of obligation – that of the civic order to itself and to its members, and of the individual to the civic order – alone makes possible the securing of the ends of the civic order, as I have set them out. Hence, the obligation of the civic order to defend itself from assault has precedence over all other obligations to the citizens whatever.

78. The self-defence of the civic order from assault from whatever source, being a precondition of the securing of the well-being of the citizen-body, is a means not an end; the purpose of the civic order is not order itself, nor order for its own sake. Moreover, its duty of self-defence is not confined merely to the repulsing of attacks upon it from within or without. The maintenance of the

coherence of its institutions under the rule of law, and their modification and renewal to the same purpose, are equally defensive means of protecting the security, liberty, and well-being of its members.

The obligation of self-defence of the civic order as a precondition for the security and liberty of the individual citizen is a fundamental principle of classical liberal thought; Locke's political philosophy, no less than Hobbes', is a theory of civic order. Furthermore, although order is not an end-in-itself of civic organisation, the physical security of the individual citizen is preferable to his insecurity and fear, the rule of law – provided that the laws are not wicked – to arbitrariness and the corruptions of power, and sovereign self-government under the rule of the principle of duty preferable to the erosion of the sovereignty of the civic order under the rule of dutiless right.

At the same time, in a democratic civic order, conflicts of interest, freely expressed, are both an inevitable and a vital component of such civic order, over which a supposed 'principle of order' as an end-in-itself, or for its own sake, cannot be permitted to hold sway. Even if it wished, an ethical civic order, itself governed by the principle of duty, cannot suppress social conflict and internal division, such as that between economic classes. But it has an equally compelling ethical obligation, in the interests of the civic order as a whole, to prevent such conflict and division taking violent form.

Moreover, insensate forms of refusal of co-responsibility for the well-being of the civic order, and other expressions in the corrupted liberal order of the politics of dutiless right which threaten the civic order itself, cannot be considered as mere expressions of democratic choice, freely arrived at and requiring to be defended as matters of individual right. Over such acts and expressions the principle of duty must rule, including by means of sanction, as I show in Chapter Eleven.

79. The terms *civic order* and *citizenship* are, in the first instance, derived from, and refer to, not the nation but the city; just as the word 'Zion' is derived from, and refers to, not a nation or a people but a city, the city of Jerusalem. Such derivation points also to one of the main traditional concerns of political philosophy in the matter of the civic order: the 'problem of scale'.

That is, beyond a certain size of territory or population, so it is argued, there can be no 'real' civic order. 'If the number [sc. of citizens in the civic order] increases to one hundred thousand,' Aristotle declares (*Ethics*, IX, 1170b), 'it is not any longer a community'; the round figure of 'one hundred thousand', albeit plucked from the air, signifies to Aristotle a total from which a coherent civic order cannot be composed.

'An excessively large number [of people] cannot take on any degree of order,' Aristotle likewise insists in his *Politics* (VII, iv, 1326a); 'we know of no state with a reputation for a well-run constitution that does not restrict its numbers.' Why? Because, in Aristotle's judgment, 'in order to give decisions on matters of justice and for the purpose of distributing offices on merit, it is necessary that the citizens should know each other and know what kind of people they are' (ibid., 1326b).

Indeed, the Greek civic order, or 'city-state', like the medieval Italian city-republic, was of the scale of the modern municipality in extent; the civic order in the scale of the modern nation did not exist. 'The city,' said Plato of his own ideal (*Republic*, IV, iii), 'can be allowed to go on growing so long as it preserves its unity: thus far and no further . . . Only so will the city continue to be one city, and not a mere conglomeration of people.'

In his *Social Contract* (Bk. II, Chap. IX), Rousseau adopted a similar principle. 'The social bond is enfeebled by extension; in general a small state is proportionally stronger than a great one.' And, in an early critique of modern bureaucracy, Rousseau adds (ibid.) that 'administration . . . becomes more oppressive in proportion to its increasing distance. The chiefs, fatigued by a multiplicity of affairs, see nothing for themselves; and clerks govern the State . . . A body too large for its own constitution . . . perishes under the weight.' It has been a further orthodoxy among some modern theorists of democracy that such democracy is weakened, or even rendered nugatory, without effective participation by the individual citizen in the system of government and administration of the civic order.

If it is also true, as Rousseau argues (ibid., Bk. III, Chap. IV), that in a democracy 'each citizen must be in a position to know all of his neighbours', then the democratic maintenance of the civic bond (and thus of the civic order) cannot be secured under modern conditions; the megalith of the metropolis, in particular, must either be ruled by draconian measures or abandoned to disaggregation.

80. But it is not so. There is in principle in the civic order, as I define it, and in most of its possible political forms, a civic place and role for all its citizens, notwithstanding the 'problem of scale'.

For all citizens, quite apart from the fundamental (but not absolute) rights which they possess, normally and in principle require to preserve their self-esteem in the eyes of their fellow citizens, community neighbours, and family members; a self-esteem which, even in the most corrupted liberal orders, continues to be damaged and lost by acts which offend civic, community, or family feeling.

Hence, without imposition of law (and even without knowledge of the very existence of the civic order), the individual citizen in general remains morally susceptible to the demands, explicit or implicit, of the principle of duty. Moreover, there are relatively few able-bodied citizens in any civic order who *cannot* in practice, and if put to it, 'render a good service to the city', in Pericles' words (Thucydides, *History of the Peloponnesian War*, Bk. II, 137); and few citizens so estranged from their fellows in the corrupted liberal order as to be *unable*, in practice, to fulfil their duties to their neighbours, whether such neighbours are familiars to them or not.

In addition, the abandonment of the civic order, whether of nation or city, to its own tendencies towards disaggregation would represent abandonment by the civic order itself of a fundamental obligation to its members, dictated by the principle of duty. It would also import the negation of the civic bond, without the preservation of which the civic order itself must gradually founder.

81. Conflicts of interest, freely-expressed, being a component part of the life of a democratic civic order, it follows, too, that the voluntary organisation of such interest – including interests of party, and cultural, ethnic, professional, and trade union interests – is also a part of the life of such civic order; and that, in a democratic

civic order, whether of nation or city, its citizens possess a right (albeit not absolute) so to organise themselves.

The voluntary organisation and expression of such interests is also, in general, and in principle, ethically and practically distinct from that pursuit of dutiless right and demand-satisfaction which carries the corrupted liberal order towards disaggregation. For they are among the principal means by which the civic bond, and thus the civic order itself, is preserved in conditions otherwise beset by the 'problem of scale'. All such organised but voluntary expressions of interest within the civic order contribute to the well-being of the civic order itself, provided that they are in accord with its general ethical direction.

They should, therefore, in principle be regarded, each in its turn, as a microcosm of the civic order; should be vested with the maximum degree of civic autonomy and authority which is compatible with the sovereignty and well-being of the civic order as a whole; but remain always subject to the latter, and governed by the overarching principle of duty. Provided that they are not permitted oppressively to command the absolute loyalty of their members, they themselves also serve as schools of the principle of civic duty.

82. However, such (voluntary) organisation of particular interest in microcosms of the civic order is insufficient in itself to meet the 'problem of scale'. Therefore, the duties and rights with which the citizen is vested are required to be made in other ways as immediate, and as direct, as can be practically achieved. In the interests of the civic order as a whole, and in the effort to halt and reverse the process of civic disaggregation, the citizen's privileges, benefits, and rights – as well as his duties – must in principle be as closely attached to locality, and to their local exercise, as is possible, including for the purposes of serving as sanctions of the principle of duty; a subject I discuss further in Chapter Eleven.

Thus, to the rights of local suffrage attached to residence must be added other rights, privileges, and benefits specific to increasingly formal membership, or citizenship, of the local civic order. Likewise, to duties of (for example) local jury service or taxation, wider formal responsibilities for the well-being of the local civic order, enforceable under the principle of duty, must be added.

Furthermore, the civic order, whether of nation or city, however large in scale, is always capable of regional, provincial, and zonal subdivision in such ways that the duties and rights of the individual citizen can be given practical local meaning, and be exercised to practical local effect. The duties owed by the civic order to its members – including the duty of the self-protection of the civic order – also dictate that such practical and ethical solutions to the 'problem of scale' be found.

83. Under whatever form of political rule, the national civic order is sovereign; in a democratic civic order, the citizen-body of the nation is sovereign. In such democratic order, both the state and government – as well as other public institutions – are merely among the instruments of such sovereignty of the citizen-body, and not themselves the embodiment of, or the replacements for, it. It is a sovereignty which in a democratic civic order cannot be usurped by state or government, or by other institution, without in principle giving ethical entitlement to rebellion to such citizen-body.

If, for the Greeks, or for Rousseau, the 'civic order' and 'the state' were synonyms, or convertible terms, the principle of duty dictates to the individual citizen of a democratic order not duty to the state but to the civic order to which he belongs. The civic order is both ethically and historically prior to the state, whose interests the latter must serve; and the moral status of the citizen-body and its collective power greater than that of the state, however armed. For the state, like the government, is, in a democratic order, no more than an association of citizens vested with powers and functions by the citizen-body, powers and functions which the latter can withdraw.

But the aggregate of citizens in a sovereign civic order is an association which embraces all other associations within its bounds, including that of the state itself.

84. In conditions of civic disaggregation, as in the corrupted liberal order, the civic order gradually ceases to be sovereign. Its sovereignty may be usurped by the state or government itself, by a supranational body, by neglect of the principle of duty, or by all of them together. Where the state, government or supranational body have usurped the sovereignty of the civic order, the powers and

rights of such civic order can begin to be restored only by the radical strengthening of the civic bond, and the enforcement of the principle of duty.

In such crisis, rescue is not available through pursuit of the establishment of a transcendent or abstract civic order, incapable of doing wrong, possessed of a corporate personality and a single will and expressing itself through one political or socio-economic form only. Likewise, and whether believed to be divinely inspired or guided by reason, no panacea or Utopian schema, libertarian or socialist, can restore or redeem a civic order in process of disaggregation.

Indeed, the sovereignty and practical cohesion of the civic order rest not upon the rational or other perfection of its form, nor upon the powers of its passing rulers, but upon the strength of the civic bond. It is a strength, both ethical and practical, which is that of the citizens themselves. Only in observing the principle of duty, as it applies to the obligations of the citizens to themselves, their fellows, and the civic order, can the sovereignty of the civic order be restored.

85. This sovereignty is not only political and practical, but moral. The sovereign civic order, as it is constituted in principle, is, among other things, an ethical order, insofar as it depends upon, and has an obligation to enforce, the fulfilment of the citizen's practical and ethical duties to it of co-responsibility for its well-being. Similarly, the citizen is a 'moral person' or 'moral being' rather than a mere 'bundle of legal rights', being part, even if involuntarily, of a web of moral (as well as of political) relations [sect. 1]; and is vested with ethical duties of co-responsibility for the well-being of the civic order, some of which – as I discuss further in Chapter Eleven – can be enforced against him.

The civic order, being the ordering of that life which is shared with others in the community, is thus a moral as well as an economic 'commonwealth'. The notion of the 'civic', as in the terms 'civic sense' or 'civic behaviour', is an ethical as well as an administrative-political notion; and the civic order as a whole, for all that it may contain 'microcosms' [sect. 81] of itself in the form of voluntary organisations of the citizens' particular interests, is a moral (as well as a political) association of the aggregate of citizens, an association which embraces and has *ethical precedence* over all others within its bounds.

86. The civic order, being a moral order, owes its ethical responsibilities in the last analysis to its members, as I show further in Chapter Nine. They are responsibilities which do not give rise to absolute rights in the latter, and which are essential to the maintenance of the civic bond.

Thus, exploitation and abuse – economic, social or sexual, for instance – of the vulnerable and weak members of the civic order by the strong, since they threaten the well-being of the civic order as a whole, fall ethically to the civic order to prevent, by education, protective laws, and the enforcement of sanction.

Similarly, while conflicts of interest, freely expressed, are a component part of the life of a democratic civic order, where such conflicts derive, for example, from circumstances of economic exploitation, material hardship or abuse by the citizen of the politics of dutiless right – and particularly where such conflicts harm the well-being of the civic order as a whole – it is *prima facie* the ethical duty of the civic order to seek to remedy the causes of such conflict and harm.

Above all, as I show further in Chapter Eight, it is the obligation of the civic order, being a moral order, to prevent the reduction, as a result of its own default or neglect, of any citizen to a condition of life in which the self-regard of such citizen is lost, or cannot be sustained; and in which the fact of citizenship is deprived of dignity, meaning, and substance, or becomes indistinct from the condition of the non-citizen stranger.

It is also the obligation of the civic order, as a moral order, to ensure that avoidable conflict between citizens which damages the well-being of the civic order as a whole does not go unresolved; that the fundamental rights of the citizen are protected in their exercise; and that the principle of duty is not permitted to go untaught in the civic order, or to be flouted by members of the civic order without consequence or sanction.

87. In the civic order, as it is constituted in principle, the individual member plays the citizen's part, actively fulfilling his duties and exercising his rights. Belief that he ought to do so, expectation that he will do so, and ethical assumption that in so doing he acts the 'moral person' or 'moral being' are the characteristic expressions of a civic morality itself, especially in the democratic civic order.

Such civic morality may be defined as the ethical and practical embodiment of the citizens' collective self-respect as members of an association which embraces all others. It is manifested in the individual citizen as civic consciousness or civic sense, which takes practical form in the acting of the citizen's part in a civic order which is also a moral order, and in particular by the *voluntary observance of the principle of duty*.

To act so, despite its being an ethical and (in some circumstances) also a legal obligation of citizenship, is deserving of merit, whether rewarded in fact or not. Moreover, the degree to which the civic order flourishes as a moral order can in large part be measured by the extent to which the principle of duty is voluntarily accepted, and voluntary service – morally preferable always to service under duress – to the civic order is performed. That is, it may be measured by the extent to which time and thought are voluntarily expended upon the well-being of one's fellows, and therefore upon the well-being of the civic order as a whole.

It is not, however, the case that 'the better a State is constituted, the more do public affairs intrude upon private affairs in the minds of the citizens', as Rousseau would have it (*Social Contract*, Bk. III, Chap. 15). In the corrupted liberal order, in particular, resistance to the politics of dutiless right and to the accelerating process of civic disaggregation demands not the conflation of the domains of the public and private, of the elision of the latter in favour of the former, but the observance of the citizen's duties to himself, his fellows and the civic order in the interests both of public well-being and the liberty of the individual.

In circumstances in which real or sufficient effect is not given, by the voluntary practice of individual citizens, to the civic morality to which I have referred, the civic bond must come increasingly to be maintained by force of law and sanction.

88. That the civic order is, as well as a political, a moral order does not exclude the fulfilment of the principle of duty, on the part of

the individual citizen, from motives of self-interest alone. Between fulfilment of duty by choice, and fulfilment of duty under sanction, self-interest may make its own ethical and practical demands upon the individual.

Just as in the old Italian city-state the 'truly Italian sense of well-calculated interest' might dictate the 'sentiment of duty', as Burckhardt tells us (*The Civilization of the Renaissance in Italy*, p. 50), so in the modern civic order the fulfilment of the citizen's co-responsibility for its well-being may be dictated to him not by moral scruple but by similar calculation of interest, or in order only to avoid sanction.

But in the effort to halt and reverse the process of civic disaggregation, observance of the principle of duty from self-interested motives is itself ethically preferable to the non-observance or refusal of the principle of duty, or its observance only after the suffering of sanction.

Moreover, as Kant observes (*Lectures on Ethics*, p. 72), 'a man whose actions have *rectitudo juridica* [sc. are correct in the eyes of the law] may be a good citizen without necessarily being a virtuous man'. A civic morality which is manifested 'merely' in 'correct' actions on the part of the individual, or is expressed in habitual conduct without moral conviction, is again ethically preferable to an absence of such actions and conduct; and, in our circumstances in the corrupted liberal orders, could even be considered (if not by a Kant) virtuous in itself.

89. The civic order, even where the co-responsibility of individual citizens for its well-being is for the most part expressed in habitual action, action from mere self-interest, or action in avoidance of sanction, remains – whether actually or only potentially – the great school of education which Protagoras described it to be (Plato, *Protagoras*, tr. J. Wright, London, 1910, pp. 248–50).

It is so, too, whether or not vitiated by the defects [**sect. 86**] which it is the duty of the civic order to prevent and cure; whether or not ridden with conflict; whether or not in process of accelerating disaggregation. Life in the civic order is both the only ordered political life that men know and the only possible such life. It is the locus both for the practice of the virtues required in an association which embraces all others, and for the exercise of the individual citizen's rights.

Moreover, most citizens – unless they are 'out of their senses', as the *Protagoras* (ibid., p. 249) has it, or are otherwise disabled – possess both the will and the capacity to understand the nature of the principle of duty. Hence, as I argue further in Chapter Nine, it is the obligation of the civic order, in accord with the principle of duty itself, to *educate* the individual members of such civic order to their citizen parts, to instruct them upon the history, laws, and customs of the civic order to which they belong, and to encourage and promote the development of a civic morality within them.

The true end of such education, carried out by or on behalf of the civic order, is to render the object of it fit to be a citizen among citizens by 'forming his mind for the civil state' in Kant's words (*Lectures on Ethics*, p. 248). Without such education, the nature of the civic bond, upon which the civic order rests, cannot be fully known or understood.

90. The civic order is also the 'great school of education' in other than a literal sense, although such literal sense must be given urgent ethical and practical priority in conditions of civic disaggregation. Wherever a 'certain and regular method', as Cicero puts it (*Offices*, II, iv), is 'laid down for the conduct of men's lives' – not only by formal civic education, but by law and custom, the coherence of institutions, and the existence in the civic order of a common ethical direction – the 'natural roughness of men's tempers' is 'filed off', their greater mutual security is achieved, and their well-being is advanced.

But where, in the name of such well-being, the imposition upon men's lives within the civic order of a 'certain and regular method' is oppressive, put to wicked or chimerical political purpose, or becomes an end in itself – as when its end is lost sight of – such civic order ceases to be a 'school of education'. Instead, the civic bond is undermined, and, where mere order for its own sake remains, order itself is ultimately lost.

91. The civic order, as I have thus far defined and described it, is not only a moral order but a *practical social order*, the right principles of which I have termed a 'civic social-ism'. The new civic social-

ism, which I discuss further in Chapter Twelve, can, like the old [sects. 27–28], be grounded only in an ethical and practical judgment as to what is the prior or most urgent 'social question' of the day: in our time, especially in the corrupted liberal order, the question of how to protect and maintain the civic order itself, and not, as in the mid-nineteenth century, the question of how to alleviate or end the inequalities and injustices to be found within the civic order.

Hence, in accordance with my argument, the new civic social-ism I speak of is a social-ism of the civic bond, a social-ism which insists upon the principle of duty and its fulfilment. New socialists, whether of old 'left' or old 'right' in provenance and belief, constitute the party-of-the-civic-bond.

The principle of duty, the existence of the civic bond, and the dependence of the civic order for its well-being on both, were, from the beginning of the nineteenth century, gradually lost from view in the twin pursuit of (and resistance to) the *utopia* of the 'greatest happiness of the greatest number' and the socialist *chimera*, what-ever practical and ethical benefits each of them may be said to have brought to the citizen.

In particular, the organising principle of class deformed and displaced understanding of citizenship itself, of its duties and of the limits of its rights; militants of the 'class struggle' challenged and sought to replace the 'aggression of property or money' with the 'aggression of labour' (Amiel, *Ethics and Legality in Jewish Law*, p. 124). In aberrant interruption of the modern evolution of a politics and ethics of the civic order, old socialism sought instead to 'crumble the Golden Calf into small scraps and distribute them to all of mankind in equal measure' (ibid., p. 126). Both ethically and in practice the principles underlying such aspirations, however rational-seeming in many instances, failed.

A great and progressive renewal of civic morality is now called for. But if old socialists are to adopt and espouse a new social-ism of the civic bond and of the principle of duty – the duty of the citizen to himself, his fellows, and the civic order, and the duty of the civic order to its members – they will require to recognise that their authoritarian, egalitarian, redistributive, and welfare principles caused damage in practice both to community and to civic order; that in their communist party-state form they came near, in many countries, to destroying both; that the politics of dutiless right, of dutiless entitlement to benefit, and of pressure to extend the scope of both, is damaging to the civic bond and, therefore, to the civic order; and that a new social-ism, neither of 'left' nor 'right', can alone arrest and reverse the process of civic disaggregation in the corrupted liberal orders.

92. The citizen, as well as a 'moral being', is, as a member of a family, a community and a civic order, a *practical social being*, to whom the new social-ism of the civic bond and of the principle of duty is directed. His citizenship, sought by him in some instances but involuntary or unchosen in most, is generally the product of accident of birth and residence. But it nevertheless gives rise to determinate and necessary social interests – interests of the individual *qua* citizen – in the well-being of the civic order. It gives rise, similarly, to duties which are in their nature and implication social: duties to oneself *qua* citizen, and to one's fellows *qua* citizens of the same civic order.

The citizen, as a social being, has much on which he relies, and therefore much which he has a duty to protect and defend, in the civic order to which he belongs, however imperfect such civic order may be. The value – moral, practical, material, cultural, emotional – of such belonging may have been lost from sight, or its recognition be wilfully refused by the citizen, or even be discouraged in the corrupted liberal orders. But its value, an inestimable value, remains.

In the political vocabulary of mankind in all times but these, the very language of distinction between the civic and the non-civic, the city-dweller and the country-man, and the citizen and the stranger denotes such value: the value of the civic bond and of the civic order, perceived both as ethical values-in-themselves, and as values of a practical, cultural and material kind.

Thus, the Greek word for 'citizen', already discussed in another context [sect. 75], is πολίτης (*polites*), or member of the civic order. But the word for a 'private person', close enough to our 'individual', is ἰδιώτης (*idiotes*); a word also meaning 'layman', an 'ill-informed, ordinary fellow', and, by further extension, 'idiot'. Its derivation is from ἴδιος (*idios*), meaning 'personal', 'private', 'one's own', and, by extension, 'particular', 'separate', 'distinct', and by further extension 'peculiar' or 'strange'.

In fourteenth-and fifteenth-century Florence and Venice, for example, some two hundred to six hundred men at most were enfranchised in each city, and the power of officials was already such as to have begun to usurp the exercise of citizen right. Yet it is plain from contemporary sources that the nature of the civic order, the values and virtues of citizenship, the distinction between *cittadino* (citizen) and *contadino* (countryman), and the dangers of civic disaggregation were widely and fully understood. The history of such civic knowledge – a history whose evolution has only recently been brought to an end in the corrupted liberal orders – is the history of the civic order itself.

At the heart of this history stands the etymology of the word 'civic'. Its root is in the Latin verb *ciere*, to summon. The 'citizen' is *he who is summoned* by the principle of duty to assemble and take counsel with his fellows upon the safety and well-being of the ordered community to which he belongs. The 'city' is the place of such summons to duty; the 'civic' is that which pertains to, and flows from, such summons; 'citizenship' is the constellation of further duties, rights, and privileges which attach to the individual thus summoned.

The first or root meaning of πολίτης (*polites*), the Greek citizen, is not dissimilarly the *defender of the citadel* or πόλις (*polis*), which by extension came to signify the city as a whole; the ἀγορά (*agora*), or place of assembly of the πολίτεις (*politeis*), is derived from the word ἀγείρειν (*ageirein*), to collect together.

In both Greek and Latin, the citizen, 'summoned' or with others 'collected together', is identified by his active co-responsibility for the security and well-being of the civic order, which is at the same time the source and guarantee of his privileges and rights: duty is citizenship's first term, right its second. Such citizen must, by definition, also possess the predisposition and capacity to exercise responsibility when called upon – as by giving counsel to the citizen-body, or otherwise protecting the civic order – for, without

these virtues, such a concept of citizenship has neither substance
nor effect; eligibility for office was regarded as a defining characteristic of Greek, Roman and Italian citizenship, and even as synonymous with it.

But in any civic order whatever, ancient or modern, citizenship
requires the virtues which become a citizen, among them sufficient
knowledge to act the citizen's part. When 'citizenship' itself
signifies the possession of such virtue, to be a citizen is a proud
boast; those who in his day falsely pretended to such citizenship,
Epictetus tells us (*Discourses*, II, xxiv, 2), could even be punished.

Moreover, from the root meaning of 'civic' derives that adjective
of virtue, 'civil'. Thus, in Latin, civilis at first meant, neutrally,
'that which relates to a citizen'. It soon came, however, to signify
'befitting a citizen'; and, by further extension, 'affable', 'courteous',
and 'popular'. The sixteenth- to eighteenth-century evolution of
the English 'civil' followed a similar pattern. In 1494, it has the
meaning 'pertaining to the community of citizens'; in 1526, 'befitting a citizen'; in 1606, 'polite'; in 1684, 'human'; in 1691, 'decent';
in 1716, 'educated' or 'refined'.

But in the twentieth century, and in the corrupted liberal order
in particular, citizenship has lost such association with the extended
meanings of 'civil'; to be a citizen and to be 'uncivil' are not
contradictions in terms, for all that the ethic of neighbourliness
may, against the odds, survive. Nor could the specific notion of
civic virtue, known to all times but these, prosper in conditions in
which an individual may become a citizen by the mere issue to him
of a passport.

Not only to an Aristotle ought it to be preposterous that civic
rights may be bestowed gratis, without ceremony or oath, and
without correlative duty, *upon any individual whatever*; preposterous
that any citizen whatever should take his place in the civic order, in
conditions of accelerating civic disaggregation, *without civic education*; and preposterous that, in the corrupted liberal order, little
ethical or practical distinction should be made between the rights,
benefits, licences, and privileges of citizenship, but that all should
be conflated as 'rights' under the rule of the politics of dutiless

right, demand-satisfaction and self-realisation through unimpeded freedom of action.

The perception (in the citizen's own eyes) of citizenship as a privilege or prize is therefore ever harder to sustain. So, too, is the ethical and practical distinction between the civic and the non-civic, the citizen and the non-citizen, and civic right and civic wrong. 'Our conceptions of what a good citizen should be are all at sixes and sevens', wrote H. G. Wells in 1914 ('The Ideal Citizen', *An Englishman Looks at the World*, London, 1914, p. 336). 'No two people will be found to agree . . . upon what is necessary, what is permissible (and) what is unforgivable to him.' But such a judgment was already a consequence, and further intellectual cause, of the gathering pace of corruption of the liberal order. A citizen in 1914 was what he always is: a member of a civic order, more than a mere inhabitant or stranger, and subject to the principle of duty, whatever the politics of dutiless right in the corrupted liberal orders might appear to license.

Nor is a title to citizenship gained by the individual who, in Locke's words (*Two Treatises of Civil Government*, Bk. II, para. 122), merely finds it 'convenient to abide for some time' in a particular place. Likewise, 'submitting to the laws of any country, living quietly and enjoying privileges and protection under them, makes not a man a member of that society' (ibid.). The civic order, as it is constituted in principle [sect. 4], is not composed of a passive or inert aggregate of citizens but an active association of citizens which embraces all others, fashioned, modified, and renewed through time by its members, acting with institutional coherence and a common ethical direction; and resting upon the civic bond.

Moreover, citizenship is vested not only with fundamental and universal (but not absolute) rights, but with particular and valuable privileges and benefits, the suspension or removal of which – as I argue in Chapter Eleven – must once more become a sanction for anti-civic conduct. Citizenship, as membership of the civic order in the form of the nation or the city, cannot be prized, nor civic virtue be promoted, nor the civic bond strengthened, except where citizenship's rights, privileges, and benefits are plainly seen to attach to it, and where their suspension or removal represents a marked and felt loss to the individual.

For citizenship, like the civic order itself, is an ethical institution, and the citizen an ethical being. Both, therefore, must be subject to ethical rule, which penalises civic misconduct and breach of the principle of duty – including on the part of the civic order itself – in the interests of the civic order as a whole. By the same token, citizenship, being an ethical institution, cannot be vested only with rights, privileges, and benefits; thus reduced, it loses much of its ethical substance. As the ancient truths of the civic order disclose, it is not merely by exercising his rights, but in discharging his duties to the civic order, that the individual becomes a citizen at all. Conversely, to evoke in the individual a sense of co-responsibility for the well-being of the civic order, the civic order, as well as being a source of benefit and right, must possess a moral value in his eyes.

93. The civic sensibility which expresses itself most characteristically in the voluntary and spontaneous acceptance of the principle of duty is termed 'civic consciousness' [sect. 6]. Or, as Epictetus asserts (*Fragments*, LXXVII), 'cities are made good habitations by the sentiments of those who live in them, not by wood and stone'. At its simplest, such 'civic consciousness' is the 'sense of community' writ large in civic form; a consciousness that the individual is, in Aristotle's words (*Politics*, VIII, i, 1337a), 'part of the whole' and not an isolate atom.

But this consciousness is at the same time complex in its provenance – in family training, in community affiliation, in religious faith, in civic education, in moral emulation of others' example, among other sources – and may take diverse forms. 'Every single Jew', thus declares Amiel (*Ethics and Legality in Jewish Law*, p. 82), 'has within himself the central source of existence of the whole nation'; in this case, a consciousness of identity with a community, or people, which is emotionally and historically prior to, but an ethical component of, the civic consciousness of the Jewish citizen of a particular civic order.

Such consciousness of community, or of belonging to a particular community among the communities which compose the civic order, may in some circumstances make more difficult the vesting of the civic order with a common ethical direction. But it may equally serve as the means to a deeper understanding of the ethic of the civic bond, without the support of which no civic order can prosper. It is also as much the secret of the Jews' survival as it is of the survival of the civic order.

Civic sensibility, or civic consciousness, is also derived from and composed of *knowledge* of the civic order to which the individual belongs; of this knowledge, historic memory and familiarity-with-place are commonly parts. In particular, respect for place is both a source and an expression of civic sensibility, a respect which dictates protectiveness towards its appearance and aesthetic, as well as a desire for its maintenance, salvation from rapine, adaptation, and improvement.

In Pericles' funeral oration for the Athenians who had fallen in the first year of the Peloponnesian War (Thucydides, *History*, Bk. II, 38), he praises Athens for the beauty of its private buildings, a beauty to 'cheer the heart and delight the eye day by day'. Similarly, the citizens of thirteenth-century Siena declared it to be 'a matter of honour' that its officials should occupy 'beautiful and honourable buildings'. In Parma, the *piazza* was considered, under the city's ancient rules, a place of dignity deserving special protection; nor was 'respect for pure language and pronunciation', as Burckhardt (*Civilization of the Renaissance in Italy*, pp. 241–3) tells us, the least of such cities' civic concerns. In the time of the Italian city-states (and in modern times too), pride in the city's appearance and individuality was (and is) an expression of civic sensibility, or civic spirit.

The possession of such consciousness implies more than a passive awareness of whatever beautiful and good things the civic order has inherited as a legacy from the past. It also dictates a custodial duty – if necessary, to be reinforced by sanction – to pass on such inheritance, unravaged, to the following generation. Moreover, since the civic order, whether of nation or city, is an ethical order, its moral repute also requires to be jealously guarded in the interests both of the self-esteem of the individual citizen and the honour-in-the-world of the civic order to which such citizen belongs.

For without such forms of civic sensibility as I have discussed, it is not only the civic order as a whole which is diminished, but the individual citizen also; just as, without a sense of ethical and practical co-responsibility for the well-being of the civic order, the individual's sense of purpose is, in general, less. Conversely, when the individual citizen, conscious of his membership of the civic order – however flawed the civic order may be – no longer perceives such civic order merely as a means, his moral status too is enhanced.

This civic sense predisposes us to, and even informs us of, the principle of duty. It induces in us the desire for the well-being of the civic order, at best for its own sake, and at least in our own interest. It teaches the golden rule, either in its Christian form that the citizen should treat his neighbour as he would have the latter treat him, or, a higher ethic still, in its Jewish form: 'what is hateful to you', declared Rabbi Hillel, 'do not do unto your fellow-man' – the moral basis of the civic bond. 'This is the law,' he added, 'the rest is commentary; study it' (*Shabbat*, 31a; cited Amiel, *Ethics and Legality in Jewish Law*, p. 30). Jewish ethics does not consider it sufficient for us merely to 'do unto others as we would have them do unto ourselves'. For there is both egotism and calculation in this formulation, which, as Amiel puts it (ibid., p. 32), 'attempts to satisfy others with that which one considers good for oneself.'

For Hans Jonas (*Il Principio Responsabilità*, passim), the civic sense is, above all, a sense of co-responsibility for *the future*; that is, for the natural-physical environment upon which the very life of such order depends. ('Human beings are sentinels on earth', also declared Kant (*Lectures on Ethics*, p. 154), 'and may not leave their posts until relieved by another beneficent hand.') Enunciating an ethical principle close to that asserted by Aristotle (*Politics*, III, iv, 1276b) as to the responsibility of all citizens for the σωτηρία (*soteria*), or keeping safe, of the civic order, Jonas assumes that whatever is conducive now to the individual's general well-being and safety is likely to be so for future generations of similar human beings (ibid., p. 154); and that whatever intrinsic good is to be found *in rerum natura* and in the present state of things will also be found so, and needed, by future citizens yet unborn.

To possess such sense is, at its best, to possess an habitual attitude of civic awareness, an awareness which is required of every good citizen and which can be produced only with the aid of early training and education. But it may also be found in citizens who are otherwise less than paragons of virtue: 'free as he was in speech and morals', Burckhardt (*Civilization of the Renaissance in Italy*, p. 72) declares of Machiavelli, yet the welfare of the civic order was his 'first and last thought'.

In the civic order as it is constituted in principle, it is an awareness which may justly be expected of almost all its members. Moreover, if Florentine historians such as Guicciardini were 'citizens who wrote for citizens', then today's political philosophers must learn to write as citizens too.

94. This civic sense or awareness can justly be expected, in principle, of the citizen, but it cannot be presumed that it will be acted upon in practice. Moreover, insofar as it is a sense which derives in part from a rational understanding of the relation between citizen and civic order, to make such an assumption, the assumption of reason, is to commit the very error upon which (among others) the corrupted liberal order rests, and from which the politics of dutiless right derives.

In our conditions, the civic ideal of rational self-rule and voluntary observance of the principle of duty cannot be attained by wishful thinking, and without civic education and sanction. A Locke might suppose the citizen who has reached the years of adult discretion to be 'capable to know that law [sc. the law of Nature], that so he might keep his actions within the bounds of it' (*Two Treatises of Civil Government*, Bk. II, para. 59), and that 'when he has acquired that state [sc. of maturity], he is presumed to know how far that law is to be his guide, and how far he may make use of his freedom and so he comes to have it [sc. freedom]' (ibid.). This is the liberal assumption of reason in archetypal form, and applicable to all but children, 'lunatics and idiots' (ibid., para. 60).

Hobbes had no such illusion as to the rationality and civic sense of his *homme moyen*. 'Ignorance of the sovereign power in the place of a man's ordinary residence excuseth him not', he roughly declares (*Leviathan*, Chap. XXVII), 'because he ought to take notice of the power, by which he hath been protected here'; that is, in the civic order to which he belongs.

Now, taboo deters such bluntness. Worse, in the corrupted liberal order, the assumption of reason in the citizen, as a principle or article of faith of the civic order, itself goes hand-in-hand with ethically inert responses to assault upon the civic bond and, simultaneously, with the undeterred promotion of the politics of dutiless right. In other societies and other times, reproach of, and the use of sanction against, the a-civic and anti-civic were themselves marks of the civic sense.

The a-civic, or those with no regard for the well-being of the civic order, 'we consider not as unconcerned', declared Pericles (Thucydides, *History*, Bk. II, 40), 'but as useless'. *Ἀχρεῖοι* (*achreioi*), with its sense of being unserviceable to others, is a word of truly civic judgment. Conversely, 'whoever conducts himself well', thought Kant (*Lectures on Ethics*, p. 7), '*is happy*'; and to live as a citizen, or in civic fashion – *cittadinescamente viveasi*, Boccaccio called it (*Decameron*, Bk. II, 3) – was, until our times, seen as a means to such happiness.

Instead, the citizen, especially in the corrupted liberal orders, has been increasingly turned into a stranger not only to his fellows but to the civic order to which he belongs. With such estrangement, made profounder by neglect of the principle of duty as it applies to the citizen's duties to himself, his fellows, and to the civic order, the civic order itself must begin to fail.

FIVE

The Civic Order
in Crisis

Distinctions between the citizen and non-citizen – the civic bond
under stress – the ethical stranger and the forms of his behaviour –
the inviolability of citizenship and the 'new citizen' –
classical tradition and modern taboo – the universal plebeian defined –
the condition of civic disaggregation – the welfare state
and welfare-subject – losing the sense of the civic order.

95. Without distinctions of substance between citizen and non-citizen, or stranger, citizenship can have no significant meaning, civic morality and civic sense are diminished, and the civic bond and civic order are weakened together. In such circumstances, a further ground is given to the transformation, whether involuntary or wilful, of the citizen into a stranger to the civic order; and, from this and other related causes, the majority of the civic order may ultimately become strangers to one another, and live in a condition which I have termed *civic disaggregation* [**sect. 7**].

This condition in turn creates and promotes further degrees of estrangement of the citizens from one another and from the civic order to which they belong, and, in circumstances which conduce to it, may also arouse increased animus in the citizen towards the stranger. On this ground, among others, the significance of citizenship must be enhanced, especially in the corrupted liberal orders, and its content be restored, *inter alia* by the reassertion of the principle of duty.

96. It is a premise of my argument, as I have made clear, that every civic order rests upon the civic bond [sect. 5], and that it cannot rest upon relations of widespread mutual estrangement between citizen and citizen. Moreover, the civic bond, being an ethic shared by members of the civic order, and which dictates to them that they compose a single civic order (whether of nation or city) to which they are affiliated and bound by the principle of duty, and for whose well-being they are responsible in their common interest, can even less prosper in conditions of mutual strife or hatred.

Further, where, as in the corrupted liberal orders and under the rule of the politics of dutiless right, the very distinction between citizen and non-citizen comes to be regarded by many with disfavour – or may even be attempted to be set aside – the civic order, already under other and related destructive pressures, must come essentially to exist only in name: shorn of sovereignty, its authority usurped by its instrument the state, and its former existence unknown to its members.

97. Distinction between citizen and non-citizen (whether of nation or city) is not only a fundamental element of any civic order whatever [sect. 4], but rests upon historically universal means for establishing the integrity of the civic order as a body politic, and the identity of the members who compose it.

Such distinction was not only a constituent part of the civic consciousness of citizens of the ancient Greek and Roman worlds, and of the Italian city-states in medieval and Renaissance times, but in all societies until our times it remained – in one form and another, and with varied implication and consequence – the basis of the civic order itself.

Thus, Hobbes (*Leviathan*, Chap. XIX) defined 'strangers' as 'men not used to live under the same government nor speaking the same language'; Locke (*Two Treatises of Civil Government*, Bk. II, para. 122) distinguished between 'foreigners' and 'members of a society', comparing the former, as I have already noted [sect. 92], with those who find it 'convenient to abide for some time' in the 'family' of another. In ancient Greece, as in all times and places, residence alone did not confer citizenship; in medieval Italy non-citizen residents were called mere *habitatores*, inhabitants. Athenians of the Periclean age might claim that there was 'equality' between full citizens and 'resident aliens', but the latter remained non-citizens – disallowed from owning land, but liable for military service and paying certain taxes – unless citizenship was specifically granted. If it was not granted, the resident alien or μέτοικος (*metic*), although sharing some of the citizen's obligations and privileges, and benefiting from the protection of the civic order, was not considered a full citizen since he was not vested with the latter's civic duties and rights.

Indeed, the very word μέτοικος signified an individual who had changed his abode and settled elsewhere, just as the Roman *inquilinus* signified one who dwelt 'in a place not his own', whether a citizen or not. That is, they were both considered settlers, or biblical sojourners, although they might in due course be granted citizenship; in Athens they paid a special tax, the μετοίκιον (*metoikion*), for the privilege of settlement in the civic order of their choice. It is to be noted, too, that in the earlier times of Solon, foreigners might acquire Athenian citizenship but only on their special merits and to aid the civic order, as when they possessed a special skill and intended to settle permanently in Athens in order to exercise it. A variant regulation in Plato's Laws (VIII, 850) provides that metics could remain as residents in Athens for twenty years without paying the μετοίκιον (*metoikion*) on condition that they continued to practise their skill, and might stay for life if the civic order agreed to it.

But everywhere and in all times, a form of civic guardedness, just and unjust, may be found. 'It is the duty of strangers and sojourners in a place,' Cicero – who was himself a citizen *inquilinus* – declares (*Offices*, I, xxiv), 'to follow their own business and not intermeddle with anyone else's; not to take upon them what in no way concerns them, nor to be curious in prying into the secrets of a state with which they have nothing to do.'

Likewise, in *Deuteronomy* (XIV, 21), the Jew, contrary to the ethic discussed earlier [sect. 92], is instructed that 'ye shall not eat anything that dieth of itself [sc. from natural causes]. Thou shalt give it unto a stranger that is in thy gates that he may eat it, or thou mayest sell it unto an alien; for thou art an holy people unto the Lord thy God.' A not dissimilar discrimination is at work in More's

Utopia, where the citizens have 'treasure' set aside for the purpose of 'hir[ing] therewith, and that for unreasonable great wages, strange soldiers' at times of 'extreme jeopardies or in sudden dangers.' For, More explains (*Utopia*, Bk. II, Chap. 6), 'they had rather put strangers in jeopardy than their own countrymen.'

An interesting example in Hobbes of such moral distinction made between citizens and strangers is equally rough, but to the civic point, the point of the civic bond: 'If a man come from the Indies hither,' he declares (*Leviathan*, Chap. XXVII), 'and . . . teach them [sc. the indigenous citizens] anything that tendeth to disobedience of the laws of this country, he commits a crime . . . because he does that which he would not approve in another . . . coming [sc. to the Indies] from hence.'

At the same time, although, in Cicero's words, 'we should make a distinction between citizens and strangers' (*Offices*, I, xli), 'it is no small credit and reputation to the public that strangers never fail to meet with hospitality and liberality in our city' (ibid., II, xviii); he also calls such conduct towards strangers a 'bounty'. Likewise, the Greek word ξένος (*xenos*) meant not only 'passing stranger' but 'guest' and 'friend', even if Plato (*Laws*, XII, 952) thought that ξένοι (*xenoi*) who came to Athens in summer for trade should carry on such trade 'in the suburbs' only, and, after the summer, move on. For Cicero, however, it was to 'do ill' to 'banish all strangers and forbid them the city'; to 'exclude them from having anything to do there is plainly against the dictates and laws of humanity' (*Offices*, III, xi). Yet the civic distinction must remain; 'it is not fair', he declares, 'that he who is no citizen should have the privileges of those who are' (ibid.).

Moreover, the fact that such distinctions have served, sometimes cruelly, to dissever from the civic order the 'barbarian' and 'metic' in ancient Athens, the 'non-Aryan' in the Third Reich (with genocidal effect), or the 'alien', the 'immigrant' and the 'guest worker' in present times, cannot alter the nature of the *civic bond*, which remains one of the principal preconditions for the existence of any civic order whatever. However plural the constituents of such civic order, it is grounded not only in its institutional coherence and possession of a common ethical direction, but in its composition by a body of persons with determinate duties and rights, privileges and benefits, which – whether in whole or in part – do not belong to non-members of such civic order.

By not possessing them, they are distinguished from those who do, thus giving to the latter their identity as citizens, and particularity and integrity to the civic order to which they belong. At the same time, however benignly the non-citizen may and should be treated, according to the principle of duty, in an order which is ethical as well as practical, such non-citizens' circumstance must remain distinct in substance from that of the members of the civic order; not least so that the sanctions of duty, such as I describe in Chapter Eleven, may possess due force.

However, the distinctions established in the civic order between citizen and non-citizen are without prejudice to the entitlement, or otherwise, of non-citizen residents to become citizens themselves; a matter which nevertheless must remain within the sovereign discretion of the civic order itself.

98. 'He who is no citizen', or a stranger, is not merely the non-citizen who does not possess, or who has not yet acquired, the responsibilities and privileges, duties and rights, of the citizen. The stranger is also he who, whether formally a citizen or not, is estranged from the ethic of the civic bond and the purposes of the civic order in which he finds himself. Conversely, he who is not formally a citizen may be less a stranger to such ethic and purposes than he who is formally a citizen.

Thus, the merely ostensible citizen who exhibits an asocial hostility towards, or passive unconcern with, the civic order to which he formally belongs becomes a stranger among strangers, whether they be fellow-citizens or not, indigenous or migrant, familiars or 'aliens'. Since a citizen is an individual who, among other things, knows enough of his own society to act the citizen's part, a refusal, unwillingness, or inability to acquire such knowledge must also make him a stranger to the civic order; certainly, he should know more of it than the actual, or literal, stranger who is, or once was, recognised as a stranger precisely because of his lack of knowledge of the community to which he has come.

The citizen does not, however, become a stranger to the civic order merely because he opposes the particular politico-economic system under which the civic order chances to live. Indeed, where such system – as in the corrupted liberal order under the rule of the politics of dutiless right, or in the totalitarian socialist order under the rule of the party-state – bids to destroy the civic bond itself, the citizen who opposes such system may be a truer friend of his fellow-citizens than he who supports or serves it. It is those citizens who deny and damage the civic bond, and thus the well-being of the civic order itself, who are the veritable 'foreigners among citizens', as Rousseau (*Social Contract*, Bk. IV, ii) described those who opposed his (fictional, or metaphysical) 'social compact'.

Equally citizens-turned-strangers are those who, in the corrupted liberal orders, refuse or know nothing of the principle of duty, and live instead by the rule of a politics of dutiless right and the satisfaction of demand. In such circumstances the 'individual', and the egotistical 'individualism' he espouses and pursues, become ethical synonyms for 'stranger' and 'estrangement' from the civic order. *For if duties without rights make slaves, rights without duties make strangers* [sect. 23].

No less turned strangers to the civic order are those who are enabled by privilege and wealth to find retreat, or exemption, from claims to their duty on the part of the civic order to which they belong. The atrophy of the civic bond is owed no less to the desire to escape the *hoi polloi* or madding crowd, and to turn the back ethically and in practice upon the deformities of the mass civic order, than to its correlate, the moral and other retreat of the 'universal plebeian' into his own a-civic penumbra.

Both contribute to the process of civic disaggregation. So, likewise, does the exclusion from effective membership of the civic order of those citizens, otherwise willing to observe the principle of duty, who are too poor or deprived to claim and exercise their citizen rights, an exclusion which is in breach of the civic order's own fundamental duty to its members, as I discuss further in Chapter Eight. In more serious estrangement from the civic order are those who reject the principle of duty – to self, to their fellows, and to the civic order as a whole – and are at the same time victims of the civic order's failure of duty to them; they are caught in a many-sided civic failure. These, though formally citizens, are also 'no-citizens', or strangers to the civic order. Only the general assertion and enforcement of the principle of duty, as it applies *both* to the civic order's responsibilities to the citizen and the citizen's responsibility to the civic order, can break this vicious circle.

99. Equally strange to the civic order are those citizens who, while claiming its rights, privileges, licences and benefits, refuse the ethic of the civic bond by denying, or even seeking to destroy, the common ethical direction of the civic order to which they belong; to refuse to recognise its rule of law is a comparable refusal. Thus, when the newly-made citizen of the civic order – such as the stranger-turned-citizen who was previously, in Hobbes' description, 'not used to live under the same government, nor speaking the same language' [sect. 97] – does not accept, despite his citizenship, that he is bound by the common ethical direction of the civic order he has joined, he remains a stranger to it and contributes to its disaggregation.

But in the corrupted liberal orders, it is often denied, falsely, that the civic order in question has such common ethical direction, or even asserted, more falsely still, that it would be beneficial to the members of such order if it had not. Or, equally, there may be little concern in the civic order with, or knowledge of, such ethical matters at all, so that the citizen's refusal – whether his citizenship be newly acquired or not – of the ethic of the civic bond and the civic order is regarded with equanimity, lack of interest, or resignation.

Yet the citizen (whether indigenous or by origin immigrant, 'alien', refugee, invitee, or other category) can be no true citizen, nor properly consider himself to be a citizen, unless he possesses at least a will to share the values – and not merely the rights and benefits – of the civic order of which he is a member. Nor is it a sufficient ground for objection that the civic order in question is ethically or otherwise wanting. Where, as in the most corrupted liberal orders, the politics of dutiless right and of demand-satisfaction suffuse and taint the entire civic order, the principle of duty nevertheless continues to dictate an obligation to uphold the ethic of the civic bond, as I set it out. For it is a principle which is governed by respect for the ethical virtues and practical necessities of civic association itself; unchanging virtues and necessities which are common to every civic order, however misgoverned, and never more to be defended than in conditions of civic disaggregation. 100. Refusal of the ethic of the civic bond is also refusal of the truth that, in the words of De Tocqueville (*Democracy in America*, p. 372), 'society can exist only when a great number of men consider a great number of things in the same point of view; when they hold the same opinions among many subjects, and when the same occurrences suggest the same thoughts and impressions to their minds.' It follows, too, that without some discrimination in the civic order as to the priority of certain ethical values over others, in particular when those values are clearly incompatible with each other, there can be no coherent body of values, or common ethical direction, at all.

In the corrupted liberal order, the rule of the politics of dutiless right helplessly permits not only the just dissent of a free civic society but the predatory egoism of a society without a governing ethic, in which the civic bond is discounted. That is, it permits not only the multiplicities and diversities of free association, opinion, and belief but the moral estrangement of substantial numbers of citizens – as many as a majority – from the civic order, to whose rights, benefits, and privileges they nonetheless at the same time claim dutiless title.

'Agreeing together mutually to enter one community and make one body politic', Locke declares in his account of the metaphorical compact upon which he believed the civic order to be founded, 'puts an end to the state of Nature between men' (*Two Treatises of Civil Government*, Bk. II, para. 14). But in the corrupted liberal order, the 'body politic' ceases to be 'one', and the aggregate of citizens of which it is composed ceases to be an association which embraces all other associations within its bounds. In consequence, and in relation to the embattled civic bond, many citizens remain in a 'state of Nature'; a large (and increasing) degree of civic disaggregation coexists with the maintenance of the civic order in form, if not in ethical substance; opposition to the civic bond – as on the ground of 'ethnic' particularity – is erected to the status of a civic principle itself; and the civic order becomes increasingly a plural association not of citizens but of mutual strangers.

101. In the name of the liberal toleration of diversity, rights to difference become, in the corrupted liberal order, rights to reject the civic bond itself; the rejection of the civic bond contributes to the loss in the citizen-body of its sense of a common ethical direction in the civic order; and, with a lost sense of ethical direction, even the most assertive acts of civic estrangement may come to arouse little or no civic response. In conditions where such acts of civic estrangement, as on the part of a militant minority of citizens, come to be feared by others, social peace may be purchased – by those fearful of offending minority opinion – at the price of the well-being of the civic order itself.

Moreover, as Hobbes forewarned [sect. 97], the new citizen in particular, emboldened by the lost sense of ethical direction which he finds in the civic order as a whole, and confirmed in his estrangement by the like-minded, may press social claims and moral demands (under the rule of the politics of dutiless right) upon the corrupted liberal order which he would not allow himself if the positions were reversed – that is, he the representative of the civic order and another the claimant.

In a further derogation from the civic bond, and in a moral world remote from the principle of duty, such individual may mount his ethical and practical pressures not only against a civic order which shows bias against him, but to which he does not himself wish to belong except upon ethical and other terms of his own choosing. In the corrupted liberal order, under the rule of the politics of dutiless right and demand-satisfaction, matters may come to a further pass still, in which the individual may confidently insist both upon his citizenship *and* his estrangement; and demand, from a civic order which he does not himself respect, that both his estrangement and his citizenship be respected.

And when such ostensible citizen feels most threatened by the just civic hostility which he has aroused, if he arouses it, he is likely to insist further upon, and even make a fetish of, his estrangement, openly asserting his rejection of the civic order to which he continues to belong.

102. Such parodic abuses of the civic relation, insofar as they flout the civic bond and threaten the integrity of the civic order itself, can be prevented from damaging the well-being of the citizen-body as a whole only by the enforcement of the principle of duty and by the use of civic sanction, as I discuss further in Chapter Eleven. Indeed, unless the civic bond is thus enforced, and reinforced, any civic order, simultaneously beset by this and other pressures which accelerate the process of disaggregation, may come to be morally overwhelmed by them; in the corrupted liberal order such process is furthest advanced.

103. It is the *ethical* stranger, not the *ethnic* stranger, who is the true foe, actual or potential, of the civic order. Ethnic identity, being inescapable and unchangeable, cannot be foresworn, and may make its own moral and practical demands upon the individual. But the claims and demands of civic identity – the identity of the individual as a member of a civic order which is the guarantee of his physical and legal rights – are morally prior.

In all circumstances, the ethical tie between men, the tie formed by their common humanity, has moral precedence over the ethnic bond, strong as the latter may be. The Jew, while being the world's archetype of the *ethnic* stranger and carrying his Jewish identity about with him – but not knowing when a next expulsion from the civic order might come – has (in general) sought not to be an *ethical* stranger in the civic order to which he belongs. Moreover, since the Jews' ethical principles, such as those laid down in the Mosaic Decalogue, have helped to form part of the commonly accepted ethical principles of the civic bond itself, the Jews themselves have had a moral predisposition to accept the principle of duty in the form in which I set it out in Chapter Seven. They have thus been able, whatever the civic animus which may (or may not) have been demonstrated towards them, to avoid at least some of the sense of estrangement which the applicant and new citizen may otherwise feel in an adoptive civic order.

But when the individual *ethnic* stranger is also an *ethical* stranger to the civic order of which he is a member or which he seeks to join – that is, a stranger to its form of the civic bond, common ethic, and civic sense, however atrophied – and, worse, insists upon such estrangement, the civic order will justly react against him. Indeed, a civic order in decline and disaggregation, provided that it is not also in a condition of moral inertia as to its composition, will be likely to defend its own particularity against such stranger with more ardour (and even hatred) than would a cohering civic order, confident of its ethical direction and future.

104. It is the ethical stranger, whatever his provenance, who remains the enemy of the civic order. The 'anti-social citizen', the citizen who rejects and acts against the civic bond, is a contradiction in terms.

Such a citizen, or citizen-turned-stranger, shows himself to oppose the common interest which brings men together in the civic order; he offends both the 'desire for life together', as Aristotle put it, and the prospects for that 'good life' which can only be secured in and through the civic order. In the corrupted liberal order, action taken by the individual against the well-being of the civic order as a whole, or anti-social action, is generally the expression of 'private strength' [sect. 30] – physical or brute strength, economic strength, political strength – exercised against the public good; that is, against the good of fellow-members of the civic order, and in breach of the principle of duty.

In the case of the individual, to act anti-socially and asocially is (inter alia) to be dutiless and to think nothing of it; in the case of the civic order, which may also act anti-socially through its representatives and in breach of the principle of duty, it is (inter alia) to permit, encourage, or turn an ethically blind eye to dutilessness and the flouting of duty on the part of members of the civic order.

It includes the condition in which the citizen does not know, and does not care that he does not know, 'how far he may make use of his freedom', as Locke put it (Two Treatises of Civil Government, Bk. II, para. 59) [sect. 94]. That is, he does not merely fail to 'keep his actions within the bounds of the law' (ibid.), but, oblivious, often wilfully, of the principle of duty, is unconcerned to know what such bounds might be. In such a condition – a relative commonplace in the corrupted liberal order – it is not merely the individual citizen's ungoverned exercise of his liberties which threatens the liberty of others, and therefore of the civic order itself, but ungoverned acts which are at the same time *unconcerned* acts; that is, acts which are not only anti-social but amoral.

105. The forms in which estrangement from the civic bond and from the common ethical direction of the civic order may express themselves are not confined to ungoverned and unconcerned acts which break the law.

In the corrupted liberal order, in particular, such forms are manifold, as may be expected under the rule of dutiless right and in conditions in which the 'gamble of liberty' is being lost. They include the refusal and abuse by the citizen-turned-stranger of the very privileges, benefits, and licences furnished to him by the corrupted liberal order itself; the refusal of work; the refusal and abuse of opportunities for education and training; the refusal and abuse of opportunities to be healthy and to live a healthy life; the wilful or neglectful spoiling of facilities established by the civic order for the public good; and many other similar or related forms, some of them involving the use of violence.

In most, perhaps all, of them, the 'assumption of reason' [**sects. 40–46**] can be seen to be falsified; in most, perhaps all, of them, the principle of duty can be seen to go unenforced; in many, the citizen-turned-stranger can be seen to be unable, without the prompting of sanction, to protect himself from himself, to his own harm and that of the civic order as a whole.

At worst, especially where violence is used against fellow-citizens in pursuit of individual interest (however misperceived), the 'lawless wild-beast nature which is in all of us', even in 'good men', as Plato holds (*Republic*, IX, 572), is made manifest; 'some men are hardly any better than wild animals', Aristotle similarly declares (*Politics*, III, xi, 1281b). In extremes of unreason, the citizen-turned-stranger may even *pride himself* upon his aggressive hostility to the civic order to which he belongs, and from which he continues to gain his security and his rights. 'Is there not [in men] honour, fidelity, justice?' Epictetus inquires (*Discourses*, III, xiv, 5). 'Then show yourself the better in these, that you may be better as a man. But if you tell me you can kick violently, I will tell you that you value yourself on the property of an ass.'

That some men may be 'transformed into mere brutes', as Cicero puts it, has always dogged the civic order. 'Some such there are,' he declares (*Offices*, I, xxx), 'who are men in name and not in reality'; and accordingly asks (ibid., III, xx), 'Where is the great difference between altering our shapes and becoming real beasts, and carrying the nature and fierceness of beasts though under the outsides and figures of men?' Sir Thomas More (*Utopia*, Bk. II, Chap. 9) likewise refers to the individual who 'hath availed [sc. made over] the high nature of his soul to the vileness of brute beasts' bodies.'

In the writings of political and moral philosophers until the present times of the corrupted liberal orders, extremes of ethical estrangement from the civic bond have been perceived as offences against reason. Thus, Locke describes the violation by citizens of the very laws of the civic order which provide for the preservation of their 'life and liberty', or 'mutual security', or 'security from injury and violence', as a 'varying from the right rule of reason . . . whereby a man so far becomes degenerate, and declares himself to quit the principles of human nature and to be a noxious creature' (*Two Treatises of Civil Government*, Bk. II, para. 10). Such are 'void of reason and brutish' (ibid., para. 163); violence among fellow-citizens is described as the 'way of beasts' (ibid., para. 180). Aristotle (*Ethics*, VII, 1145a) likewise contrasts 'self-mastery' with 'brutishness'. Indeed, at all times but these, times of civic disaggregation, ethical thought has engaged itself with the *beast-in-man* as a threat to the well-being of the civic order.

Not infrequently, also, such brutishness is ascribed to the failure of the civic order to educate the citizen correctly. 'Man can become the most savage beast on earth if he lacks training, or is badly educated', Plato declares (*Laws*, VI, 766); 'we must keep all that is of inferior quality unfamiliar to the young, particularly things with an ingredient of wickedness and hostility', Aristotle instructs (*Politics*, VII, xvii, 1336b); 'we must also forbid them to gaze at debased paintings and stories,' he adds (ibid.). But Aristotle's old fear of 'familiarity with wickedness', or of a 'gazing' at 'debasement', has now become youth's habituation, under the rule of demand-satisfaction, to the electronic enactment of violence, while the constraint which Aristotle proposed is itself the subject of corrupted liberal taboo.

106. The citizen-turned-stranger who anti-socially rejects and acts against the civic bond may not merely break the law. He is also the *unjust* individual who by his deeds, whatever their motive or explanation, offends Rabbi Hillel's injunction not to 'do unto others what is hateful to you' [sect. 93]. It is such ethic which informs Hobbes' judgment (*Leviathan*, Chap. XV) that 'he that, having sufficient security that others shall observe the same laws towards him, observes them not himself, seeketh not peace but war'.

That is, in unilaterally refusing the reciprocity of the civic bond [sect. 5], the citizen-turned-stranger threatens the civic order itself, whether knowingly or, as is common in the corrupted liberal order, without ethical concern for the consequences of his actions. For in the absence of a civic will to enforce the principle of duty, the acts of civic estrangement to which I have referred must gradually carry the civic order – despite the combined efforts of fellow-citizens to prevent it – to that condition which Locke also described as 'a state of enmity, malice, violence and mutual destruction' (*Two Treatises of Civil Government*, Bk. II, para. 19), whose extreme archetype was Cain's fratricide of Abel.

'In transgressing the law of Nature' – as by 'taking away or impairing the life, or what tends to the preservation of the life, . . . of another' – 'the offender', says Locke, 'declares himself to live by another rule than that of reason and common equity . . . and so he becomes dangerous to mankind' and to its 'peace and safety' (ibid., para. 8). Such 'other rule' in the corrupted liberal order is the rule of dutiless right and demand-satisfaction, expressed *in extremis* by means of acts of violent self-assertion. In these acts not only are aggression and moral unconcern typically combined, but the violent act is itself often thought by the actor to be justified by the common ethical direction (as he perceives it) of the civic order to which he belongs.

107. Thus, in the corrupted liberal order, it is believed by some – with resignation, out of apathy, or as a form of 'principle' itself– to be possible to accept ethically that a certain level of crime and certain forms of crime, now including the most heinous, constitute

both an inevitable and a tolerable norm. Alternatively, it is believed that no significant distinction can be drawn between present and past in relation to the frequency of type of assault on the civic order; but, alternatively again, that the risk of a Hobbesian 'war of every man against every man' (*Leviathan*, Chap. XIII) can be forestalled by the employment of ever increasing oppressive force, such as by means of enhanced levels of surveillance of the citizen-body, greater recourse to incarceration, and, even, resort to draconian forms of physical punishment, including the execution of those who most offend the civic order.

In the corrupted and confused liberal order, with the civic bond increasingly set at nought and a common ethical direction of the civic order increasingly denied to be desirable – or to exist at all – Plato's 'wild beast' in man is variously perceived as a phantom of the apocalyptic imagination, as an eternal presence, as a controllable social product, or, less commonly, as a significant threat to the civic order; and, equally variously, to be dismissed as mere fancy, accepted as an incubus, tamed or cured by social development, or crushed by repression. He is not, however, seen in general as the extreme type of citizen-turned-stranger who, in violently rejecting or assaulting the civic order, rejects his own citizenship, and its rights, privileges, licences, and benefits, as well as its responsibilities and duties.

108. In all times, save these, the citizen-turned-stranger has been the constant object of systematic ethical and practical thought upon the civic order, and upon the means of its self-defence.

Thus, to the Greeks, the anti-civic and non-civic citizen was ἀχρεῖος (*achreios*), without use, unprofitable to the community, unserviceable to others [sect. 94]; that is, an individual whose non-civic or anti-civic acts were *not needed* by others. Locke terms the 'corrupt and vicious' not merely 'degenerate men' (*Two Treatises of Civil Government*, Bk. II, para. 128), men who have lost the qualities proper to man, but 'delinquents' (ibid., para. 136): a word, whose full sense is now lost, which signifies those who fail in civic duty or obligation, and which only by extension comes to have the general meaning of 'criminals' or 'offenders'.

To act anti-civically, particularly if such action is physically violent, has, until present times, been to act in self-exclusion from the civic order. Thus, for Rousseau (*Social Contract*, Bk. II, Chap. 5), the 'malefactor' who violates his nation's laws – Rousseau is thinking of serious crime, including murder – 'ceases to be a member of it [sc. the nation]' and is 'not a moral person'. By his anti-civic acts, especially of violence against his fellow-citizens, 'any man, in what station soever', may take himself 'out of the bounds of civic society', as Locke puts it (*Two Treatises of Civil Government*, Bk. II, para. 94). For Mill, even 'despotism' was a 'legitimate mode of government in dealing with barbarians, provided the end be their improvement' (*On Liberty*, p. 23).

But, today, in the corrupted liberal order, the Greeks' ἀχρεῖοι (*achreioi*), Locke's 'degenerate men', those who to Rousseau were 'not moral persons', Mill's 'barbarians' and all those others who by their acts declare themselves not to be members of the civic order are protected by taboo from civic exclusion. Subject as may be to punishment (much of it gratuitously cruel and without ethical or practical effect), their citizenship remains inviolate, their dutiless right secure, the principle of duty unenforced against them.

109. In the corrupted liberal order, the ethical stranger not only may remain a citizen, armed with dutiless right and claiming title to the satisfaction of his demands, but bids to be – and is gradually becoming – the pattern of the citizen as such. This archetype of the 'new citizen' *is* the citizen-turned-stranger who remains a citizen while ceasing to be a 'moral person'; who rejects the civic bond, refuses the principle of duty, and by his acts excludes himself ethically from the civic order, yet remains a citizen for all that. He is also the egotistical 'individual', licensed by the politics of dutiless right, who, although no more than a self-interested unit in a civic order which he helps (with millions of others) to reduce to a mere 'conglomeration of people', continues unthwarted as a citizen of such civic order; the 'no-citizen' who is not only a citizen but secure in his citizen right.

Such 'new citizens' are of all classes and none, alike the 'universal plebeian' and the privileged purchaser of exemption from the principle of duty; alike the claimant of right to dutiless demand-satisfaction and the claimant of right to a dutiless free market, or to the economic exploitation of fellow-members of the civic order. 'Like so many cattle,' Plato harshly declares (*Republic*, IX, 586) of those for whom neither the civic bond nor the civic order exists, 'they keep their eyes downward, and pass their days consumed with insatiable desires'.

But, in the corrupted liberal order, the pursuit of insatiable desires to the point of rejection of the ethics of the civic bond is no bar to civic belonging. Indeed, especially for the already-privileged, the successful pursuit of such desires may become an additional badge of civic honour, whatever its consequences for the civic order as a whole.

110. In our circumstances, where the corrupted liberal order (whether of nation, region, or metropolis) is now generally of vast scale, the politics of dutiless right and demand-satisfaction has further encouraged and magnified the scale of such desires. Even in the diminutive city-states of ancient Greece their pursuit and satisfaction set tests for the civic bond, and for the common ethical direction of the civic order, which can be recognised today, not least in the disdain which was aroused centuries ago for the preferences of the *hoi polloi*.

Thus, 'in the theatre', declares Aristotle (*Politics*, VIII, vii, 1342a), 'there are two types of audience, the one consisting of educated free men, the other of common persons drawn from the mechanics, hired workers and such like . . . Each group finds pleasure in that which is akin to its nature . . . For the relaxation of the latter class competitions and spectacles must be provided.' Not dissimilarly, Epictetus (*Enchiridion*, XXXIII) speaks of the topics of 'gladiators, horse-races, athletic champions and feasts' as 'common subjects' and 'vulgar topics of conversation'.

In such philosophers' distinctions – over-fastidious, or just, according to judgment – a deeper apriorism lurks: the assumption that the educated are capable, almost by definition, of the self-mastery upon which the strength of the civic bond in part depends, and that the rest, the *hoi polloi* set to their base desires, are not. (A further moral assumption about the 'lower orders' in the Greek world resided in the very word βάναυσος (*banausos*), or 'mechanic', with its meanings both of 'working by the fire', and, by extension, 'illiberal'.) From such premises it followed that the 'lower orders' were perceived to require instruction in their duties to the civic order, most generally in the form of duty to obey the law.

'The vulgar sort of people', says Sir Thomas More (*Utopia*, Bk. II, Chap. 7), writing within this classical tradition, are 'most in number and have most need to know their duties.' Hobbes (*Leviathan*, Chap. XXX) similarly thought that the 'common people' should have 'some certain times set apart from their ordinary labour', in which 'they may attend those that are appointed to instruct them'; the alternative was the 'miserable and horrible calamities' which attend 'that dissolute condition of masterless men [who are] without subjection to laws' (ibid., Chap. XVIII).

But it is not only in the works of classical or traditional political thought that such sentiments – once glibly dismissed as mere 'class judgments' – are to be found. They are inscribed in every culture, and expressed in a multitude of related forms, both as reflex disparagement and salutary caution. 'The bulk of mankind,' declares Don Quixote, 'who have neither had a good beginning, *nor a rational continuance*, and whose ending shall therefore be obscure – such are the common people, the plebeian race' (my emphasis). To Burke (*Thoughts on the Cause of the Present Discontents*, p. 35), 'the opinion of the meer vulgar' was 'a miserable rule even with regard to themselves, on account of their violence and instability . . . so that if you were to gratify them in their humour today, that very gratification would be a ground of their dissatisfaction on the next'. Burke's 'swinish multitude' is Hegel's 'mob' and De Tocqueville's 'formidable rabble' in New York; it is also Marx's and Engels' violently (and even pathologically) described 'lumpenproletariat', or 'dangerous class, the social scum, that passively rotting mass thrown off by the lowest layers of old society' (*Communist Manifesto*, Part 1, *Collected Works*, vol. 6, London, 1976, p. 494). 'The mob, high class and low, judges by appearances, by the facade, the immediate result', Marx also wrote in a private letter (Feb. 4, 1871; ibid., vol. 44, p. 110) to his friend Ludwig Kugelmann; a judgment which, despite the careful insertion of 'high class', is in linear intellectual descent from that of Aristotle upon the tastes of 'common persons'.

Taboo in the corrupted liberal orders now forbids all such terms, and conceals the thoughts and experiences which have always underlain them.

111. In our conditions of civic disaggregation, in particular, such taboo – whether the thoughts it conceals be largely just or unjust, largely true or false – inhibits free civic debate and thus disables the civic order itself. Indeed, the corrupted liberal order now restrains a wide range of public sentiments and judgments upon its own defects while simultaneously giving licence to the politics of dutiless right and demand-satisfaction; and justifies both the restraint and the licence in the name of the classical liberal ideal which it has itself imperilled.

Moreover, without a free ethical critique of the forms of anti-civic behaviour no practical amendment of them is possible, nor can the civic sense be educated. No longer can a Hegel declare that 'when a great mass . . . suffers a loss of the sense of right of self-respect and of honour which arise out of one's own activity and work, this brings forth the mob' (*Philosophy of Right*, Third Part, sub-section 2, para. 244). Only in oblique and dilute terms – in meek reservations as to the 'tyranny of the majority', for example – is Hegel's argument permitted to be heard in the corrupted liberal order. 'Mass media', for example, is considered an acceptable term, but the 'mass-man' of the 1930s, for all that he is present in larger numbers than ever, has vanished. And with the failure of communism, which was ideologically less squeamish about its 'proletarians' and 'lumpens', so too have 'the masses'. But the 'individual' and the citizen-turned-stranger remain (in their millions) as asocial archetypes of the citizen himself.

To the taboo now laid upon criticism of the Greek βάναυσος (*banausos*) or illiberal mechanic, Hobbes' 'common people', or Hegel's, Burke's, and Marx's 'mob', the practice of old socialism in the corrupted liberal order also made its stifling contribution. Once a Heine could openly express anxiety over the '*wilden Heer des Proletariats*', the 'savage army of the proletariat' (*Collected Works*, Munich, 1968–76, vol. V, p. 185), and presciently declare that he had a 'great fear of the atrociousness of proletarian rule'. ('Had I not torn the crown [sc. either of King David, or the poet's laurel] from my head, and thrown it away, had I not donned a plebeian smock', Heine wrote ironically of his adoption of a left persona in the 1840s, 'they would have cut my head off' [letter to August Varnhagen von Ense, Jan. 3, 1846, cited in Prawer, *Heine's Jewish Comedy*, Oxford, 1983, p. 512].)

Old socialism's naive divinisation of 'the working class' has left its ethical mark. Today, despite the fact that Heine's fears have been borne out in the corrupted liberal orders, the taboo is intact. Mill, too, in the heyday of the Victorian liberal ideal, could refer to 'masses of merely average men' (*On Liberty*, p. 120); the ethically sterner Marx did not hesitate, in May 1850, to assail as 'plebeian' the hostility towards intellectuals being manifested in the nascent communist movement (*Collected Works*, vol. 7, p. 266). Now, the plebeian 'average man' of all classes and none is both a universal, and an increasingly prominent, figure in the corrupted liberal order; its archetypal citizen-turned-stranger and claimant of dutiless right. To declare so, however, still falls under corrupted liberal taboo.

112. The leading characteristic of the 'universal plebeian', of all classes and none, is a lack of civic consciousness or civic sense [sect. 6], and a consequent lack of respect for the civic bond and therefore for the civic order which rests upon it. In particular, such plebeianism is expressed in refusal, whether wilful, casual, or unknowing, of the principle of duty, whether in part or in whole, as it applies to duty to self, duty to family members (including to one's own children), and duty to share ethical and practical responsibility for the well-being of the civic order as a whole.

At the ethically-uneducated heart of the refusal of the principle of duty, and of the absence of civic sense in general, is a lack of sense of boundary and obligation, as well as diminishing respect for place and regard for the rights of others. Expressed and fostered by the rule of dutiless right and demand-satisfaction, it is the politics both of the corrupted liberal order and of the universal plebeian. The universal plebeian, a figure of all provenances both indigenous and 'alien', is the type of the 'ethical stranger' to the civic order to whom I have referred [sect. 103]; who, although a citizen, does not

play the citizen's part; and whose non-civic, and sometimes pur-
posefully anti-civic, conduct flouts the ethic of the civic bond and
damages the civic order.

113. Furthermore, the conscienceless universal plebeian, whether
male or female, whether black or white, and whether prosperous or
poor, having generally been formed in societies dominated by
masculinist values, for the most part perceives the virile self-
assertion of individual right as a form of 'strength', and observance
of the principle of duty as a form of 'weakness', or a surrender to
the rights and claims of others.

The increasing prominence in the corrupted liberal order of such
universal plebeian ethic threatens gradually to infuse the civic
order. Unless resisted by the enforcement of the principle of duty,
the universal plebeian's contempt for the civic bond threatens to
become that of the civic order as a whole.

114. The universal plebeian – today's civic correlate and heir of
yesterday's 'common persons' (Aristotle), 'mob' (Hegel), 'meer
vulgar' (Burke), 'formidable rabble' (De Tocqueville), and 'dangerous class' (Marx) – is, unlike his predecessors, set to become, unless
resisted, the representative 'citizen' of the civic order to which he
belongs and which he harms. For in the corrupted liberal order he
is protected by the legitimacy of the politics of dutiless right and
demand-satisfaction, which is his politics also; and this whether the
demand to be satisfied relates to welfare provision, to consumption,
or to the economic exploitation of others in the 'free market'.

Such legitimacy is one consequence among many of the misplaced 'assumption of reason' [**sects. 45–6**]; a legitimacy which, as
I show in Chapter Twelve, a new civic social-ism would deny. But
it also represents a corrupted liberal concession to the modern civic
order's new 'dangerous class', whose earlier plebeian incarnations
played volatile and unpredictable, but generally retrogressive and
sometimes violent, roles in the histories of their respective civic
orders. The acts of commission and omission of today's asocial
universal plebeian, licensed under the rule of dutiless right, may
justly be counted to be as harmful to the civic bond and civic order
as the readiness of his precedessors, changing with the political

tide, to take up the cudgels either in defence of the civic order or in assault upon it.

Now, the 'dangerous class' is constituted by the increasingly vast cohort, pacific or otherwise, of citizens-turned-strangers, whose dutiless actions and inertias are directed to the satisfaction of wants without sense of the reciprocity, or mutuality, of relations between fellow-members of the same civic order, or of their co-responsibility for its well-being.

Indeed, such citizens-turned-strangers in general possess an undiscriminating sense both of right and justification – a parody of the civic sense – which extends equally to actually existing rights, claimed rights, imaginary rights (as, for example, to a 'free market' or to public provision without limit), discretionary benefits, and other contingent privileges of the civic order to which they belong.

115. This sense of right, a further mark of the universal plebeian, was once perceived as the historic mainspring of civic liberty and progress. But it can no longer be considered as conducive to, and even less be considered as synonymous with, the common benefit or public good. For the sense of right of the universal plebeian is dutiless right, and (being ethically uneducated) is exercised without concern for the effect of such exercise upon the well-being of the civic order as a whole.

116. This lack of ethical concern is not attributable simply to moral fault, or defect, in the citizen-turned-stranger and universal plebeian. For civic consciousness, or civic sense, requires to be educated into existence by the civic order in fulfilment of its own obligations to its members, as I argue further in Chapter Nine.

Moreover, where such civic sense is nascent in the individual citizen it requires to be nurtured by the civic order, and, where made manifest in civic action, respected and honoured.

117. Even those corrupted liberal orders of which the number of citizens-turned-strangers composes a large and increasingly assertive part, and in which the ethics of the universal plebeian hold increasing sway, remain capable of observing the principle of duty as it applies to their obligation to provide a civic education to their members. Furthermore, the citizen as a 'moral being' continues, embattled, to survive. The existence of the civic bond, under

whatever pressure it may be brought, remains known to a large (if shrinking) proportion of members of the civic order; and the well-being of the civic order as a whole is understood by many to be the precondition of the well-being, material and ethical, of the individual citizens who compose it.

In addition, however prominent and increasingly legitimated the values and preferences, demands and tastes, of the universal plebeian – in particular, in the educational system and the mass media of the corrupted liberal orders – these values, preferences, demands, and tastes continue to be held by many in ethical and practical discredit. The criteria for discriminating within the civic order between the ethical and the unethical, the civic and non-civic or anti-civic, the social and the anti-social, the educated and the uneducated, also continue – even if with gradually decreasing success – to disable and to disqualify at least some of the presumptive rights and asocial claims-to-satisfaction of the universal plebeian.

Nevertheless, the plebeian armies, the armies of the civic night, continue to grow within the corrupted liberal orders. Creatures of the quickening speed of technical and cultural change and evolution, penalised by such change but also architects of their own misfortunes, they now constitute in almost every corrupted liberal order the new (but unnameable) 'masses'. Both contributory cause and effect of civic disaggregation, they are its symbol and symptom, citizens-turned-strangers in droves, conglomerations of people.

If the archetypal proletarian was, more often than not, employed, skilled, organised, free-standing, proud, respectful of education, and predisposed to the principle of duty to self and others, the typical plebeian is too often unemployed, unskilled, unorganised, not free-standing – but quick, rather, to transfer responsibility from self to others – demoralised and lacking in self-regard, disrespectful of education, hostile to the providers of public benefit, and not predisposed to the principle of duty.

118. *Civic disaggregation* [**sect. 7**] thus has many and interconnected causes. Among them are the lost sense of the significance of membership of the civic order, national and local; the flux and heterogeneity of populations; the scale of the civic order; the diminished sovereignty of the civic order and its usurpation by the state and supranational bodies; the failure of the civic order to fulfil certain of its ethical and practical obligations to the citizen-body, to be discussed further in Chapter Nine; the strength and secrecy of bureaucracy and the remoteness and inaccessibility of authority in the civic order; the obstacles and difficulties put in the way of the civically-minded who wish to play the citizen's part; the failure and absence of civic education; the discrediting of civic morality and the civic bond; the gradual transformation of the citizenry and its common civic interests into a constellation of minorities and minority interests; the transformation of many free citizens into welfare-subjects; violence and the fear of violence, including of random violence in the public places and thoroughfares of the civic order; and, as both cause and further consequence of such con-ditions, the rule in the corrupted liberal orders of the universal plebeian politics of dutiless right and demand-satisfaction, whether such demand be for free benefit, free market or other freedom from the principle of duty.

119. In such conditions, particularly those marked by flux and heterogeneity of population in a large-scale civic order where sense of citizenship is lost, where civic authority is remote, and where the politics of dutiless right prevails, most citizens, or ostensible citizens, are strangers to each other in an increasingly strange land, and the passer-by an atom with neither local habitation nor name.

Where, in addition to such flux and mutual estrangement, there is random aggression, large-scale family breakdown, long-term unemployment and lost respect for place, the civic order gradually becomes a shadow of itself and loses its meaning. In such conditions – described by Hobbes (*Leviathan*, Chap. XXIX) as the 'irregular jostling and hewing [of] one another' – the citizen's 'true self' or 'identity', thought by Aristotle to be discoverable only in the civic order through association *with* others, comes to require protection by the civic order *from* others. Yet it is precisely in such conditions that the civic order finds growing difficulty in providing such protection.

120. But, as I have already pointed out [sect. 117], in the most unpromising circumstances the civic bond, wearing out or attenuated

as may be, generally holds. It does not break; the civic minority continues to repair and maintain it. *In extremis*, community, fellowship, and civic association survive, against the odds; community and fellowship may even flourish as the civic order staggers. However, it is also in such conditions that the civic order is under its greatest obligation to the civic-minded minority which supports it to enforce the principle of duty upon all; and in such conditions that the civic order, in particular the corrupted liberal order, appears least able, and even least willing, to do so.

121. This paralysis of will in the corrupted liberal order is both contributory cause and further consequence of the process of civic disaggregation. But it is only part of a more general ethical paraplegia in such civic order, in which non-observance of the principle of duty afflicts equally both citizen and civic order.

A ground of this complex reciprocal failure, in which citizen and civic order cease to act ethically towards one another, can often be found in the usurpation of the sovereignty of the civic order, earlier referred to [sects. 29, 83–5]. For one of the principal consequences of such usurpation is to supplant the true relationship between the citizen and the civic order, governed by the civic bond, with a non-civic and anti-civic relation between the citizen and the state, the latter the mere instrument of the civic order when the civic order is sovereign.

This process of displacement of the relationship between the citizen and the civic order had already been noted by Mill in the mid-nineteenth century, when he referred (*On Liberty*, p. 201) to the condition under which 'the public, accustomed to expect everything to be done for them by the State, or at least to do nothing for themselves without asking from the State not only leave to do it but even how it is to be done, naturally hold the State responsible for all evil which befalls them.' In such detachment of the citizen from the civic bond and from the civic order which it upholds, a process which simultaneously undermines the sovereignty of the civic order, a new and anti-civic relation is commonly established, especially in the corrupted liberal order and more particularly when it is in economic crisis or decline: that between *the state and the social victim*.

Old socialism helped mightily to draw the veil of further taboo over such process of asocialisation, even if Engels, for example, was not reticent on the subject. In 1833, the Poor Law Commissioners issued a harsh (and largely unjust) criticism of the maintenance of the poor and the unemployed on the rates, describing the system as a 'national provision for discouraging the honest and industrious, and [for] protecting the lazy, vicious and improvident'. It was also, they declared, 'calculated to destroy the bonds of family life . . . and ruin the taxpayers'.

To this declaration Engels responded in *The Condition of the Working Class in England* (Leipzig, 1845, London, 1892, p. 286). *'This description of the action of the old Poor Law is certainly correct; relief fosters laziness* [my emphasis]', he asserted; and, 'under present social conditions' – or, as we might say, under the rule of the politics of dutiless right and satisfaction of demand – 'it is perfectly clear that the poor man is compelled to be an egotist and, when he can choose, living equally well in either case, prefers doing nothing to working. But what follows therefrom? That our present social conditions are good for nothing.'

122. The ethic of the 'welfare state' is, confusingly, part expression of the civic bond and part (now the greater part) a displacement of it. That is, it displaces the relation between citizen and civic order with that between the ostensible citizen, often no more than a welfare-subject, and the bureaucratic officials of the state.

By assuming responsibility for wide areas of traditional personal obligation, once governed by the principle of duty as it applies to responsibilities to self, to one's familiars, to one's fellow-citizens, and to the civic order as a whole, such officials have served as further solvents of the principle of duty itself. Moreover, when the servants of a state – its nurses, social workers, home visitors, probation officers, and many other personnel – begin to live the absolved citizen's own moral life for him, to that extent such citizen may cease himself to be a 'moral being', arid thus become less, not more, of a citizen than he was before.

123. In conditions of civic disaggregation, some forms of welfare provision are also employed by the state, and welcomed by the state's welfare-subjects, as compensations for the very civic

disaggregation to which such provision contributes. Moreover, despite the practical necessity and ethical justice of much of this provision, which the principle of duty makes it obligatory for the civic order to furnish to those citizens who are in need of it – but not otherwise – such provision is perceived by many of its recipients as a mere object of dutiless consumer-demand. That is, in corrupted liberal orders welfare provision is often seen as an object of the politics of dutiless right and demand-satisfaction.

124. As early as the mid-1830s, De Tocqueville (*Democracy in America*, p. 310) described, or foresaw, a condition of democracy in which 'every citizen, being . . . equally dependent, has only his personal impotence to oppose to the organised force of the Government'; a condition which he further compared (ibid.) with those in which citizens could 'no longer protect themselves'. It is in such circumstances, present in corrupted liberal orders, that the sovereignty of the free citizen, and therefore of the civic order to which he belongs – but not the strength of the state – is weakened or lost; that the powers of the free citizen, enhanced by some forms of public provision but diminished by others, come to be the powers, such as they are, of the welfare-subject; and that the civic order and the citizen lose what the state and the state official gain.

125. In the flux and heterogeneity of populations, and amid the civic disaggregation to which they contribute, the mechanism of public provision also serves, for many citizens-turned-strangers, as the only point of contact between themselves and the civic order, albeit mediated through minor officials of the state. Needed or unneeded, it becomes a symbol of continuity and regularity in the prevailing uncertainty and disarray.

For those who do not regard such provision as a mere object of dutiless right and demand-satisfaction, it also serves as a substantial practical expression of the ethic of the civic bond. Where the citizen-body is being transformed by pressures-to-civic-disaggregation into an increasingly randomly associated mass of individuals, the common receipt of the benefits of public provision constitutes a form of moral tie, however tenuous, between them.

Moreover, in circumstances in which meretriciousness, empty sensation-mongering, and what the historian Burckhardt called

(*Briefe*, p. 518) *effekthascherei* – a taste for cheap effects – lead to the smallest trifles being treated as if they were the weightiest matters, and all are encouraged to be in a 'perpetual state of feverish agitation' (De Tocqueville, *Democracy in America*, p. 405) over events and persons without ethical or practical significance for the well-being of the civic order, the very rationality – where they are rational – and practicality of the mechanisms of public provision may be considered an ethical good in themselves.

126. Nevertheless, the same regularities of public provision, when the habituated beneficiaries of it, being dutiless, hold such provision in low ethical esteem, also come to be seen as the debts which a corrupted liberal order is paying for the demoralisation of its members.

In such conditions, the due weighing of the common good cannot prosper when the citizen-turned-stranger can barely weigh his own. Moreover, in the corrupted liberal order, ethical perception, additionally ruled by a diet of substanceless sensation, is subordinated to the rule of dutiless right and demand-satisfaction: the well-being both of the self and of the civic order is lost from view in continuous distraction of mind and unfulfilled desire.

By the early nineteenth century, the acutest sensibilities of the emergent liberal civic orders were already aware of it. Thus, in 1826, William Hazlitt declared of the Londoner ('On Londoners and Country People', *Collected Works*, London, 1931, vol. 2, pp. 66–8) that 'time and space are lost to him . . . The world turns round, and his head with it, like a roundabout at a fair, till he becomes stunned and giddy with the motion. Figures glide by as in a *camera obscura*. There is a glare, a perpetual hubbub, a noise, a crowd about him . . . Nothing dwells long enough in his mind to produce an interest . . . He regards an obligation you confer upon him as a species of imposition . . . He talks about everything, for he has heard something about it; and . . . concludes he has as good a right as you.'

Now, the 'figures in the *camera obscura*', electronically reproduced, are seen simultaneously in every corner of the civic order. Or, the same shadows-on-the-wall are watched, alone, by nearly all

146

citizens, increasing both their demoralisation and their distance from the civic order.

127. It is in such conditions, in the midst (often) of an inordinate excess of population and (often) struggling with economic stress, that 'individuals', deprived of a sense of co-responsibility for the well-being of the civic order to which they ostensibly belong, must make their way. Conversely, it is with such citizens, or ostensible citizens, that the civic order must seek to compose itself upon the basis of a shared sense of the civic bond.

Furthermore, it is in such conditions, and others earlier described, that some – the protagonists of the process of civic disaggregation – can be heard arguing for the enhancement and extension of dutiless individual right, generally in the name of citizenship and the civic order themselves. But no civic order whatever can be composed of mere aggregations of dutiless individuals possessed of rights (and more rights), and rights alone. Nor can a civic order rest upon a civic bond degraded by ever greedier expectation of entitlement, on the ostensible citizen's part, to free benefit, the free market, unrestrained consumption, self-realisation through unimpeded freedom of action, and the free exploitation of others; and upon the manipulation of such expectations and desires by ephemeral politicians, pursuing their own electoral interests.

128. Moreover, in these conditions, *humanitas* – in Kant's sense, the habit of harmony and sociability [sect. 69] – is undermined and undone, or repressed by anxiety and fear. As the process of civic disaggregation continues, and accelerates, Kant's assumption of reason, which dictates that ratiocination alone is capable of revealing the moral law to us, becomes falsified on an ever wider scale, threatening, even, to be whittled away to nothing. And when the very elements of the moral world become arbitrary and indeterminate, and ordinary capacities to distinguish between good and evil falter, the survival of the civic bond itself is put at risk.

Nonetheless, every salutary movement of moral objection to such a state of affairs – objection frequently scoffed at by old socialism as a symptom of 'moral panic' – discloses that Kant's *humanitas* is still alive. So, too, are civic sense and the readiness to play the citizen's part. But pitted against *humanitas* is the refusal of the citizen-turned-stranger to take personal moral responsibility for his actions, whether they affect him, his familiars, or the wider well-being of the civic order to which he belongs; against *humanitas*, also, is the failure of the civic order, and of its instrument the state, to avert the increasing need of the citizen to protect himself by his 'private strength' (Hobbes, *Leviathan*, Chap. XVIII) [sects. 30, 104] from the injuries of others; and against *humanitas* is the 'apathetic' or depressed retreat of the citizen-turned-stranger from all concern or involvement with the civic order which is not to his own immediate interest or advantage.

'Under a bad government,' wrote Rousseau (*Social Contract*, Bk. III, Chap. 15), 'in the end every man turns his attention to his own domestic affairs . . . When once you hear someone remark, speaking of the State' – or, as I should say, the civic order – '"What is it to me?", you may give over the State for lost.' Today, in the corrupted liberal order, the citizen has more excuses, but not grounds, for such moral insouciance and civic retreat than ever. Among them is the incoherent sense he possesses of his own persona in relation to others, and to the civic order in general; a persona increasingly preoccupied with, and anxious for, self; a persona easily lost in a multiplicity of fragmentary roles, both active and passive, as family member, householder, wage-or salary-earner or welfare-subject, as taxpayer, 'voter', 'consumer', or 'viewer', or as mere anonymous passer-by in the flux of the city.

129. To such persona, association with others, including in intimate personal and familial relations, may come to appear, and to be, increasingly casual and random. The focus of the individual's existence may come to appear, and to be, increasingly lost; the citizen's life, even where it is not also so in fact, may appear to be spent in egotistical self-preoccupation *in vacuo*, or in a non-civic limbo, where the only remaining community – that of the millions and tens of millions separately watching the 'figures in the *camera obscura*' – is synthetic.

If much of this randomness, or sense of randomness, can be attributed to the 'benefits of free choice' in a liberal order, it is also the outcome of the corruption of the liberal ideal, and of the failure of the principle of duty. Casual, or casual-seeming, forms of association in some relations concern only those engaged in them. But in other relations – such as the marriage-relation, or the relation between parents and children – they go to the heart of the well-being, or otherwise, of the civic order itself.

130. The range and heterogeneity, as well as the fragmentariness, of the affiliations, private and public, of the citizen-turned-stranger, especially in conditions of mass population and plural culture, not only render the citizen-turned-stranger's sense of himself increasingly incoherent and unstable, but make of the civic order a hydra-headed body, duty towards which comes itself to be considered an incoherent notion. Where the citizen-turned-stranger belongs, equally casually, to everything and nothing, the very idea of responsibility for self, family, place, or civic order comes to have ever-diminishing meaning.

The weakening of such forms of responsibility and the neglect of the principle of duty in the corrupted liberal orders have damaged individual happiness and the well-being of the civic order together. In particular, the retreat from obligation under the rules of the politics of dutiless right has, in many societies, increasingly con-signed the government and administration of the civic order to some of its least scrupulous and disinterested members; in the worst of cases, into the hands of the corrupt and the violent, whose individual interests become the interests of the civic order as a whole.

SIX

Law, Justice, and
Civic Order

The unjust individual – the principle of duty and the law –
political obligation and obedience – knowledge of the law –
law and peace – the rule of law – Utopian forms of justice –
old socialism and 'bourgeois' law – the code of law and the civic bond –
law and a common rule – law and civic sense – law and toleration –
law and equal justice – justice and desert, or merit – law and violence –
law, liberty and duty.

131. To help retrace the steps taken by the civic order into that ethical cul-de-sac which is marked by refusal and neglect of the principle of duty is one of the tasks of the law. 'The duties of knowledge and searching after truth,' asserts Cicero (*Offices*, I, xliii), 'are obliged to give way to the duties of justice, which consist in upholding society among men', the precondition for the pursuit of all human purposes whatever.

The individual who acts as a hostile or neglectful stranger to the civic bond I have thus far termed, in general, the asocial or anti-social individual; he is the unjust individual also [**sect. 106**]. For the well-being of the civic order is a precondition for the safety and well-being of its individual members; to assail or harm the first is to imperil the second, and *prima facie* constitutes an act of injustice against fellow-citizens in breach of the civic bond, the ethic of which dictates that all citizens are responsible, and justly responsible, in their common interest, for the well-being of the civic order to which they together belong.

132. Moreover, the civic order (whether of nation or city), built through time by the citizen-body in self-protection and as an expression of *humanitas*, and inherited anew in each generation, owes much of its durability, such as it is, to the law: which, declares Hans Jonas (*Il Principio Responsabilità*, p. 6) in Hebraic fashion, it is man's 'duty to honour'. Even in circumstances in which law and justice are not synonymous, the maintenance of the civic bond – and therefore of the civic order which rests upon it – requires that the law, and especially the rule of law as a principle, be respected; provided that such law is known, is not arbitrarily made, can be modified, and is not itself destructive of the civic bond and the integrity of the civic order.

Above all, since the principle of duty cannot, in many of its aspects, be enforced without the ultimate sanction of law, it is in the interest of every citizen that the status of law as such be not compromised, whether by those who discredit or betray it 'from within' – lawmakers, judges, advocates, policemen, prison officers and others – or by those who, for whatever motives, would have it discredited or overthrown. This is without prejudice to the right of the citizen in a democratic civic order to object openly to, and to seek to change, laws regarded by such citizen as objectionable.

133. In conditions of civic disaggregation under the rule of the politics of dutiless right, existing laws which uphold the principle of duty, and impose its specific obligations upon the civic order and the individual citizen, require in particular to be observed. Where they have fallen into desuetude, they require, provided that they remain appropriate to the defence of the civic order, to be revived; and where they are inadequate in scope, they require to be extended, as I discuss further in Chapters Ten and Eleven.

In respect of these tasks, many past notions of 'political obligation', insofar as they have to do with mere obedience to government and to power-holders rather than with the ethical and practical obligations of citizens to their fellows, including that of co-responsibility for the well-being of the civic order as a whole, are wanting. 'Every man that hath any possession or enjoyment of any part of the dominions of any government', says Locke (*Two Treatises of Civil Government*, Bk. II, para. 119) in this manner, 'doth thereby give his tacit consent, and is as far forth obliged, to obedience to the laws of that government.' But it is the interest of the civic order and of the citizens who constitute it, and not that of government nor of any particular system of power, which now commands *not* the political obedience of the subject but the civic duty of the individual citizen-member.

Even less is it a passive obedience to power which the principle of duty, enforced by law, dictates, as I further argue in Chapter Eight; rather, it is an active awareness of the existence of the civic bond, and recognition by the citizen of his practical obligations to the civic order to which he belongs. Moreover, it is not the teaching of obedience to power which is the purpose of civic education, but the procuring in the citizen of awareness of the civic bond and the voluntary observance by him of his obligations to the civic order.

134. Indeed, there can be no true (or just) civic education which fails to provide the citizen, as it fails in the corrupted liberal orders, with at least elementary knowledge of the laws which govern the civic order, the laws which govern the conduct, private and public, of its members, and the laws which govern their duties and rights as citizens.

As I have already shown [sect. 94], Locke declares it as a principle, in accord with his 'assumption of reason', that the citizen is 'supposed capable to know the law, that so he might keep his actions within the bounds of it' (*Two Treatises of Civil Government*, Bk. II, para. 59); but, where a citizen does not know, or does not yet know, the law, 'somebody else must guide him' (ibid.). The absence of provision for such guidance in the corrupted liberal orders is a failure of education; and such failure is itself a breach by the civic order of the principle of duty, as it applies to the responsibilities of the civic order to its members, as I discuss further in Chapter Nine.

135. The law, whether in the form of the rule of law as such or in the form of particular laws, is not a matter only of narrow negation and prohibition. Both the rule of law in general and its particular laws are an expression of the interest of the civic order – and of the past generations of citizens who have made such laws – in its own preservation as an association of citizens which embraces all others,

and in the practical preservation of the security and well-being of its members.

Law, whether its ground be found by some in 'God's will' and by others in 'natural justice', or historic covenant, or utilitarian dictate, is the outcome of men's efforts to raise themselves above the animal condition and above the promptings of mere instinct. It is also, in the words of Winstanley (*The Law of Freedom in a Platform*, p. 374), 'a rule whereby man and other creatures are governed in their actions for the preservation of the common peace'. Indeed, the very idea of law has at its heart – as in the Decalogue, in the provisions of Roman Law, and in the principles of English common law, among other ancient codes – the purpose of *peace*, as well as of justice; the 'outlaw', deserving of the reproaches of God and man alike, is he who puts himself outside the law by *breaking the peace*.

But for the law to be able to draw ethical bounds around human behaviour it must itself be respected and be deserving of respect. Where the citizen, in conditions of accelerating civic disaggregation, as in the corrupted liberal orders, comes (whether cynically or with reason) to doubt the justice of the law, or possesses an inward and passive contempt for the law, or actively repudiates its restraints, or commits crime with increasing impunity, the law gradually ceases to keep the peace; a consequence and further cause of the process of civic disaggregation.

136. The sovereignty of the civic order as a body, which is one of the principal ends to be secured by enforcement of the principle of duty [sect. 24], itself depends, especially in a democratic order, upon the rule of law.

For the rule of law is not only a means by which the civic bond is sustained but also one of the expressions of such civic bond, as well as the guarantor that the institutional coherence and common ethical direction of the civic order will be protected.

But where, as in the corrupted liberal orders, the ethical rule of the politics of dutiless right and demand-satisfaction not only leads to the repudiation of the restraints of the law but begins to take precedence even over the rule of law itself, then the sovereignty of the civic order – increasingly composed of citizens-turned-strangers

– is imperilled. Law, as well as being the antithesis of the promptings of mere instinct, is the antithesis of arbitrary personal will; that will which the politics of dutiless right does much to encourage, and which it ratifies by its neglect of the principle of duty.

In the struggle of the civic order against such will, even arbitrary laws might, *in extremis*, be considered ethically preferable to the flouting of all law save the law of the jungle, and to civic dissolution.

137. If it is in the general nature of the law, in the form both of the rule of law and of particular laws, to seek to maintain the coherence of the civic order, the same cannot be said of the pursuit of all forms of justice, above all the vain pursuit of absolute and Utopian forms of it. Their very unattainability – beguiling to some – draws men, as it drew old socialism, towards excess, harm, crime, and even destruction of the very civic orders which they seek to redeem.

Indeed, old socialism contributed much to the process of corruption of the liberal order by diagnosing the latter's system of law as merely 'bourgeois' or class-based, and observance of such law as a form of ethical compromise with it, a compromise which was *prima facie* to be resisted. This was to create yet another cohort of citizens-turned-strangers living under the rule of dutiless right; that is, claiming and gaining rights, benefits, and privileges from a civic order whose legitimacy they professed to doubt, and duties towards which they refused (generally in bad faith) to acknowledge.

Some among them there were, and still are, who regard – or profess to regard – all law as, in some sort, a derogation from the right of the individual; itself an extreme form of the politics of dutiless right and demand-satisfaction, but vested in ethical garb. But a 'government without laws' is, in the words of Locke (*Two Treatises of Civil Government*, Bk. II, para. 219), a 'mystery in politics inconceivable to human capacity, and inconsistent with human society.'

If not all responsibilities which are dictated to the citizen by the principle of duty can be made subject to sanction, as I argue further in Chapter Ten, the ethic of the civic bond and the obligations of the principle of duty, whether or not voluntarily assumed by the individual, nonetheless require to be generally sustained and reinforced by law.

138. The 'design and end' of such law, as Cicero put it (*Offices*, III, v), is to 'keep up agreement and union amongst citizens' as a precondition for the fulfilment of their other ends, and under whatever passing politico-economic system the particular civic order may live. 'By civil laws', declared Hobbes (*Leviathan*, Chap. XXVI), 'I understand the laws that men are . . . bound to observe because they are members not of this or that commonwealth, but of *a* commonwealth' (my emphasis). That is, by virtue of living in a civic order, men are bound, subject to proviso [**sects. 132–3**], to observe its laws.

'The laws', Rousseau similarly states (*Social Contract*, Bk. II, Chap. VI), 'are properly but the conditions of civil association', or the terms under which its members are vested with citizenship's duties and rights, and the means by which the civic order is maintained. Such duties and rights could have neither ethical substance nor practical effect except in a civic order so maintained; nor could the individual citizen fulfil such duties and exercise such rights except where the maintenance of the civic order took ethical and practical precedence, especially in the last resort, over his own claims, liberties, grievances, and objections.

Thus, 'for the attaining of peace and conservation of themselves thereby', in Hobbes' words (*Leviathan*, Chap. XXI), men have 'made artificial chains called civil laws', chains which may be changed, replaced or even removed, but (in a democratic order) only by the members of the civic order themselves, acting in their common interest and in the exercise of their sovereign powers.

139. It is only under the rule of law, and in a democratic civic order, that mutual observance of the principle of duty can be justly expected of its citizen-members. Without the rule of law, such mutuality – in which the individual citizen's duty to himself, his fellows and the civic order is reciprocated by other citizens – cannot be guaranteed, and the principle of duty must itself be cast into suspicion and fail.

Moreover, because the voluntary observance by the individual of the principle of duty falters under conditions in which the civic bond is increasingly flouted or ignored by others, the sanction of law requires to be reasserted in order that the principle be secured, and the civic bond maintained. Nor, without the presence of sanction, can the voluntary fulfilment of duty to others, and to the civic order in general, be reasonably expected of citizens when such duty becomes increasingly difficult, and even dangerous, to fulfil in practice; as when, in conditions of accelerating civic disaggregation, dutiless right pits itself against dutiless right in an a-civic struggle – increasingly armed, in some corrupted liberal orders – for the survival of the fittest.

Then, the enforcement of the principle of duty under sanction of law alone can break the ethical and practical vicious circle, in which the refusal of such duty is both consequence and further cause of civic disaggregation. But even in settled civic conditions, the civic bond requires to be reinforced by sanction; in particular, no civic order composed of free citizens can be sustained except under the rule of law.

140. Indeed, a legal code is a precondition of civic order itself. The Jews would even argue that, in their case, the Mosaic Decalogue preceded the civic order in time, as well as having ethical priority over it. The term used for 'the state' in Hebrew, *medinah*, derives from the word *din*, or law; and of the seven Noachide commandments to the world according to the rabbinic tradition, six were moral prohibitions and the seventh – the only positive commandment – was to 'establish a legal system'.

But not every particular of a legal code, nor every legal code, is entitled to equivalent moral regard; the Germans' 'Aryan' legal code, or the South Africans' 'apartheid' code, was not entitled to moral regard at all. The 'positive law' must be in accord with the 'moral law', or law of humanity, that law dictated by the 'conscience', God, or a 'sense of justice', which, as the world's legal and moral codes have shown with great consistency, is also at its heart a law of the civic bond and the defence of the civic order.

At the same time, especially in conditions of civic disaggregation, claims of individual conscience cannot be permitted such ethical priority as to prevent the enforcement of the principle of duty. For the first task of any legal code which is at the same time a civic code is the preservation of the civic order in the interests of its members as a whole.

141. It is a commonplace anti-social judgment of citizens-turned-strangers in the corrupted liberal orders, as I have indicated [**sect. 137**], that the law, even in the form of such civic code, and even where its particular laws are fully in accord with the moral law, is incompatible with personal freedom. 'Although free', declared the wiser Demaratos of the Spartans (Herodotus, *History*, Bk. VII, sect. 104), 'they are not absolutely free; for they have a master over them, the law.'

Such 'mastery', a mastery which is a precondition of personal freedom, is also no more, and no less, than an expression of the sovereignty of the civic order; a sovereignty undermined not only by civic disaggregation and the refusal of the principle of duty, as I have explained, but also by ethical disregard for the law on the part of the citizen-turned-stranger on the one hand, and maladministration of the law or miscarriage of justice on the other.

Without the sovereignty of the civic order, law cannot be made binding; but without respect for and observance of the law, the sovereignty of the civic order itself cannot be maintained. It is also ethically preferable, as the Jews argue, to be servants of the law than of the wills of men.

142. Moreover, if the members of any civic order whatever are to play their citizen's parts, there is required a common rule [**sect. 4**]; that is, the common rule, under law, of the principle of duty as it applies to the citizen's responsibilities to the civic order, and the civic order's responsibilities to its members. This is not the common rule of a Hobbesian tyrant, to keep the citizens 'in awe' (*Leviathan*, Chap. XVII), but the common rule of the civic sense, enforceable by sanction.

Yet the politics of dutiless right and demand-satisfaction in the corrupted liberal orders constantly challenges and subverts such common rule of civic sense. It challenges both the positive and the moral law, elevating the practical benefits of egoism, greed, and exploitation not only over the 'harm of their punishment', as Hobbes puts it (ibid., Chap. XXVII), but over the diminishing risk of their punishment as the enforcement of law itself staggers to a fall.

In such conditions, the citizen-turned-stranger is decreasingly disposed to serve God or to respect man, to abide by law or to value custom. Indeed, the corrupted liberal order increasingly legitimates, and at the same time is driven to pacify by public provision, a condition of ethical rebellion against the civic bond and the civic order itself.

143. To frame good laws, that is laws which are conducive to the well-being of the citizen and the civic order to which he belongs, and to secure the observance of such laws, is not enough in itself to sustain the civic bond. As I argue further in Chapter Nine, the principle of duty imposes upon the civic order a number of practical responsibilities to its citizen-members of which the maintenance of the rule of law is merely one.

However, the civic bond [sect. 5], voluntarily assumed but sustained by law, is in the first instance dependent for its force upon the civic consciousness, or civic sense [sect. 6], and not upon imposition. Civic consciousness is at best a matter of habit, the product of education, and a vindication of the assumption of reason. Insofar as such civic consciousness, or civic sense, is also an expression of a sense of justice, it is additionally predisposed to the principle of duty, which dictates that each member of the civic order should reciprocally and mutually fulfil his obligations to his fellows, and, in so doing, do what he ought to do: the ethic of the civic bond in practice.

The legal code complements such acceptance of moral co-responsibility for the well-being of the civic order by making each citizen juridically responsible for certain of his actions in regard to his fellows. It cannot, however, displace or replace the civic sense itself, nor even attempt to do so, without causing harm to the civic bond and to the civic order which rests upon it. But failure on the part of law to sustain the civic sense, as by failure or unwillingness to enforce and extend the application of the principle of duty, is equally harmful to the civic bond and civic order. The price of such failure is further civic disaggregation.

144. The liberal ideal of toleration – which dictates that that which

is not specifically forbidden by the law should be regarded as ethically and in practice permissible to the individual – has also made a substantial contribution both to the corruption of the liberal order itself and to the process of civic disaggregation. It is a principle too passive in conditions of many-sided social crisis; it provides a substantial part of the ethical ground for the politics of dutiless right and demand-satisfaction; and it has thus helped to undermine the principle of duty, and to harm the civic bond.

Moreover, that it is the positive function of law to *command what should be done*, in the manner of a minority of the commandments of the Decalogue, as well as to forbid what should not be done, is a proposition generally rejected by the corrupted liberal order as an unwarrantable intrusion upon the liberty of the individual.

The function of law, rather – or so the corrupted liberal ideal illiberally dictates – is, whilst forbidding what should not be done, merely to entitle, permit, and oversee what may be done. Under such ethic, law is perceived less (or not at all) as a means to remind the citizen of his duties than as a means to secure, protect, and give effect to his rights; rights limited only by the practical need, not ethical duty, to respect the same rights in others.

Such a view of the law's purpose is not only ethically insufficient but the civil law in practice becomes largely directed to the reconciling of competing wills and conflicting wants, often without regard to, and even at the expense of, the well-being of the civic order as a whole. In the adjudication of such conflicts, the principle of duty has generally been lost from sight, or has had no status in law in the instant case; the presumptions and claims of dutiless right have been both taken for granted and confirmed; and the liberal ideal has thus been further corrupted. Only the extension and enforcement of the principle of duty, tempering the passive liberal ideal of toleration, can rescue the liberal order itself.

145. Similarly, the corrupted liberal ideal of equal justice, which dictates that all citizens possess the right to equal respect as moral beings in the eyes of the law, has, in its passivity before the circumstances of civic disaggregation, also contributed to these circumstances. For such ideal, whose reach is long, has helped to prevent acknowledgment, in civic practice, that even if such moral

respect is owed *prima facie* to all, it is no longer owed to those citizens-turned-strangers whom the due process of law – provided it be fairly conducted – has found, for example, to have acted violently and unwarrantedly against the well-being of fellow-members of the civic order. Indeed, this same ideal has its ethic undermined by the increasingly common refusal in the corrupted liberal order to permit practical discrimination at all between the moral and amoral, for fear of infringing the claims, become absolute, of 'equal justice'. The very notion that there is an ethic and a canon of just civic behaviour may come, in such conditions, to be denied or lost from view; and all behaviour, harmful or not to the well-being of the civic order, may (in an ethical *reductio ad absurdum*) ultimately come to seem equally just.

146. Suppressed, too, under the rule of the corrupted liberal ideal of equal justice is the sense that in every form of justice, *desert*, or that which is deserved by and therefore due to the individual [sect. 57], must stand at its heart, if justice itself is to continue to bear meaning. That which is deserved by, and therefore done to, the individual may comport both reward and penalty; but, without reward or penalty according to desert, the *doing of justice* has neither significance nor purpose. To live in a civic order where justice is done is to live in a civic order where that which is deserved, or merited, is done; as in Campanella's City of the Sun, where *nessuno ottenga più di quanto meriti*, 'no one obtains more than he deserves' (*La Città del Sole*, 1602, Rome, 1993, p. 80).

Moreover, such principle of *desert* is a social principle, and the only possible principle of a new civic social-ism.

147. The suppression of the concept of justice-as-desert, a suppression aided by old socialism's refusal of the principle of merit, has also done much to displace and discredit the very idea – an ethical and civic idea – of worth and unworthiness in citizen conduct. To the support of the discrediting of the idea of worth has come, in the corrupted liberal order, the cynicism which illiberally decrees that worth, like good, cannot be objectively measured; and that the 'common good' of the civic order, which such citizen-worth would advance and unworthiness harm, is incapable of definition.

In such an ethical limbo, the politics of dutiless right and demand-satisfaction acquires both a value-free and a certain mean-ing; desert, merit, worth and, most dangerously, justice itself, being 'merely' ethical categories, are at cynical worst considered to have no meaning at all. While, once, a Cicero could declare it to be 'injustice' for a man to 'forsake the common good and society of mankind' (Offices, I, ix), now, for some, not one of his terms possesses significant meaning, the word 'society' included; and where, once, fiat justitia, ruat coelum! – let justice be done, though heaven fall! – proclaimed the existence of a civic order, now both 'justice' and 'heaven' are mere abracadabra to the amoral semioti-cian or the academic logic-chopper.

Now, few could or would simply say, without risking the scorn of the wise or the indifference of the citizen-turned-stranger, that justice is the 'most admirable of virtues', as did Cicero (ibid., II, xi); or, that it is the 'strongest and surest bond of a commonwealth', as did Thomas More in his Utopia (Bk. II, Chap. 7). Indeed, the very consideration of the ethical purposes of law and government, as instruments of the civic order, has fallen under that taboo of embarrassment and silence which the corrupted liberal order has imposed upon 'abstract' concern for moral means and moral ends.

Yet, without such concern, no notion at all of right and wrong, or of just and unjust, civic conduct can be fruitfully discussed in the civic order, let alone established in consensual practice as a means of defence of the civic bond. In such conditions, which are both consequence and further cause of the disaggregation of the corrupted liberal order, the most ethically-minded of citizens begins to live, morally, from hand-to-mouth; the least ethically-minded becomes no citizen at all.

148. Under the rule of dutiless right, law, blinded to its ethical tasks, may lose its way even with the basest of crimes; even when man turns beast, and the assumption of reason fails, law – checked in its stride by the corrupted liberal ideal – may falter. In other ways, too, the very doing of justice, when the principles both of desert and of duty have lost their moral status, may become an increasingly arbitrary and ethically unanchored thing. The right of the citizen-turned-stranger to demand satisfaction or insist upon freedom of choice may command, even in law, the authority which

is denied to the principle of duty, the plea of the victim, or the interest of the civic order as a whole.

Thus it was only by a narrow majority (of three Lords of Appeal against two) that the House of Lords, sitting as a court in Regina vs Brown and others (1993, 2 All E.R., pp. 75–124), dismissed the appeals against conviction of men found guilty of unlawful wounding in a case involving sado-masochistic genital torture, branding, and blood-letting 'for fun', or in exercise of their individual rights in a corrupted liberal order.

Lord Templeman was 'not prepared to invent a defence of consent for sado-masochistic encounters' which 'glorified cruelty' (ibid., p. 83). Society was 'entitled and bound to protect itself against a cult of violence. Pleasure derived from the infliction of pain is an evil thing', he declared, using moral terms which run against the tide in such corrupted order; 'cruelty is uncivilised', he added, in like fashion (ibid., p. 84). To my Lords Slynn of Hadley and Mustill, however, this was the intrusion of 'policy' and 'public interest' into the realm of private and – in Mill's phrase – merely self-regarding action; it was an act of 'paternalism', even, so to intrude (ibid., p. 124).

In this case, the interest of the civic order was asserted over the ethics of dutiless right and infinite demand-satisfaction; the beast-in-man was briefly caged by law. The voices of reproach for the decision, as constituting a denial of 'individual freedom', were those not of citizens as ethical beings, but of citizens-turned-strangers to the civic order. The decision itself, however, for all that it momentarily asserted the ethical priority of *humanitas* [sect. 69] over the right to take pleasure in violence, was not the less arbitrary, random and ethically unanchored; and was swiftly swept away on the tide of event (and greater crime), leaving little moral trace behind it.

149. Under the rule of dutiless right, it is the mark upon the forehead of the citizen-turned-stranger that he does not know, or does not accept, that law, flawed as may be, is applicable to all and sovereign in a sovereign civic order; that it is bound to set limits to the freedoms of the citizen – and of those who hold power or office in such civic order – in the interests of all; and that, although it must provide each citizen with protection for the exercise of his rights, it must also enforce a system of sanctions by which to inhibit the same citizen's offences against the civic order.

Hence, in addition to the existing equality of rights to exercise the will, which the law seeks to police against mounting odds in the corrupted liberal orders, equality in enforceable individual duty – dictated by the principle of duty – must increasingly become the law's business in the interests of the civic order as a whole. For the purpose of law remains as Hobbes (*Leviathan*, Chap. XVIII) defined it: that is, *inter alia*, to 'encourage men to serve the commonwealth or deter them from doing disservice to the same'. Or, as More 'discovered' in his *Utopia* (Bk. II, Chap. 7), 'all laws (say they) be made and published only to the intent that, by them, every man should be put in remembrance of his duty'.

But in the corrupted liberal order this connection between law and duty, a connection as old as civic order itself, must be relearned; knowledge of the connection between law and right is not enough. **150.** The connection between law and duty has not to do, in a democratic civic order, with the citizen's obeisance to power – as I explain further in Chapter Eight – but with the law's civic purpose in creating the conditions for the individual citizen's well-being and for the secure exercise of his rights within the civic order to which he belongs. To this end, law must, as Hobbes declares (*Leviathan*, Chap. XXVI), 'limit the natural liberty of particular [sc. individual] men, in such manner as they might not hurt but assist one another'.

This 'assistance', dictated by the principle of duty as it applies to the citizen's responsibilities to his fellows, the sanction of law must sustain and reinforce. The 'limits' upon the 'natural liberty' of man – which, if not set, permit the corrupted liberal order's toleration of *licence* – are a just derogation equally from the rule of dutiless right and from the presumption of the absolute rights of man; the maintenance of the rule of law, and the interest of the well-being of the civic order as a whole, forbid such licence.

It is, therefore, not the function of the law and other civic institutions – and cannot be permitted to be their function in the liberal order, if its corruption is to be halted – to seek to secure for the individual the maximum practical degree of free self-assertion as a sovereign end in itself. To pursue this end is merely to contribute to that process of civic disaggregation which transforms such free self-assertion into a struggle for the survival of the fittest. Instead, the principle of duty beckons. Under its rule, supported by law, the limits to free self-assertion imposed by duty to self, to one's fellows, and to the civic order make possible the return to moral being of the citizen-turned-stranger, and hence the strengthening of the civic bond.

But it is not the function of the law and of the rule of law to displace the civic bond, nor must law and the rule of law be imposed gratuitously upon the citizen to the denial of his freedoms. Rather, their purpose is to reinforce the civic bond by reinforcing just relations – another term for justice itself – between the members of the civic order; 'upholding society among men' by giving sanction, in particular, to the principle of duty.

151. This is the law's prior ethical task. But just relations between citizens cannot be secured unless the law protects citizens from each other not only (say) in respect of acts of violence, but also in respect of other, non-violent acts of oppression, including acts carried out by those who command the instruments of power, both political and economic.

Thus, the principle of duty, as I have already stated, demands not only the fulfilment of the citizen's duties to self, to fellows, and to the civic order, but also the fulfilment of the duties of the civic order, and of its instrument the state, to the members of such civic order. The law is required to help enforce both sets of duties in the interests of just relations in the civic order as a whole.

152. When the attempted securing of such just relations is seen and known to be the care of the law and other civic institutions, it serves also to vindicate and sustain civic consciousness, or civic sense. Conversely, such civic sense is harmed and diminished the less ethical concern for justice there is felt to be in the institutions of the civic order, those of the administration and enforcement of the law chief among them.

Furthermore, the civic order of the nation cannot be an effective sovereign body when riven by unjust, or amendable but unamended, relations among its citizens, as in conditions of unchecked, or inadequately checked, violence, licence, political oppression, or economic exploitation. Just relations are those relations, as Aristotle declares (*Politics*, III, xii, 1282b), which are 'for the benefit of the whole community'; such just relations, or justice itself, it is the ethical and practical task of the law and other civic institutions to seek.

153. Under the unchecked rule of dutiless right and demand-satisfaction, just civic relations, or justice itself, cannot be found. In particular, the corrupted liberal doctrine that the liberty of each is limited only by the like liberty of all – a doctrine of egoism fitting for the citizen-turned-stranger – contains no civic ethic whatever.

Just relations, or justice itself, have to do *in the civic order* not with relations between strangers but between citizens. Rival and conflicting expressions of free, self-interested assertion, for all that they must be constantly adjudicated – and as justly as possible – in the corrupted liberal order, cannot be permitted to be of equivalent moral status with expressions of the civic sense and with the enforcement of the principle of duty, if the civic order is to resist the process of civic disaggregation.

Instead, justice itself demands acknowledgment that there is a limit in any civic order to what may be allowed to individual wants and wills. Only within such limit is civic order made possible at all. Without individual entitlement, as I have argued [sects. 23, 98], the citizen is a slave; but without the principle of duty, sustained by law, there can be no civic order.

SEVEN

The Principle of Duty
in General (1)

*The principle of duty defined – duty and liberty –
self-restraint and self-harm – duty to self and to others –
reciprocal obligation – duties to the civic order in general –
duties to nature and to the past – duties of public service –
democracy and active citizenship – Jerusalem and Athens –
arguments of the religious – duty and right – the principle of duty
as an ethical principle – the moral sense and moral knowledge –
duty, reason and utility – civic coherence – equity –
summary of argument – rejection of idea of covenant or contract –
duty voluntarily undertaken and duty by imposition.*

154. The principle of duty, the sovereign ethical principle of the civic order, demands both general and particular duties of the citizen – to himself, to his fellows, and to the civic order as a whole – and, likewise, general and particular duties of the civic order, and of its instrument the state, to its members. Such duties have their ground in ethics, reason, and utility. In their application to the citizen, they comport not obedience to power but co-responsibility for the well-being of others and of the civic order in general; have ethical precedence over the rights, benefits, and privileges with which the citizen is vested as a member of such civic order; and, fulfilled, signify that the individual who fulfils them is playing his citizen's part.

The principle of duty is, in the first instance, that principle which regulates the relation between citizen and citizen, and the relation between the citizen and the civic order to which he belongs.

It is, further, the fundamental principle of the civic bond and the heart of its ethic; that ethic, voluntarily assumed but sustained by law, which dictates to citizens that they compose a single civic order for whose well-being they are responsible in the common interest. The function of the principle of duty, whether its dictates are voluntarily assumed or enforced and reinforced by law, is the protection and maintenance of such civic bond, and thus of the civic order which it in turn upholds.

155. To observe the ethical and practical dictates of the principle of duty as they apply to the citizen is neither weakness nor strength in such citizen, but a moral imperative, a rational undertaking, and a practical necessity. For such observance is a precondition of any civic order whatever. In conditions of accelerating civic disaggregation, as in the corrupted liberal order, the imperative of the principle of duty is greatly increased; even where such conditions do not exist, the principle of duty is required to be observed, as the ground of the moral and practical relations between citizen and civic order. But where consciousness of the civic bond has waned, where citizens have turned strangers by the thousands and millions, and where obligation of all kinds – to oneself, to one's familiars, to the community, to the civic order – is contemplated with increasing discomfort, or is neglected, or is refused entirely, the resurrection of the principle of duty, that great neglected rule, itself becomes a civic obligation.

Here, I emphasise such principle, but do not invent it; in fulfilment of my own duty, remind the civic order and its members of it; and give such principle its due place within a general political and moral theory of the civic order.

156. In the corrupted liberal order, under the present rule of dutiless right, it could be argued that such reassertion of the principle of duty is a *minimum in extremis*; and, as a 'mere' moral notion, can provide in itself no more than what Hegel called the 'inkling of right ethical life' as it applies to individual conduct in the civic order. But, as I show in Chapters Nine and Ten, such moral principle dictates particular and practical duties; and, as I show in Chapter Eleven, many of such duties can, and must, be enforced and reinforced by sanction. Moreover, as I show in

Chapter Twelve, the principle of duty must stand at the centre of a new civic social-ist doctrine and movement, capable of arresting the process of civic disaggregation in the corrupted liberal orders.

The political and moral lessons taught us by the ancients and their early modern legatees, cited here, can guide us only so far; for all their philosophical and practical preoccupations with the well-being of the civic order, they do not provide us with a systematic theory of duty in and to such civic order. Antique fidelities and pieties, for all their ethical example and practical force, do not provide an adequate model for a modern political theory of duty in the corrupted and disaggregating liberal orders. Nor can the obligations of the citizen which have been left to him after the democratic supersession and just overthrow of feudal authority – as to pay taxes, to take out licences, (in some civic orders) to vote, or (in some cases) to serve for a limited period in the armed forces – be themselves the ground of a sufficient civic relation between citizen and civic order.

157. The principle of duty, the 'great neglected rule' and sovereign ethical principle of the civic order, is an expression of the *constraints of membership of the civic order*. The duties which such principle dictates constitute the first, and main, limitation upon the citizen's claims to dutiless right. Moreover, the principle of duty, sustained by law, not only helps to define the bounds of licence but, in so doing, simultaneously to demarcate the proper scope of individual freedom and to protect it.

The principle of duty is also an ethical and practical cheek to the risks posed to the civic order by the 'losing gamble of liberty' [sect. 30], and a similar counterweight to the disappointments of the assumption of reason [sects. 40–6]. Further, the power (not right) of 'free choice' in the corrupted liberal order is limited by constraints, which the principle of duty dictates, upon what, and how much, may be chosen. The principle of duty additionally aids the cure of that extreme form of 'individualism', or egoism, which is found in the citizens of the corrupted liberal orders, and which deprives such citizens of civic sense; that is, of a sense of duty to their fellows and to the civic order, and even, paradoxically, of a sense of duty to themselves.

158. The principle of duty becomes a principle of compulsion only where the individual's duty to self, others and the civic order to which he belongs is not fulfilled of his own free will; as when such individual is moved to comply with it not from conscience or from within, but from fear of sanction.

As Kant argues (*Lectures on Ethics*, p. 48), to carry out an obligation which is dictated by the principle of duty is not an unfree act; the fulfilment of a moral obligation is not, in itself, a restraint upon the free will, but may be, and is at its best, the fullest expression of it. Indeed, the assumption and fulfilment of obligation on the part of the individual not only presupposes such individual's exercise of freedom, but, in contributing to the maintenance of the civic bond, enhances the possibility of liberty in the civic order.

159. The individual's observance of the principle of duty represents such individual's contribution to the common ethical direction of the civic order to which he belongs, and as such is a further practical contribution to the conditions necessary to his own and others' exercise of the citizen's rights and freedoms. Hence, the principle of duty is not merely compatible with the (uncorrupted) liberal ideal but essential to its preservation; as it is fitted also to be the main constituent of a new social-ist ethics and practice, or civic social-ism.

Moreover, in observing the principle of duty, and not only in exercising his rights, the citizen acts the citizen's part. And in accepting, whether voluntarily or under sanction, the bounds to licence and the limits upon his own freedom which the principle of duty dictates, the citizen helps to make real not only the civic sense but the sense of proportion and limit which is of the essence of justice.

160. Of the universal duties to self which the citizen-member of a civic order owes, the duty of self-restraint in the making of demands upon such civic order stands at the head.

For the virtues and advantages to be found in civic association themselves demand, if such virtues and advantages are to be sustained to the well-being of all, the moderation of our desires in regard to them; we not only must, but can, so moderate them. As Locke declared (*Two Treatises of Civil Government*, Bk. II, para.

44), man is 'master of himself and proprietor of his own person and the actions or labour of it'; he has, therefore, the power to do what the principle of duty commands in this respect.

Furthermore, it is only under the rule of such self-restraint that the imposition of the civic order's prohibitions can be averted, and that in a free society the exercise of freedom can be 'in harmony with itself', as Kant puts it (*Lectures on Ethics*, p. 124), and not 'come into collision with itself'. It is, above all, lack of civic sense which makes us blind to the relationship between our self-restraint and the well-being of the civic order as a whole; lack of awareness of where our 'private' interest lies plays a related part.

Nor are we any more permitted by the principle of duty to harm ourselves, as members of the civic order, than we are permitted to harm the civic order to which we belong. 'I have set before you life and death, blessing and cursing', it is declared in *Deuteronomy* (XXX, 19), 'therefore choose life, that both thou and thy seed may live'; both an ethical injunction and an early acknowledgment of free will. 'We shrink in horror from suicide', argues Kant (*Lectures on Ethics*, pp. 150-1), 'because all nature seeks its own preservation . . . How, then, could man make of his freedom, which is the acme of his life and constitutes its worth, a principle for his own destruction? Nothing more terrible can be imagined . . . humanity in one's person is something inviolable.' But if a man may not ethically 'use his freedom against himself', and, in particular, not in order to 'destroy himself', no more may he use his freedom against his fellows, or in order to destroy the civic order to which he belongs.

'It is obvious', Kant further argues (ibid., p. 118), 'that nothing can be expected from a man who dishonours his own person. He who transgresses against himself' – as occurs on an increasing scale under the rule of dutiless right and demand-satisfaction in the corrupted liberal orders – 'becomes incapable of doing his duty towards his fellows . . . The prior conditions of our duty to others is our duty to ourselves.' The citizen-turned-stranger who has lost his citizen identity and, often in the persona of the universal plebeian, has also lost his self-esteem – that same self-esteem which Kant believed 'should be the principle of our duties to ourselves' (ibid.) – can only be brought back to both his civic sense and his self-esteem by the imposition of the principle of duty. Having 'cast away his personality', as Kant puts it (ibid., p. 121), or made himself an 'object of contempt' (*The Metaphysics of Morals*, tr. M. Gregor, Cambridge, 1991, p. 217), he will not otherwise or voluntarily fulfil such duty.

161. It is a further moral aspect of the duty of self-restraint in the member of the civic order that he should judge himself by a strict standard. ('Even if the whole world tells you that you are a *tsadik* [righteous person]', declares Amiel (*Ethics and Legality in Jewish Law*, p. 26), 'you should view yourself as a *rasha* [wicked person].') Egoism, and (worse) that which is animal-in-man – being given increasing freedom and legitimacy under the helpless rule of dutiless right and in conditions of accelerating civic disaggregation – must be tempered not only by the imposition of the principle of duty but by the restraint, if necessary under sanction, of individual claims and material demands made as if of right, and from habit, upon the civic order; that is, claims and demands made upon fellow-members of the civic order.

This is without derogation from the principle of duty as it applies to the responsibilities of the civic order, and its instrument the state, for the well-being of its citizen-members.

162. The moral and practical nexus between duty to self and duty to others in the civic order is plain. 'It is wisdom that thou look to thine own wealth', says Thomas More (*Utopia*, Bk. II, Chap. 6), 'and to do the same for the commonwealth is no less than thy duty, if thou bearest any reverent love or any natural zeal and affection to thy native country.' Or, 'while you are of the same community and the same kindred with me, shall you be careless of yourself', asks Epictetus (*Discourses*, III. i, 4), 'and show yourself a bad citizen to the city, a bad kinsman to your kindred, and a bad neighbour to your neighbourhood?'

Under the principle of duty, there are many instances where duty to self and duty to others dictate the same actions. The duties, for example, to pursue a livelihood and to make oneself informed (as far as possible) are duties both to self and to others. Moreover, the fulfilment of our ethical and practical duties to ourselves is not only conducive to the raising of our own self-esteem, but of that of others also. Conversely, as Kant argues harshly, 'the less inner worth a man has, the less esteem does he deserve . . . We should so conduct ourselves as to be worthy of honour' (*Lectures on Ethics*, p. 49). Such self-respect is enhanced not only in those to whom respect is shown, but is itself a possible, and even probable, effect of having shown respect to others. Thus, to fulfil duty to self may fulfil, at the same time, a duty to others; duty to others fulfilled, in enhancing respect for self, fulfils a duty to self also.

163. Duties to self which are also duties to others are duties which, in Cicero's words, 'flow from society' (*Offices*, I, lxiii), albeit that they may appear to flow, or be argued to flow, from an autonomous moral imperative alone. The duty to work and to pursue a livelihood is one such duty which 'flows from society', as is made clear even in the most Hebraic of ascriptions of such duty to 'God's will'. Thus, Locke's declarations (*Two Treatises of Civil Government*, Bk. II, paras. 32, 34) that 'God when He gave the world in common to mankind, commanded man also to labour' and that 'He gave it to the use of the industrious and rational' contain a plain social injunction; that is, an injunction derived from the general interest of the civic order and its well-being. So derived, likewise, is the Jewish proverb: 'If each one sweeps before his own door, the whole street is cleaned.'

164. Indeed, Cicero thought (*Offices*, I, lxiii) that duties to others which 'flowed from society' were 'certainly the greatest' of all the duties which the individual was required to fulfil. Among such duties which are derived from society Cicero included familial duties, the family being for him a social microcosm of the civic order as a whole. Active socially-derived duties were also contrasted by him with, for example, duties to self which demanded only intellectual or theoretical activities of a passive and contemplative kind. 'The duties belonging to human society should in reason take priority over those which relate to inactive knowledge', he declared (ibid., I, xliv). Much of the work of modern academe, when conducted under the rule of dutiless right and without ethical purpose, practical significance, or, sometimes, discernible meaning,

is the production of 'inactive knowledge' of this kind – when it is
productive at all.

165. The archetype of individual obligation to others is to be found
in the ethical and practical responsibility of parents for the well-
being of their children who, with their parents, compose the first
association of human beings in which the individual is destined to
find himself. The sense, or knowledge, of the individual citizen's
moral and practical duty to his fellows – at its simplest and most
fundamental the duty to help them – is derived from experience
(whether as parent or child, or both) of this association.

'Thou shalt not see thy brother's ox or his sheep go astray, and
hide thyself from them: thou shalt in any case bring them again
unto thy brother', instructs *Deuteronomy* (XXII, 1). Here, duty to
one's familiars and to non-familiars is equally inscribed; all are
brothers under the skin. The obligation to 'honour thy father and
thy mother' (*Exodus*, XX, 12) – a duty closely bound to duty to
self, since to fail in it is to 'cast away one's own personality' and to
dishonour oneself [**sect. 160**] – is, in like ethical fashion, also a duty
of more general respect for seniority and age, whether of familiars
or not.

Epictetus (*Discourses*, II, xvii, 2) sets out a hierarchy of individual
obligation to others – he speaks of 'my duty to God, to my parents,
to my relations, to my community and to strangers' – but of which
obligation to familiars is at the origin and heart. 'We should pay the
first regard to our country and parents,' similarly declares Cicero
(*Offices*, I, xvii), endowing parents and country with parity of
esteem, 'from whom we have received the most endearing obligations', and to whom 'we most of all owe what is necessary for their
subsistence'.

That such reciprocal obligation *among familiars* is the basis of
wider notions of respect for others is plain in Cicero. 'Each age', he
declares (ibid., I, xxxiv), 'has its respective duties . . . It is required
of the younger sort of people that they pay due reverence to those
that are old, and choose out the best and most approved among
them by whose counsel and direction they may steer their lives';
and, reciprocally, 'as for old men, it is their duty . . . by prudent
and wise counsels to do what good they can to the younger sort of

people, to their friends and dependants, and more especially to the republic'; or, as I should say, to the civic order.

The principle of respect for parents and for old age, a constituent part of the principle of duty, has been largely lost from sight in the corrupted liberal orders, just as the sense of ethical and practical responsibility in parents for the well-being and education of their children is gradually diminishing among citizens-turned-strangers, who may flout, neglect, or reject the principle of duty in other respects also.

166. The individual citizen, in addition to such duties to himself and to his familiars, has other duties to the civic order to which he belongs, duties which will be set out in more detail in Chapter Ten. These duties, as I have indicated, are not merely complementary, but ethically related, to his duties to himself and to his familiars, as well as being dictated by a common imperative, that of *humanitas* [sect. 69].

It is on this ground that the principle of duty dictates, for example, the general obligation of the citizen to protect and maintain the civic bond; more particularly, 'in the business of getting in his corn' to 'assist a next neighbour', as Cicero puts it (*Offices*, I, xviii), and to give aid to the stranger and the oppressed; to sustain, and not lightly to abandon, those voluntary engagements and associations, the marital relation included, into which the individual citizen enters; and in other ways to contribute as a citizen to, and bestow pains upon, the preservation of the civic order to which he belongs.

And where the asocial citizen-turned-stranger will do no such good by the civic order, it is the civic order's own obligation, in accord with the principle of duty, in the first instance to seek to prevent such citizen-turned-stranger from doing harm. 'Every man', declares Hobbes (*Leviathan*, Chap. XXVIII), is 'obliged . . . not to do the commonwealth disservice.'

167. The duties of the individual citizen and the duties of the civic order are, as I have made clear, united by an overarching ethical and practical purpose: the protection and maintenance in existence of the civic order [sect. 5] in the interests of the well-being of all. Hence, all – those holding authority in the civic order and the state

and the individual citizen alike – are under a general moral duty to respect and to safeguard the natural environment of such civic order as far as is possible and practical. This duty remains despite the dilemma presented to mankind by the forms of scientific and technological development themselves, namely that many of these forms are irreversible, that some of these forms damage nature, and that many are, for all that, necessary to the well-being of the civic order.

Nevertheless, the principle of duty, the sovereign principle of the civic order, dictates that policy, law, and conduct be directed to respect for nature; that the members of the civic order, who are as much defenders of the 'citadel' as in the times of the Athenians, be made aware by civic education that many of their resources cannot be renewed and that some cannot be replaced; and that there are certain *natural* limits both to growth and to the satisfaction of demand.

168. There is also a general civic duty, applicable alike to individual citizens and to the civic order as a whole, of conservation (insofar as it is practicable) not only of natural resources but of the historic patrimony of the civic order, a civic duty which is related to that of respect for place [sect. 93].

169. The maintenance and defence of the civic order, especially in conditions of civic disaggregation, further requires the fulfilment on the part of the individual citizen of *obligations of public service* to the civic order. The 'politike order', in the words of Montaigne (*Essays*, tr. J. Florio, 1603, London, 1910, Bk. I, Chap. III, p. 26), 'hath need of our assistance', and never more than when the civic bond is flouted and the civic order itself thrown into question.

Such public service may take many forms – from community service to representative service, service which is voluntary and service which is compelled, gratuitous service or service which is paid – but each form 'contributes something to the sustentation of the whole' as John Donne expresses it [sect. 72].

To make such contribution to the civic order is the duty of the citizen who belongs to it, and again recalls the meaning of the word citizen itself: that individual who is ready, by virtue of his citizenship, to be called upon by the civic order for assistance and service [sect. 92]. Thus, a citizen may be cited, or summoned, to military or jury service, to vote (under some constitutions), or to contribute funds to the civic order by taxation. In each case, and whether the citizen inwardly grudge it or not, they are calls to civic duty. Moreover, a summons to such civic duty, welcome or not, is rightly understood – as long as the civic bond remains – to take ethical precedence over the activities of mere private calling; in ancient Athens during the sittings of the Ecclesia, or public assembly, the market was closed and a scarlet rope drawn around it.

It is a form of service to the civic order, also, to wish to see the law which upholds it itself upheld, and to act accordingly, without prejudice to the right of the citizen in a democratic order to object to, and to seek to change, laws regarded as objectionable [sect. 132]. Many of the ordinary activities of the citizen, when fulfilled with scruple, also serve the civic order, whether with or without the conscious reflection of the individual actor as to their end. The 'principal operations belonging to man', as Epictetus called them (*Discourses*, III, vii, 3) – which he, for his part, exemplified as 'engaging in public business; marrying; the production of children; the worship of God; the care of our parents' – are, in the normal course and even where the rule of dutiless right prevails, themselves capable of serving the general well-being of the civic order.

Indeed, the civic order is maintained not only by each citizen's fulfilment of his duties to himself, to others, and to the civic order, but by the carrying out of his daily tasks, whatever they may be, provided that they are in accord with the common ethical direction of the civic order in question and carried out under the rule of law. In the corrupted liberal order, however, the right of individual self-assertion possesses a higher ethical status than the fulfilment of duty; and the carrying out of the individual's tasks takes place in decreasingly civic conditions, in which the rule of dutiless right grants rewards to a-civic egoism which are denied to civic virtue and to the discharge of obligation.

170. It is also a form of service to the civic order, as well as a duty to it, that the individual citizen not permit himself to be, or to become, an *ἰδιώτης* (*idiotes*) [sect. 92] – that is, an 'ill-informed,

ordinary fellow', incapable of defending the civic bond, and at worst, unaware of the existence, let alone the nature, of the civic order to which he belongs, and of his duties to it.

Such necessity is all the greater in a democratic civic order. 'When the right of every citizen to cooperate in the government of society is acknowledged', as De Tocqueville pointed out (*Democracy in America*, p. 163), 'every citizen must be presumed to possess the power of discriminating between the different opinions of his co-temporaries [sc. contemporaries] and of appreciating the different facts from which inferences may be drawn.' The duty of education in a democratic civic order – a duty to educate oneself, to make use of educational opportunity and, on the part of the civic order, to provide such opportunity to the citizen body – arises in large part from the presumption, itself a form of the assumption of reason, which De Tocqueville sets out.

171. All such duties of the citizen, whether to himself, his fellows, or the civic order, when fulfilled, strengthen the civic order, help to preserve its sovereignty, and in consequence serve to prevent the accretion of unaccountable power to the civic order's instrument, the state. The state is the servant of the civic order, not its master; and to secure that the state serves the well-being of the civic order and its members, the citizen must himself forswear a servile or dependent relationship towards the state and learn to act the citizen's part. It is a part which implies fulfilling duties to one's fellows and to the civic order, and not only exercising rights against, or making demands upon, them.

Active citizenship of a democratic civic order, as distinct from passive dutilessness in a corrupted liberal order, *prima facie* demands the fulfilment of duty to it. (The limits upon such duty I discuss further in Chapter Eight.) In a democratic civic order, the non-fulfilment by the individual of his duties and tasks – and, in particular, the refusal of the citizen-turned-stranger to act the citizen's part – is a derogation from democratic principles them-selves. It contributes both to the usurpation by the state of the sovereignty of the civic order and to the process of civic disaggre-gation; a process which, in turn, the state may be driven to try to arrest by recourse to increasingly anti-civic, undemocratic and authoritarian means.

Hence, both ethical principle and argument from democratic utility call upon the individual citizen to act to fulfil his responsibilities for the well-being of the civic order, in accordance with the principle of duty. Securing the fulfilment of such duties to self, to one's fellows, and to the civic order, both voluntarily and under constraint of sanction, is also the task of a new social-ist ethic and practice, which will safeguard and enlarge that which remains democratic in the corrupted liberal order.

172. But whether in a democratic system or not, the principle of duty, to whomsoever and by whomsoever owed, is the ethical basis of the social order itself. It is the 'moral tie' by another name, embodying the principle both of the moral responsibility of the individual for his actions and of his practical co-responsibility for the well-being of the civic order to which he belongs. It is 'Jerusalem and Athens', the principle of the Decalogue and the πόλις (*polis*), or civic order, together.

The principle of duty is also an expression of the moral understanding that the civic order is *a duty-demanding end before it is a right-bestowing means*; and that the duties which the citizen owes to such order, and to his fellow-members of it, stand at the heart of his general ethical obligations as a human being. Although there are limits upon such duties, the individual member of the civic order can no more be exempt from ethical co-responsibility for the condition of such civic order than he can be exempt – except where a legal infant, mentally incompetent, or suffering from certain kinds of illness – from moral responsibility for his actions.

Nor, as I shall shortly argue further, is a 'covenant', whether real, imaginary, or implied, required as the source or ground of the moral ties between the individual and the civic order to which he belongs; no more than a pact between man and his maker, or man and his conscience, is required to ground his moral responsibility for his own actions. *Humanitas* [sect. 69] is the ground of both, even if the assumption of reason often fails and the law be required to reinforce them. For the sense of justice, a gift of the same *humanitas*, not only dictates the principle of duty to us, but teaches that justice and duty (to self, familiars, fellows, and the civic order) are the same. Moreover, if justice is ethical desert – that which is merited or deserved [sect. 57] – the assumption, and imposition, of duty, whether in the form of the moral responsibility of the individual for his actions, or the co-responsibility of the individual for the well-being of the civic order, is a form of ethical desert also.

173. The religious, those who find in 'God's will' a divine injunction for the carrying out by the individual of his general ethical obligations as a human being, would place the argument on a different and generally homiletic plane. Thus, 'the path of duty in this world is the road to salvation in the next', according to the Hebrew proverb. 'You are a distinct portion of the essence of God, and contain a certain part of Him in yourself. Why, then, are you so ignorant of your noble birth? . . . You carry a god about with you, wretch, and know nothing of it', declares Epictetus (*Discourses*, II. viii, 2), enjoining a dutiful ethics upon his philosophical pupils in God's name.

But even without such forms of other-worldly promise and divine sanction, the moral life of the individual is elevated and expanded by the recognition, and acceptance, of responsibilities for self and towards others. For the citizen-turned-stranger it is the path from estrangement; the fulfilment of duty to others Mill (*On Liberty*, p. 150) makes synonymous with 'social morality', the redeeming morality which is shared with others in the interests of all. Indeed, the principle of duty flows from, and gives expression to, the fact that the citizen-*qua*-citizen is a 'moral being' and occupies a place within a 'web of moral relations' [sect. 1]; relations with the capacity to support and sustain him, ethically and practically, even when he acts against the interests of the civic order, or when such support is given against his will.

This moral relationship between the individual and his fellows corresponds ethically to that which the religious in the Judeo-Christian tradition hold to be the relationship between man and God.

174. The principle of duty, as I have already indicated, is a free-standing ethical principle in that it is not the product of a 'covenant', compact, or contract – whether between the citizen and the civic order to which he belongs or among the citizens themselves – and, as it applies to the citizen's duties, is morally prior to the possession of right. Parental duty is morally prior to, transcends, and is independent of any presumption of parental right; the citizen's duty to himself, his fellows and the civic order to which he belongs is, in the first instance, similarly owed by him as a moral being among moral beings who owe duties to one another, without benefit of covenant express or implied, and whatever such individuals' respective rights may be.

Thus, it is just that many of the duties of the citizen to himself, to his fellows, and to the civic order should be owed, ethically and in practice, by the resident non-citizen also. Moreover, duty to the civic order being morally prior to claims of right against it, such claims of right (not being absolute) may be disqualified by the neglect or refusal of duty. In conditions of civic disaggregation, in particular, the disqualification of right in circumstances of neglect or refusal of duty may become a duty of the civic order itself, in the interests of the well-being of all.

175. The principle of duty imposes this and other obligations upon the civic order as obligations to the civic order itself; their end is the preservation of the civic bond and thus of the civic order which it upholds. Thus, in addition to that obligation to disqualify right which may arise in conditions of grave neglect or refusal of duty by the citizen-turned-stranger, the civic order is similarly under a general obligation to defend itself from assault, to preserve its own sovereignty, to limit and control the powers of its instrument the state, and to prevent its own disaggregation. To these and other obligations of the civic order to its citizens I return in Chapter Nine.

176. To whomever it applies, the principle of duty is in the first place an ethical principle, even if it is also commanded by reason and practical necessity. It is neither, on the one hand, a mere bureaucratic formality – even if, where it exists, it has generally been reduced to it – nor, on the other, in its application to the citizen's duties, is it a mere liability to sanction, as Bentham would have it. For in both cases the principle of duty is (in general)

reduced to a negative and morally impoverished principle, in which the citizen's responsibility is no more than to do what he will be penalised for not doing.

Instead, the principle of duty, to whomever it applies, is a positive ethical principle through whose observance the citizen is educated to his true status as a moral being and in turn gains greater moral worth thereby; the citizen as empowered ego, under the rule of dutiless right and demand-satisfaction in the corrupted liberal order, is the less a citizen, the less educated to such status. Moreover, the citizen who observes the ethic of the principle of duty is enabled thereby to live his own moral life. But he who, for instance, delegates or attempts to shrug off duty to self and others to the professional servants of the state, or otherwise becomes a stranger to civic purpose, only seemingly gains greater moral independence by his conduct; or an independence of low moral worth which reduces the individual in his own esteem.

It is not only that the civic order, or community of the individual's fellow-citizens living under a common rule, is a worthy object of his duty *per se*; or, more practically, as the Florentine friar Remigio de' Girolami expressed it (Martines, *City States in Renaissance Italy*, p. 127), that a man 'unmoved' to the interests of the 'common weal' is 'unworthy of friendship'. The ethical implication of observance and non-observance of the principle of duty, as can be seen from the extremes of conduct of the citizen-turned-stranger in the corrupted liberal order, is much larger. Long ago, Cicero understood (*Offices*, I, ii) that 'as all the virtue and credit of our lives proceed from the due discharge of our duties, so all the baseness and turpitude of our lives result from their non-observance'.

177. As an ethical principle, the principle of duty rests upon firmer ground for being so than as a principle dictated by reason alone, or by a narrow calculation of its utility to the individual. For there is no need for great perspicuity on the part of the normal individual, nor for much philosophy or religion, for him to know – especially when instructed – what he ought to do in relation to himself and others if he is to be considered morally good. However increasingly large the obstacles set in the path of the individual, especially in the corrupted liberal orders, to his obtaining and acting upon such knowledge – obstacles I discuss in Chapter Eight – the appeal of the principle of duty to the inherent moral sense of the individual remains a securer appeal, in essence and in principle, than that which is grounded upon the assumption of reason alone.

It needs no Stoic argument that, for example, moral worth possesses an 'intrinsic beauty' to persuade a normal citizen even of a corrupted liberal order – and perhaps especially of a corrupted liberal order – that a sense of responsibility for self and co-responsibility for the well-being of others is a moral attribute of the *homme moyen*. For he knows it to be so, even if only in principle, through the promptings of his moral sense or intuition, just as he knows himself to be bound, in ethical principle, by his relationships with, and undertakings to, his familiars and immediate fellows.

This moral sense is generally reinforced in practice by knowledge gained, even by the young, from experience of the consequences for the individual of failure to act upon such moral sense or otherwise to observe its promptings. Moreover, that which the individual does not sense, or does not know directly, may be sensed and known from the sense and knowledge of others communicated to him; such vicarious experience and the moral wisdom drawn from it are the common patrimony of human association and education in the family, in the community, and in the civic order.

It is to this moral sense and moral knowledge that the principle of duty appeals. Thus, 'you will elicit from the very idea of a neighbour or citizen', Epictetus declares (*Enchiridion*, XXX), 'what the corresponding duties of citizen and neighbour are, once you accustom yourself to contemplate the various relationships in which the citizen and the neighbour are involved.' In reflection of that relation between education and moral knowledge which is being gradually lost in the corrupted liberal order, 'when we are children, our parents deliver us to the care of a tutor, to watch over us that we get no hurt', says Epictetus further (Fragment XCII, *Moral Discourses*, London, 1910, p. 291); 'when we become men, God delivers us to the guardianship of an implanted conscience'.

The 'implanted conscience' in the *homme moyen* is the source of a moral sanction which generally requires no law to bring to mind.

Moreover, it is the existence of a moral knowledge and a moral sense common to all men, and knowing no limit or boundary of time and place, which permitted Aristotle to declare, *a priori*, that 'it is *not right* . . . that any of the citizens should think that he belongs just to himself' (my emphasis) (*Politics*, VIII, i, 1337a); and, likewise, permitted him to hold the view, with other political philosophers across the ages until the present times, that for the citizen to fulfil his duties to the civic order is a manifest good in itself, requiring no special ethical pleading for it to be made out.

The same 'common moral sense' leads Epictetus (*Discourses*, II, x, 4) to insist upon the existence in us of 'natural fidelity', 'natural affection', and a 'natural disposition to mutual usefulness and mutual forbearance', all of which are also preconditions for the existence and preservation of the civic bond. 'Man's good inclination is inborn', declares Amiel (*Ethics and Legality in Jewish Law*, p. 92), rejecting the doctrine of original sin, 'and his evil inclination only incidental'; 'we are obliged to be moral', adds Kant (*Lectures on Ethics*, p. 82).

The assumption of reason is often falsified in practice, and the beast-in-man an omnipresent fact, but so too is such common moral sense, on which the principle of duty rests.

178. Modern scientific methods, categories, discoveries, and habits of mind, so some vehemently argue in the corrupted liberal orders, have swept away the basis upon which the ethical realm once stood, destroying the very idea that that which is 'not-science', with its ethics and values, can exist at all. Yet even this assertion is a moral not a scientific assertion, disclosing – albeit negatively and destructively – that the moral habit of mind survives.

Moreover, for all that the use of Zyklon-B or the violent misapplication of nuclear fission was not much curbed by ethical scruple, the ethical sense has not been, because it cannot be, destroyed. The individual's sense of responsibility for the world which he inhabits, however honoured in the breach, continues to cast its guilty shadow before the most a-civic of his actions; and if he does not observe the principle of duty himself, others can be found who will seek to observe it for him, or to impose it upon him.

Such ethical sense cannot be destroyed because it is the correlative and product of free will; invests men's actions with meanings which cannot be found in mere self-assertion as a supposed value-in-itself; and, where such sense is actively expressed in the civic order in observance and enforcement of the principle of duty, serves to regulate the use and abuse of men's powers and to maintain the civic bond.

179. The ethic of duty rests, as I have argued [sect. 177], upon the moral sense and is reinforced by moral knowledge gained from experience and education. In the acquiring of such knowledge, ratiocination and calculation play their parts. That is, the growth or development in the individual of the moral sense, and of a capacity and will for its expression in the civic order, is an objective and rational process, for all the failures of the assumption of reason. But it is also a process in which subjective feeling, emotion, and intuition help to form the moral outcome. No single element is autonomous or wholly separable from another in the formation of such ethical sense, and the ability and desire to express it in practice.

The moral sense – in the citizen, the civic sense [sect. 6] – being compounded of many elements of which rational calculation of interest is one, is by the same token susceptible to rational appeal, even if not to the same degree in all individuals, and not at all in some individuals. Thus, the argument, say, that the individual has need of obligation, or of an ethical boundary to his claims of right, if his otherwise free actions are to acquire meaning and status beyond that which attaches to self-assertion alone, is capable of rational explanation. So, too, is the argument, for all that it is at its heart an ethical argument, that the observance of the principle of duty is required to protect the individual, the civic order, and the natural world from his least reasoning and most amoral self.

180. Indeed, among the chief ethical and practical objects of an enforceable principle of duty is the arresting, by rational arguments and means, of the rule of dutiless right, and the recall (by rational means) to the civic order of the citizen-turned-stranger, whoever he might be, and whatever his personal status, means or condition.

Such recall to the civic order of the estranged and dutiless individual by rational resort to the principle of duty is a means not an end; a means, among others, to the strengthening of the civic bond, the reform of the corrupted liberal order, the protection of what remains of its freedoms and values, and above all, the arresting of the process of civic disaggregation, but without recourse to irrational, anti-social, discriminatory, draconian, or violent measures.

181. In the corrupted liberal order, the principle of duty has therefore become a practical and utilitarian 'necessity of life' in precisely the sense – and context – which Mill would have understood. 'The necessities of life', he declared in *On Liberty* (p. 185), 'continually require not indeed that we should resign our freedom but that we should consent to this and [sc. or] the other limitation of it.' Such 'necessity of life' now dictates, as Mill would have seen, the observance and enforcement of the principle of duty, resistance to the further loss of sovereignty in the civic order, objection to the rule of dutiless right and demand-satisfaction, and the arresting of other forms of corruption of the liberal ideal. In conditions of accelerating civic disaggregation, these 'necessities of life' are, on the one hand, practical and utilitarian, and, on the other, corroborate what the moral sense first enjoins.

182. In the gradual attenuation of the civic bond, which the principle of duty is required to restore, there is the greater tendency on the part of the citizen for his sense of, and desire for, obligation to be focussed upon other forms of association and belonging, among them those of race or tribe, sex, class, and sect; at worst, for the civic bond to be replaced by the bond of blood. To uphold the civic order is not to deny such other bonds and associations – provided only that they do not threaten the civic order itself – but to defend the former's ethical and practical priority over them, as the order of the aggregate of citizens which embraces and is superior to all others [**sect. 4**].

183. The observance of the principle of duty is a practical necessity also if the free citizen-turned-stranger (and not only he) is to become habituated, in the interests of the free civic order as a whole, to acting socially for the well-being of the civic order as a whole. That is, it is a social necessity, whose ulterior ethical purpose is restoration to the estranged individual, and to the civic order to which he ostensibly belongs, of his social being. Of such purposes the new civic social-ism will be made.

184. It is a further practical necessity of civic life not only that the civic order coheres and that the gradual dissolution of civic feeling in the corrupted liberal orders be halted, but that the wish of most citizens to have pride in the civic order to which they belong is requited by the actions of the civic order itself. Hence, it is also their wish that the civic order, for all that it permits the free expression of divergent and conflicting interest, should be a locus of general concord, not of increasing violence.

The principle of duty, which dictates an equal expectation of its observance by all citizens, is a principle of coherence; the principle of dutiless right is a principle of civic dissolution. In resistance to such dissolution, the dictates of the moral sense, the lessons rationally drawn from experience, and the practical necessity of civic life powerfully converge. But it is also an obligation of the civic order – as it will be the task of a new civic social-ism – to seek to secure the most general and the most *equitable* observance and enforcement of the principle of duty, if the concord citizens desire is to be coherently pursued. In conditions where fellow-citizens are largely unknown to each other, such equity is dictated with greater force. Indeed, even in conditions where the acts of obligation carried out by most citizens must remain largely unobserved by others, fulfilment of the principle of duty, provided that it is generally and equitably enforced by the civic order, can preserve and strengthen the civic bond.

185. Such equity is further dictated by the fact that the most demoralised and plebeian citizen-turned-stranger who wilfully refuses the principle of duty, and the privileged escapee from moral obligation to the civic order who seeks to use his means to evade it, threaten the civic order in different fashion but to like effect. Where the right of the free citizen expresses itself, in the corrupted liberal order, in dutiless unconcern for the well-being of others in the very locus in which such free citizen lives, it is just and equitable that the principle of duty should temper such right,

whatever the particular form such unconcern may take, and whoever may express it.

It is also the duty of the civic order to teach civic-mindedness, or civic sense, to those who do not possess it, or, possessing it, do not permit themselves to act upon it, whoever they may be. For neglect by the citizen-turned-stranger of his co-responsibility for the condition of the civic order, a neglect which knows no boundaries of personal status or circumstance in the civic order, remains an ethical ground for the enforcement of the principle of duty, *per se*. Moreover, the ethical imperative to enforce such duty has priority, in the interests of the civic order as a whole, over counter-claims to the privilege of 'free' dutiless right, whoever may make them.

186. In this respect, as in others, the principle of duty as it applies both to the duties of the citizen and of the civic order stands at the opposite pole to habits of civic neglect and inertia. It is also opposed to asocial reflexes in the citizen-turned-stranger, and especially in the universal plebeian, which dispose him to surrender responsibility for the self and for the well-being of the civic order to 'others', in particular to officials of the state.

In conditions of civic disaggregation, where the corrupted liberal order, whether of city or nation, is in process of losing much of its authority (in the case of the city) or sovereignty (in the case of the nation), a like tendency to transfer moral and practical responsibility for its present and future condition to 'others' can be found in the civic order itself. The principle of duty in its application both to citizen and to civic order, if actively enforced, is a means of restoring and enchancing responsibility-for-themselves to both citizen and civic order.

187. In sum, the principle of duty, observed and enforced, is thus directed, in particular in the corrupted liberal order, against egotistical claims to dutiless right, against the transfer of ethical and practical responsibility to 'others', against the reduction of the free citizen to a protected subject, against the assertion of 'private strength' over public good, against the usurpation of the sovereignty and authority of the civic order by the state and by supranational

bodies, and against the neglect of the civic order's own obligations to its citizen-members.

In all these respects equally, such ethical principle is also the ethical principle of a new civic social-ism, as I further show in Chapter Twelve; its moral and practical end the well-being of the civic order and its members, and the prevention of the latter's reduction to a random association of strangers.

188. Further to summarise, the principle of duty, observed and enforced, is directed to the recalling of the individual citizen to himself and to the civic order to which he belongs, by means of an (if necessary imperative) invitation to him to play the citizen's part. It is also to remind him of what he is, by disclosing to him the true nature of his relationship with the civic order to which he belongs; and, by so reminding him, to strengthen the civic bond and to recompose the civic order.

In contrast, as the present condition of many corrupted liberal orders makes plain, the rule and politics of dutiless right both conceal and deform the true nature of the citizen's relationship with the civic order, isolating such citizen in a non-civic and anti-civic limbo where egotistical self-assertion is legitimated and rewarded, and civic sense receives diminishing recognition and honour. The individual's self-development as a citizen co-responsible for the well-being of the civic order is thus impeded or stifled, and his very membership of such civic order is made opaque to himself and without ethical status.

189. The redemption of such condition does not require the prior express agreement or consent of the citizen even in a democratic civic order. For the principle of duty is the sovereign ethical principle of the civic order and the precondition of it; the citizen's consent to such principle is implied by the fact of his citizenship alone.

Moreover, each citizen-member of a civic order is morally entitled to expect that his fellow-citizens, by virtue of their citizenship, will observe the principle of duty; such expectation, a reciprocal or mutual expectation of citizenship itself, is equally not derived from any express agreement, covenant, or contract [sect. 172]. But neither can the performance of such duty by any citizen be made dependent, by that citizen, upon similar performance of it by others. Each citizen separately, but as a member of the civic order as a whole, owes obligation to it and to his fellows; the performance of such obligation is not a *quid pro quo* for the performance of it by one's fellows.

Likewise, the fulfilment of duty by the citizen, being an ethically prior obligation [sects. 10–13], cannot in itself be made by him into the ground of a claim to absolute right, to the satisfaction of his demands, or to entitlement – his duty done – to unimpeded freedom of action in other regards. No such restraint, however, rests upon the civic order as a whole, which may, under certain conditions and in certain circumstances, as I show in Chapter Eleven, make the possession of right by the citizen dependent upon the performance of duty.

190. The juristic source of the authority of the ruler, of the duties and rights of the subject, and subsequently – in the early modern period – of the rights of the citizen and the sovereignty of the people, has hitherto been found in a covenant, contract, or constitutional settlement; the first two often imaginary, or *ex post facto* intellectual constructs, and the third generally real, historic and inscribed in a constitutional code.

In the early forms of such covenant or contract idea, including the most ancient, the ruled might be held to have originally united themselves into a body politic and subjected themselves to rule, contractually or by covenant exchanging their 'natural' autonomy and insecurity for the ruler's protection; or, where the ruler had abused his trust and the faith of his subjects, a new covenant might reassert and codify the rights of the latter, curbing the authority of the ruler and making a new 'balance' between the rights and duties of the ruled; or, a new covenant again, as in the first phases of the modern evolution of democracy, might assert the entire sovereignty of the people, at the same time making the rights of the citizen, or the 'rights of man', the sovereign principle of the civic order and reducing the principle of duty to a relatively insignificant role in the 'balance' between duty and right.

The notion, a contractual notion, of the need for reciprocity or 'balance' between rights and duties has survived in the corrupted liberal order, despite the attenuation of the principle of duty in practice, but in a mutant and a-civic form: under the rule of dutiless right and demand-satisfaction, the citizen-turned-stranger insists upon his *dutiless or absolute rights as citizen*, or ostensible citizen, on the one hand and upon the *rightless duties to him of the civic order*, or of its instrument the state, on the other.

191. But the juristic ground for the principle of duty of the individual citizen as it applies to his obligations to himself, his fellows, and the civic order cannot be established in covenantal or contractual form. For such duty – not absolute, as I show in Chapter Eight – is owed among fellow-citizens (and to the civic order) without any possible contractual 'guarantee' of reciprocity or mutuality, and without the prior performance of duty to each individual from whom duty is owed. Were there to be such a 'principle', in which, say, the performance of duty by one individual awaited upon performance, or 'guarantee' of performance, of reciprocal duty by another individual (or by the civic order), duty itself would fail.

For the principle of duty, as well as being the sovereign and prior ethical principle of the civic order, is also an ethically autonomous and practically independent principle of the civic order, arising not from agreement but from the fact of citizenship itself, and from the 'necessity of life' which the civic order serves.

192. Nevertheless, a 'son of the covenant' such as I – who carries the sense of a covenant about with him – rejects with caution the notion of such covenant as the ground of the principle of civic duty. 'One who undertakes to keep the covenant', declares Amiel (*Ethics and Legality in Jewish Law*, p. 112), 'is a part of the nation, while one who leaves the covenant leaves the nation'. It is also an ethically beguiling argument that only those individuals who fulfil their notionally covenanted obligations to the civic order should be regarded and treated as citizens, and that those who do not should not.

Moreover, the conception or fancy that a covenant or contract, express or implied, is the historical charter of the modern civic order is a conception which stands at the heart of the liberal ideal, being predicated upon a constitutionalist recoil from the abuse of power. Locke, a gentile 'son of the covenant' and principal architect of the liberal ideal, in urging that the power of government 'ought not to be arbitrary' (*Two Treatises of Civil Government*, Bk. II, para. 137), held that it should be exercised only by means of 'established and promulgated laws', made in accord with the supposed principles of the founding covenant of the civic order, so that 'both the people may know their duty, and be safe and secure within the limits of the law, and the rulers, too, kept within their due bounds' (ibid.).

But the ethical force of the conception of a covenant or contract, real as such ethical force is, is not required in practice to give legitimacy to the principle of duty in itself, nor to justify its enforcement by sanction, when such sanction is found to be in the interests of the civic order as a whole. For, as I have argued, the principle of duty finds its ground, without need or benefit of prior covenant or agreement, in the circumstance of membership of the civic order itself, its ethical force in the individual's own moral sense, and its practical content in the necessity to preserve the civic order in the interests of all.

193. In the history of the liberal ideal, the conception of the covenant or contract as the source of authority, right, or sovereignty in the civic order – wherever such authority, right, or sovereignty might be vested – has also served as an ethical alternative to explanations of the origins of power in mere force, and the legitimation of such power by the fact of its imposition alone. Hence, since the principle of duty is a principle which derives not from imposition but from the fact of citizenship itself, a presumed covenant or contract to this effect between citizen and citizen, or between citizen and civic order, might again seem, ethically and in practice, to be both the plainest and the most persuasive argument by which to justify the principle of duty to the citizens themselves.

But it is, again, unnecessary. The moral sense, which, with the help of law and education, sustains the civic bond, and continues – by the efforts of a minority – to sustain it even in conditions of accelerating civic disaggregation, itself dictates to and teaches citizens that they compose a single civic order, to which they are affiliated and bound by the principle of duty.

Those who possess such moral or civic sense require no pre-sumed covenant to justify or explain it, nor to justify to themselves their ethical expectation that the principle of duty will be equitably enforced against all members of the civic order; while those who do not possess such moral or civic sense will not be persuaded to it by having the presumed existence of such covenant urged upon them.

194. Imposition of the principle of duty upon citizens, or citizens-turned-strangers, who refuse to observe such principle voluntarily is governed not by the need to preserve a supposed contractual (or any other) 'balance' between citizens' duties and rights, but by the practical need to preserve the civic bond and the civic order which it upholds.

In the heyday and under the rule of the liberal ideal, the citizen's conduct was expected to be governed less by imposition than by freely-chosen or voluntary acknowledgment of his co-responsibility for the well-being of the civic order. In the corrupted liberal orders, where such 'freedom of choice' has instead been exercised in general support and favour of the rule of dutiless right and demand-satisfaction, imposition must play a larger part if the accelerating process of civic disaggregation is to be arrested.

195. It may be argued that the imposition of civic duty upon the citizen, or the performance of such duty under the threat of sanction, can have no ethical value, or an ethical value which is much diminished in comparison with that which attaches to duty voluntarily undertaken. 'It were a great deal better', Cicero declares (*Offices*, I, ix) *à propos* a citizen's duty to his fellows – in particular the duty to 'save and protect them' – 'would they do it voluntarily. For an action, although honest, is not truly virtuous unless it be done out of choice, and with a good will.'

Similarly, says Amiel (*Ethics and Legality in Jewish Law*, p. 55), 'one cannot be forced to serve the public against one's will', even if the obligation to be charitable to others is, under Jewish law, considered court-enforceable; that is, an individual can be *compelled* to contribute to charity. But Kant insists (*Lectures on Ethics*, p. 60) that 'in the moral sphere compulsion has no place; no one can compel us' – Jewish law notwithstanding – 'to acts of kindness or charity'.

Ethically better, no doubt, that the charitable act be voluntarily undertaken; that self-restriction or self-control should govern individual citizen conduct rather than constraint imposed by others; and that the principle of duty should be willingly observed. But if the citizen will not voluntarily discharge his duties to himself, to others, and to the civic order to which he belongs, then it must be under constraint and at the risk of sanction.

Moreover, in conditions of civic crisis in the corrupted liberal orders, the moral (and immoral) significance and status of an individual citizen's acts are more justly measured by their consequences for others than by their originating motives and causes; even their consequences for the individual actor himself are becoming ethically and practically of secondary importance to their consequences for the civic order as a whole.

196. In addition, the principle of duty, as it applies to the individual's duties to himself, creates a strong *prima facie* presumption of the individual's ethical co-responsibility for his own condition in the civic order, as I shall further show in Chapter Ten. Thus, where the civic order fails, say, to discharge adequately its educational obligations to the citizen, and he in turn fails to acquire – *inter alia* through lack of such adequate educational provision to him – the knowledge which he requires to act the citizen's part, he remains *prima facie* responsible, in virtue of his duty to himself, for making good such failure, including by recourse to all available means of self-education.

Although this *prima facie* presumption of individual co-responsibility may be modified or lifted where the failure of the civic order to observe its obligations to the citizen is such as entirely to prevent him from fulfilling his own [**sects. 86, 98**], the civic order's default does not, and cannot, in the normal course exempt the citizen ethically or practically from his own duties, nor from his liability to sanction for failure or refusal to discharge his duties to himself, his fellows, and the civic order to which he belongs.

197. But, in general, the actual imposition of duty by sanction is not required to remind the citizen of the principle of duty, as I have argued; the existence in the civic order of sanctions, and the readiness to use such sanctions, are for the most part sufficient in themselves. 'The court of justice of our conscience', as Kant expresses it (*Lectures on Ethics*, p. 132), places a 'prosecutor' in our 'hearts' with or without the existence of formal legal sanction; we 'pass judgment upon ourselves in accordance with moral laws' (ibid., p. 129). Nevertheless, and particularly in the corrupted liberal orders, faith that such moral discomfort with self will alone provide an impulse to the general observance of the principle of duty is increasingly misplaced. The individual citizen knows that he can rely with confidence upon its effective operation neither in himself nor in others; it is equally a breach of the civic order's duty of self-protection, in the interests of all, to rely upon it.

Rather, the provision (where appropriate) and the use (where necessary) of sanction by the civic order in support of the principle of duty is both a spur to conscience and to the habit of unforced civic action. In conditions of civic crisis and quickening civic disaggregation, such provision and use of sanction by the civic order are both moral acts in themselves and practical fulfilments of the civic order's own duties to the citizen-body as a whole.

'If I do a thing because it is commanded, there is no question of any moral disposition', argued Kant (*Lectures on Ethics*, p. 22), on the one hand; but, on the other, 'a man who refrains from doing evil because of fear of punishment will in the long run get accustomed to it, and will feel that it is better to leave such things undone' (ibid., p. 57).

198. But, as I further show in Chapter Eleven, not all ethical duties dictated by the principle of duty – whether duties of the citizen or of the civic order – can or should be made enforceable legal obligations. Furthermore, it must always remain within the sovereign political discretion of the civic order (where it is sovereign) to choose the best methods by which to secure the observance of the principle of duty by its citizens; but without derogation from the principle of duty itself, which is the sovereign ethical principle of the civic order and by which the civic order is itself bound.

Indeed, however voluntarist the civic order and its citizens may wish observance of duty to be or to remain, the obligation of self-protection on the part of the civic order has ethical and practical priority over such preference as there may be for the unenforced performance by the citizen of his duties to himself, his fellows, and the civic order. In the corrupted liberal orders, in particular, both the assumption of reason and its cognate, the expectation of voluntary performance of ethical obligation, have contributed to the weakening of the civic bond under the pressure of the rule of dutiless right.

Therefore, although there are, and will always remain, aspects of the life of the citizen in the free civic order which cannot be made the subject of enforceable obligation, or any obligation whatever, the presumption in favour of such liberty of choice and conduct must diminish as the process of civic disaggregation accelerates, and the numbers of citizens-turned-strangers increase to the peril of all. If even acts of charity can be made enforceable under Jewish law, so too, in principle, may – and in some cases must – other expressions of co-responsibility for the well-being of the civic order, and of the acting of the citizen's part, be made subject to more than the promptings of conscience alone.

Even where not made directly enforceable, neglect or refusal of such acts by the citizen can be made disadvantageous by loss of privilege, benefit, or right. Moreover, the incurring of such disadvantage as consequence of the commission of certain kinds of anti-civic and anti-social act – to be discussed in Chapter Eleven – is to be preferred, in principle, to some forms of penalty commonly employed in the corrupted liberal orders, and which have neither positive ethical nor practical outcome.

Similarly, abuse of, or (at worst) violent damage done to, common provisions made by the civic order for the well-being of all should be visited, as I show further in Chapter Eleven, by ethically-related loss of access to such provision. Even the wilful neglect of the opportunities furnished to the citizen by such provision – as for education and self-education, or for the maintenance and improvement of the individual's health – should not go without negative consequence in the interests of the civic order as a whole [sect. 105]. In conditions of civic disaggregation, the restoration by such means of the citizen's sense of responsibility to himself, his fellows and the civic order is an obligation dictated, by the principle of duty, to the civic order itself.

Despite its virtues, ethical voluntarism becomes even more self-defeating, especially in the corrupted liberal orders, as the demoralised citizen, ruled by dutiless right and surrounded increasingly by citizens-turned-strangers, finds diminishing incentive himself for acts of conscience, abnegation, and service. Nor is ethical voluntarism, with the moral expectations upon which it rests, sufficient to safeguard nature and to provide for the future conditions of well-being of the civic order; no more than can ethical responsiveness, or civic sense, in one citizen in itself induce in others a similar responsiveness, or sense, under conditions in which the common ethical direction of the civic order is being lost. The principle of duty cannot be left to conscience alone.

199. Since the assumption of reason is also frequently found to fail, appeal to rational self-interest alone is likewise insufficient in practice to sustain observance of the principle of duty. Moreover, under the rule of dutiless right, self-interest itself comes to be perceived as synonymous with mere self-assertion against others, undermining in many the most elementary knowledge of where true interest lies. When utilitarian calculation of interest, and even the instinct for self-preservation, fail to provide the ground of duty to self – let alone to one's fellows and to the civic order as a whole – then only fear of sanction remains.

To induce fear in the citizen-turned-stranger of the consequences for himself and his familiars of civic disaggregation, to which his own acts of omission and commission contribute, is ethically justified when all other inducements and arguments fail. To make real a fear of dissolution, *in extremis*, of the civic order itself is, also *in extremis*, the duty of the civic order, or the first and last duty of self-protection. But before such condition is reached and in order that it be not reached, the preservation of a free civic order, however corrupted, demands that the civic practices by which it is to be protected are sustained by sanctions capable, at the last, of deterring the anti-civic and anti-social.

As I have already declared, it is better that the principle of duty be enforced by sanction, and be unwillingly observed, than that it be not enforced and observed at all. Whether the duties it dictates be performed under constraint – including the constraint of fear –

or from right calculation of self-interest, or from sense of ethical obligation voluntarily assumed, is less important, both ethically and in practice, than that such duties are done. The less extensive and willing the discharge of the citizen's duty to himself, his fellows and the civic order to which he belongs, the greater the necessity, in the interests of all, that such duty be compelled. For the ultimate price of the failure of ethical voluntarism in the corrupted liberal order is the failure of the civic order itself.

The Principle of Duty
in General (2)

200. The principle of duty is not a principle of duty for duty's sake
but duty for civic ends: duty which concerns the relations between
individuals as citizens, their co-responsibility for the condition of
the civic order to which they belong, and the obligation of the civic
order to them. Moreover, the principle of duty, by which the civic
bond is maintained, is the fundamental and sovereign, but not the
only, principle of the civic order. The principle of right, but not of
dutiless right, is also a principle of the civic order, by the protection
and reassertion of which the integrity and self-development of the
individual, as well as the sovereignty of the civic order, are
maintained.

Nor does the principle of duty govern all the relations and
actions of individual members of the civic order in the multiplicity
of their affiliations and purposes, but only those relations or actions
which have effects, direct or indirect, upon the well-being of the
civic order as a whole.

201. The principle of duty, for all its ethical force, rationality, and practical necessity, is impeded – though it cannot be negated – in the corrupted liberal order by the presumed counter-'principle', falsely attributed to the liberal ideal, that it is the over-arching purpose of the civic order to remove *all hindrance* to individual self-fulfilment. In consequence, duty to one's fellow-members of the civic order and to the civic order itself comes to be perceived by many in the corrupted liberal order as an obstacle to individual freedom of action. The sense of obligation may likewise be seen as an incubus born of guilt, not the fruit of conscience; service to the community a form (at worst) of personal humiliation.

The doctrine that individual self-realisation, pursued and achieved under the protection of state and law, is properly the *raison d'être* of the civic order, has hitherto commanded general assent in the now-corrupted liberal orders. Under such rubric, the model citizen is, or has hitherto been, he who, using his rights, freedoms, and capacities, 'maximises his advantages' in the civic order, to the ostensible benefit of all. Such action for the 'realisation' of self in freedom is, or has been, further perceived as productive of civic energy, variety of effort, and fruitful change.

'Self-realisation through freedom of action' is, however, not action *in vacuo*. It is action carried out within and through the civic order, upon which it simultaneously imposes itself and is dependent. Such action *may* benefit the civic order, but its negative consequences *must* be borne by the civic order, that is by fellow-citizens. The conflicts and harms which such 'self-realisation' generates require to be resolved and treated by the civic order; the duty of sustaining the civic bond falls more heavily on some, the greater the preoccupation of others to 'maximise' the extent of their 'self-realisation'; dutilessness in one is the enlargement of duty in another.

The pursuit of 'self-realisation' generally seeks, *inter alia*, the prize of the widest esteem of others, but the existence of the civic bond is the precondition for securing such esteem. Moreover, in conditions of civic disaggregation under the rule of dutiless right – in which the claimed 'right' to dutiless 'self-realisation' plays the largest part – individual aspiration can 'realise' itself only with increasing difficulty, except in its most mutant a-civic or anti-civic forms. The well-being of the civic order, as I have therefore argued, is a precondition for individual well-being; but it is more so where such individual well-being is held, or imagined, to be dependent upon, and even synonymous with, the maximum degree of personal freedom.

202. However, this corrupted liberal ideal, even as the civic disaggregation which it promotes undermines the ideal before our very eyes, continues to make the principle of duty appear antithetical to freedom itself. The very diversity and heterogeneity of affiliations and purposes which are generated by the pursuit of self-realisation through freedom of action make for what H. G. Wells called, in 1914, an 'endless multitude of social expedients and rules' (*An Englishman Looks at the World*, p. 337). 'Belonging' within the civic order is spread, but also dissipated, across a wide variety of social fidelities and loyalties (as well as infidelities and disloyalties), associations and relations, private and public, civic, a-civic, and anti-civic.

In such conditions of heterogeneity and flux, particularly in the disaggregating metropolises of the corrupted liberal orders, it is not only thought difficult but (paradoxically) oppressive-to-freedom to speak of duty to self, to one's fellows, and to the civic order. But, here, the argument levelled at the principle of duty is itself oppressive of ethical preference, and dismissive of rational calculation as to the 'necessities of life'. The flux and disaggregation of the civic order, it is maintained, cannot be halted, but, if they could be, it would only be by recourse ('in a free society') to 'unacceptably authoritarian measures'.

In the wilderness of this argument, itself conducted under the rule of dutiless right and demand-satisfaction, the principle of duty has little ethical or practical status. Moreover, where it dictates particular duties – say, to maintain a marital relation, to join a trade union, to 'sweep before one's door' – the principle of self-realisation through freedom of action, or 'choice', is on the instant vested, by one interested group or another, with ethical or practical precedence over such particular forms of duty, for all that they may be dictated by the interests of the civic order as a whole.

203. Nevertheless, despite, or because of, the harm done to civic

relations under the ethically corrupt rule of dutiless right and demand-satisfaction, there can be little doubt that many citizens-turned-strangers wish to turn citizens once more. The philosophical basis for the resumption by the estranged individual of co-responsibility for the well-being of the civic order, and for his voluntary acceptance of the claims made upon him by the principle of duty, must still reside in the presumption of free will and the assumption of reason, for all that they have been abused and falsified in the event. Moreover, the moral and practical appeal of the principle of duty as an expression of the life shared with others must also remain, as long as the voluntary association of human beings with one another itself remains.

204. It may be argued that, in general, neither the civic bond, nor even the civic order itself, possesses any remaining integrity, or wholeness, to which a civic duty can be coherently owed; in particular, that since there is, and can be, no discernible 'general interest' in a civic order which is composed of a heterogeneous plurality of interests and competing aspirations, there is, and can be, no general principle of duty applicable in, and to, such civic order.

But if this is so, and I do not concede it, it has not served as an impediment to the assertion of a general 'principle' of dutiless right, in consistent form, in the same corrupted civic orders supposedly bereft of integrity and coherence. Nor has it hitherto prevented such civic orders from bending their efforts, in equally consistent fashion, to the meeting of dutiless claims and demands. In all such efforts, a common practical will and ethical (or anti-ethical) purpose may be found, which can – and, in the interest of preserving the liberal civic order, must – be equally bent to the enforcement of the principle of duty.

Furthermore, a common civic sense, or sense of co-responsibility for the well-being of the civic order, survives in many citizens, as I have argued, for all the plurality of interests and aspirations which may be found in it. The 'implanted conscience' of the *homme moyen* [sect. 177] continues to dictate to many, even in the corrupted liberal orders, a common ethic of duty, despite the atrophying, and even supposed absence, of a common ethical direction in such civic orders. Indeed, the 'implanted conscience' is itself an expression of such ethical direction.

There can also be no civic order at all – unless in its final state of disaggregation – which does not possess, however plural its composition, a substantial measure of institutional coherence and a generally agreed ethical direction [sect. 4], under whatever pressures they may be brought at the hands of citizens-turned-strangers.

205. The principle of duty is also subject to the pressures of radical dissent, including that form of radicalism which makes a duty out of dissent itself, and even a redeeming virtue; sometimes, where the 'rebel tradition' is deeply rooted, a duty and a virtue *whatever the nature of the civic order may be*. Refusal of obligation may thus take the most varied forms, as well as having diverse ethical and practical ends. It may express the spirit of obstinacy to any rule whatever; it may proclaim the refusal of obligation to others as an ethical principle itself; it may be directed to resistance to a particular form of rule, to a particular politico-economic system, or merely to particular ideas or measures; it may express the will to self-realisation through unimpeded freedom of action.

But the principle of duty, as it applies to the citizen's duty to himself, his fellows, and the civic order, is above all challenged by the equation, made especially in the corrupted liberal orders, of duty with 'obedience', obedience with 'obedience to authority', and 'authority' – even if it is the authority of the sovereign citizen-body itself – with that which must, by definition, be rejected; and thus, duty itself must be rejected with it. In all these cases, including that of radical dissent, duty to self and to one's fellows is frequently made synonymous with loss of freedom as such; duty to the civic order, whose well-being is the precondition of the exercise of all right, made synonymous with duty to a system of power; playing the citizen's part, with obeisance; civic fellowship with collectivist imposition; the civic bond, with an ethical leg-iron. In all these cases, including forms of dissent which pretend to more 'advanced' or 'progressive' social principles than that of the principle of duty, it is the value placed upon the mere *sense* of personal freedom, without its practical substance or ethical reward, which often stands in the way of acceptance of the principle of duty.

This is not surprising, since the ethics, or anti-ethics, of the corrupted liberal order shape and beguile the ethics even of those most radically opposed to it. Indeed, the ethical value placed upon free 'self-realisation' or 'freedom of choice' – often made falsely co-terminous with 'individual freedom' as such – may also, in practice, be ascribed to free action which has no ulterior moral purpose at all, beyond that which may be dictated by the goal of 'self-realisation' itself. Under such conditions, egoism, including the egoism of the radical dissenter, is generally quick to show the principle of duty the door, as a mere slogan of reaction.

Yet the existence of the civic bond and of the civic order is common to all politico-economic systems whatever; the individual, including the radical dissenter, is a citizen of a determinate civic order; the desirable conduct of such citizen, whoever or wherever he may be, is governed, in the interests of the civic order as a whole, by the same, universal and ethically sovereign principle of duty.

206. It may also be objected that the principle of duty requires, in the form I set it out, too inquisitorial or 'authoritarian' a system of supervision for its enforcement. This is not so, as I show in Chapter Eleven. But, even if it were so, the consequences for the already-corrupted liberal orders of further failure, or refusal, to elevate and enforce the principle of duty must outweigh the 'price' – the restriction of the scope of dutiless right, for example – which the principle of duty may dictate that the members of the civic order should pay.

Instead, it is the amoral or corrupted liberal counter-assertion of a 'right' in the dutiless individual to unimpeded autonomy of action in relation to himself, his fellows, and the civic order, provided only that he does not interfere with the autonomous 'right' of other dutiless individuals to do likewise, which now bids to destroy the civic orders in which such 'autonomy' is exercised; and which invites the 'authoritarian' to intervene.

For it is in these conditions that, although the principle of duty is not itself a principle of obedience, men are 'disposed to . . . obey or disobey [only] as in their private judgments they shall think fit', as Hobbes puts it (*Leviathan*, Chap. XXIX). Moreover, the longer such conditions persist, the greater is likely to be the egotistical individual's unwillingness to accept responsibility for self and for the consequences of his actions; and the less his capacity to adapt to, or even acquire knowledge of, any other ethical principle than that dictated to him by the presumptions of dutiless right.

207. The increasingly settled habit in the corrupted liberal orders (for all their flux and incoherence) of delegation to others of responsibility for self, for the well-being of familiars and fellows, and for that of the civic order as a whole, is a powerful obstacle to the voluntary acceptance of the principle of duty. Indeed, in refusing and neglecting duty, such habit also refuses and neglects the habit of moral judgment, upon which observance of the principle of duty itself rests. Moreover, when one form or expression of civic sense falls into neglect or contempt, so generally do others; and when, at the last, duty in whatever aspect comes to be regarded by the individual with indifference, or as a matter of mere arbitrariness or personal choice, such individual ceases to be a citizen, or ethical person.

But the delegation to others of responsibility for self and for one's familiars, or of co-responsibility for the condition of one's fellows and of the civic order as a whole, is not irreversible, even if it may only be reversed, in the case of some citizens-turned-strangers, by sanction.

208. In the corrupted liberal orders, the perception of ethical principles as matters at best of subjective preference, and at worst as obstacles to self-realisation through unimpeded freedom of action, stands close to the heart of the accelerating process of civic disaggregation. Indeed, under the rule of dutiless right and demand-satisfaction, all moral ideas whatever tend to lose legitimacy and may eventually cease to be comprehensible to a majority of persons. Moreover, in the heterogeneity and flux of the metropolitan civic order, with its changing multiplicity of interests, creeds, citizen-origins, levels of education, manners, languages, occupations, and patterns of unemployment, it is easily argued that only a moral relativism of personal choice and a value-free pragmatism in civic action are possible without resort to oppression.

It is not so. The organising principles of the civic order, the

principle of duty sovereign among them, are constant; the civic
sense, even if only in a minority which shoulders the civic burden
on behalf of the rest, survives; the desire, even if only in embryo,
of many citizens-turned-strangers to play the citizen's part can be
found in the least favourable of civic conditions. And where, could
it be imagined, neither civic bond, nor other semblance of a
common ethical direction remained to the civic order (a contradiction in terms), sheer necessity – the need of individual safety and
survival – might as soon drive men to concord as to the taking up
of arms.

209. Even if it were the case that no common ethical direction
could be found in a determinate civic order, a proposition I reject *a
priori* [sect. 4], the absence of such common ethical direction could
not be the ground for a general rejection of the principle of duty,
unless the civic order had itself abandoned its duty of self-
protection and accepted its own dissolution.

210. In any civic order which, by definition [sect. 4], is constituted
of more than a random agglomeration of individuals and is, rather,
an aggregate of citizens composed, under common rule, into an
association embracing and superior to all other associations within
its bounds, there is, as long as such civic order remains, a common
ethical purpose. However atrophied, contested, or rejected, such
purpose is that of the maintenance of the civic order itself.

This ethical purpose is neither an arbitrary purpose nor a purpose
which can be subject to individual choice, even if in other matters
which concern the free citizen of a free civic order a wide range of
moral choice is permitted. Moreover, the *homme moyen*'s interest in
his self-preservation, and in the preservation of his immediate
familiars – an interest which does not require to be taught to, or
imposed upon, such individual – itself normally dictates the ethical
and practical priority of the voluntary defence of the civic order to
which he belongs, as the best means to his own preservation. If
such interest is lacking, or does not dictate such obligation, then
such obligation must be imposed upon him in enforcement of the
principle of duty.

211. It may further be objected that, under the rule of certain
political or economic systems in the civic order, or by the reason of

the defects of the passing political figures who may come to command it, the civic order may come to be flawed in such a fashion that observance by the citizen of his duties to the civic order cannot be reasonably or justly expected of him. It might be argued, for example, that command by secret, corrupt, oppressive, or cruel power over the civic order and its instrument the state, or the prevalence of severe and remediable social and economic injustices in the condition of citizens of the civic order, may not merely deter obligation to the civic order but may properly exempt some or all of the citizens from obligation to it.

In circumstances such as these, as I have already indicated [sects. 83, 132, 140] and discuss further in Chapter Eleven, it is the right of citizens to criticise, remove democratically, rebel against or, in extreme conditions, overthrow by force a particular politico-economic system in the civic order, or particular individuals who may command the civic order. Indeed, where the effect of the rule of such system or such individuals is harmful to the civic bond and to the general well-being of the civic order itself, the exercise of such right may become a civic duty, dictated by the citizen's co-responsibility for the well-being of the civic order as a whole; in a democratic civic order it may represent the assertion, or reassertion, of the sovereignty of the citizen-body.

But such civic right, and in some extreme circumstances, civic duty, can be properly exercised only in defence of the integrity of the civic bond and the preservation of the civic order; they cannot be exercised in defence of particular interest to the damage of the civic order as a whole. Nor can the flaws and defects of a particular system of government of the civic order, or of the management of its economy, justify such assault upon the civic order as would imperil its very existence, whatever the reforms which might be justly demanded and secured in its form of rule, or whatever might have been the misdeeds of the fallen individuals ousted from office or power.

For the purpose of all such civic action is not the destruction but the protection of the civic order, whose survival and well-being is the precondition of the liberties and well-being of its citizen-members.

212. Misunderstanding the nature of the civic order, confusing the civic order with its instrument the state, and falsely conceiving of the principle of citizen-duty as a principle of obedience to power, old socialism (especially, but not exclusively, in its communist form) promoted hostility to the very idea of citizen-obligation, except that which might be owed to fellow class-members, to a class party, and to the socialist state. 'Duty' was compromised as a term; the 'citizen' gave way to the 'comrade' and 'brother' [sect. 22]. The primacy of the civic order over the passing politico-economic system was lost from sight; class sense gained the ethical priority which belongs to civic sense alone; the concepts of justice and equity were invested with a narrow economic meaning.

The defeat of old socialism has halted and overturned (but not ended) such confusions and reductions. It has also made possible, at last, the recognition, by all, of the true nature of the *civic bond* and the primacy of the *civic order*; and opened the way, as I show in Chapter Twelve, to a new civic social-ism whose cause is the defence of both in the interests of all.

213. It may also be objected that since the defects of the civic order are more easily recognised than its virtues, the principle of duty – a principle of defence of the civic order – is less likely to be embraced with ardour in any circumstances whatever than the citizen's (dutiless) claims, objections, grievances, and demands are likely to be pursued without remission, in particular in the corrupted liberal order.

But the same recognition of the defects of the civic order may equally impel other citizens to a greater sense of co-responsibility for the overcoming and cure of such defects; to a greater determination to challenge and deny the claims of dutiless right, in the knowledge that such claims contribute to the disaggregation of the civic order; and to a more certain civic sense of the ethical sovereignty of the principle of duty.

214. The relative simplicity and convenience to the individual of his claims to dutiless right, to self-realisation through unimpeded freedom of action, and to the satisfaction of his demands are, so it may be further argued, in deterrent contrast to the relative complexity and inconvenience to the individual of the observance of his duties to himself, his fellows and the civic order. Or, as Rousseau declared (*Social Contract*, Bk. III, Chap. 15), 'everything that is not in the course of nature has its attendant inconveniences, and civic society most of all'.

But the 'inconvenience' of a general or widespread failure to observe the principle of civic duty, whether in respect of the individual's duties to himself and to others or the civic order's duties to him, is greater by far. Where the 'inconvenient' consequence of failure by a defaulting individual to observe the principle of duty is not manifest to the latter, only sanction may make it so.

215. It may further be objected, as I have shown [sects. 40–6], that the voluntary observance by the citizen of the principle of duty, insofar as it implies an acceptance of ethical co-responsibility for the condition of the civic order, is dependent upon the validity of the *assumption of reason*; an unreliable assumption, frequently falsified in the outcome, in particular in respect to the citizen-turned-stranger and the universal plebeian. But, as I have also shown [sects. 154, 177], it is not reason alone which impels to such duty; the more frequently falsified by some, the greater the anxiety and will-to-duty of others, even if only of a minority; and the less observed in general, the greater the compensating need for the enforcement of the principle of duty by sanction, and its reinstatement as the sovereign ethical principle of the civic order.

216. It may equally be argued that it is not in the interests of the civic order itself for the citizen to observe the principle of duty; that, rather, his a-civic passivity, inertia, and 'non-interference' are a precondition, especially in conditions of accelerating civic disaggregation, for the effective and unimpeded administration, by representatives of the civic order and officials of its instrument the state, of the interests of the citizen-body as a whole.

But it is precisely such conditions in which the citizen does not play the citizen's part – because he is unable or unwilling to do so, or is prevented from doing so – that lead to the usurpation of the sovereignty of the civic order, the transformation of the citizen into the stranger, and the disaggregation of the civic order itself. Moreover, it is the unimpeded administration, by officials, of the interests of a passive and inert citizen-body in a corrupted liberal order which it is one of the governing purposes of the restoration of the principle of duty to prevent.

217. I now turn to the question of the proper limits upon the principle of duty, both as it applies to the citizen's duties to the civic order, and to the civic order's duties to him. I have already made it clear [sects. 132–3, 140] that citizen-duty is not obeisance to power, whether such power be that of the state, a particular politico-economic system or a particular ruler. Nor is it duty to class, kith, or clan, important as such duties may be in their own (private) right. For citizen-duty is duty to uphold and defend the civic order, and is co-responsibility for the well-being of the civic order as a whole.

Where the principle of duty dictates to a citizen obligation to the self and to others, it is duty to the self and to others as *citizens-in-common* of the same civic order, whether of the city or nation, and not as *subjects-in-common* of a state or administrative power, nor as common feudatories or tributaries of a supranational bureaucratic order. The duty which is owed to fellow-citizens is a duty owed to the sovereignty of the civic body as a whole, the fulfilment of which duty is itself a precondition of the retention of sovereignty by such civic body.

Even less is duty a form of fealty, submissiveness or bondage, since they are incompatible with citizenship and the ethical nature of the civic order, through which the citizen is vested, by virtue of his membership of such civic order, with determinate duties and rights. Moreover, fealty, submissiveness, and bondage to authority of whatever kind demand and imply an ethically offensive 'spirit of idolatry, found within the worship of power by a human being' (Amiel, *Ethics and Legality in Jewish Law*, p. 107). Judaism, in particular, says Amiel, 'hates the slave, witness the fact that the ears of the latter' – the Jew who prefers servitude to freedom – 'were pierced with an awl (*Exodus*, XXI, 5–6) as a sign of the ignominy of their voluntary prolonged period of bondage' (ibid., p. 106).

Hence, just as there are, and can be, no absolute rights vested in the citizen which are untempered by duty, so there can be no absolute duties, untempered by right, imposed upon him; notwithstanding the fact that the principle of duty is the sovereign ethical principle of the civic order, and is a principle enforceable against the citizen by sanction in respect of some of the duties which it enjoins.

218. There must always be limits placed upon and exceptions allowed to duty, as in the case of right. 'The categorical imperative', declares T. H. Green (*Prolegomena to Ethics*, Chap. 2, sect. B, para. 197), 'can enjoin nothing *without liability to exception*' (emphasis in original); as is exemplified by the exception to the duty to defend the civic order with arms, an exception which conscientious objection brings.

Nor can citizenship of any free civic order be defined by its duties alone; 'it is almost as bad to have nothing but duties as it is to have no duties at all', as F. H. Bradley puts it (*Ethical Studies*, Oxford, 1927, p. 210). For citizenship is an amalgam of duties, rights, privileges, responsibilities, and benefits. Moreover, as the principle of duty is the sovereign ethical principle of the civic order, so the citizen-body (of the democratic civic order in the form of the nation) is its sovereign political power; a power which entitles such citizen-body to determine, in the interests of the civic order, how the principle of duty as it applies to individual citizens should be enforced, which of the particular duties of the citizen should attract sanction, and what such sanctions should be.

Just as it is not obeisance to power, so *civic duty is not blind duty*, but is an expression, at best, of civic sense, self-restraint, and voluntary co-responsibility for the well-being of the civic order. In a democratic civic order, furthermore, the general rules of application and enforcement of the principle of duty must be democratically determined. In addition, although the principle of duty applies to all, it must be applied equitably; in some cases, as I discuss further in Chapter Eleven, the circumstances, means, and powers of the individual citizen will determine the scope of his duties.

Above all, the imposition of duty on the citizen must serve the well-being of the civic order as a whole, and not the particular interests of those who at any time command the political and economic instruments of such civic order.

219. Since civic duty is not, and cannot be permitted to become, blind duty – blind duty being objectionable ethically, in reason, and from considerations of utility also – it is the duty of the civic order itself to ensure that the citizen is educated not only to know what his duties are and by what sanctions they may be enforced, but, as far as is possible, to understand their ethical ground and practical purpose.

Montaigne, following Xenophon, approves the latter's assertion that the 'worthiest and best science' in the young is the 'knowledge how to obey' (*Essays*, tr. J. Florio, Bk. I, Chap. XXIV, p. 147). Yet Montaigne plainly perceived the fulfilment of duty more as a matter of 'conscience and virtue' (Bk. I, Chap. XXV, p. 162) than of blind obedience to authority and command. The former is at best the moral expression of duty to self, one's fellows and the sovereign civic order, subject to limits and tempered by right, even if such right is not absolute; the latter is, at worst, duty for duty's sake, subject at worst to no limits, arbitrary and untempered by civic right.

The principle of duty as a principle of obedience to the power of *command* is not a citizen-principle, but a principle which makes of the individual a subject or even servant – ear pierced by an awl – of such power. The principle of duty as a principle of co-responsibility for the civic order sustains the civic bond, restores the citizen to himself, and helps to preserve the sovereignty of such civic order. For the citizen to owe a duty to the civic order to which he belongs is not to be subject to it; on the contrary, to fulfil such duty is to play the citizen's part, and to cease to be a stranger.

220. The principle of duty as it applies to the citizen is also not a principle of fidelity and devotion, but of ethical, rational, and practical *self-command*, a self-command which, in the form of civic sense, dictates duty to the individual. The principle of duty, to be vested with ethical meaning, requires no bended knee; no mystical abandonment of command-of-self to an order held to stand above the individuals who compose it; no act of personal surrender save that of the egotistical claim to dutiless right.

Nor is the principle of duty, for all that it is the sovereign principle of the civic order, a principle which demands an exclusive concern for the civic order's well-being. '*Tutti per comune* [all for the commune, or community]', as Brunetto Latini, the Florentine poet and mentor of Dante, urged – on the grounds that such dedication was conducive to '*pace . . . e ben fare*', or peace and well-being – is not enjoined by the principle of duty. Rather, the principle of duty dictates to the individual that 'contribution' of 'some sustentation to the whole' which John Donne urged (*Complete Poetry and Selected Prose*, p. 456) [sect. 72], in the belief that 'to be no part of any body is to be nothing'.

221. Exclusive devotion to the civic order, even if it were possible, is not desirable either ethically or in practice. Furthermore, even if, as Epictetus declared, 'the whole is superior to a part, and the city to the citizen' (*Discourses*, II, x, 1), devotion of the part to the whole, and of the citizen to the city, or civic order, cannot be exclusive of other duty and other affiliation. Nor do citizens so 'belong' to the civic order, whether of nation or city, as to suggest, with Aristotle (*Politics*, VIII, i, 1337a) that they are in some sense the possessions of such civic order. Rather, the association of citizens living under common rule in the civic order embraces, and is superior to, all other associations within its bounds [sect. 4], but does not, and cannot, demand the extinction, suppression or constriction of the existence and rights of the latter unless they are a threat to the well-being of the civic order itself.

Likewise, the principle of duty, as it applies to the citizen's obligations to the civic order, is the sovereign but not exclusive principle of the civic order. That is, it is a principle which has precedence over others; and thus, when the principle of duty comes into conflict with other principles of the civic order, has *prima facie* ethical and practical priority in such conflict.

Just as the citizen does not 'belong' exclusively to, nor is the 'possession' of, the civic order, so the principle of duty, as I have already made clear, is neither absolute nor exclusive. The civic order cannot, in its own interest, command an excess of duty to itself which is beyond the capacity or interest of the citizen to give; an excess which is the ethical counterpart of the citizen's unrestrained claims to dutiless right in the corrupted liberal order. Nor does the principle of duty command the citizen to spring to attention at every beck and call of the civic order, or of its instrument the state. 'All the services which a citizen can render to the State ought to be rendered as soon as the Sovereign demands them', Rousseau declares in the *Social Contract* (Bk. II, Chap. 4), 'but the Sovereign cannot . . . impose any burden upon its subjects which are useless to the community'.

The obligation to preserve the free civic order, by rendering unto Caesar that which is Caesar's, can be carried out only by free citizens whose own integrity is preserved. Thus, the citizen's duty to himself, which the principle of duty dictates, is a duty to act in a fashion such as to enhance, not reduce, the citizen's dignity, self-regard, and self-command; that is, to restore the citizen-turned-stranger to himself, and thus to end his exclusion from the purposes of the civic order.

222. Indeed, the precondition of the fulfilment of the citizen's obligation to the civic order is that he fulfil his duties to himself and his fellows. By means of the fulfilment of his duties to himself – duties which I particularise in Chapter Ten – the citizen acquires the capacity to fulfil his duties to others; in fulfilling his duties to others, he fulfils a large part of his duties to the civic order as a whole. In such priority of duty to self, as dictated by the principle of duty rather than by the 'right' to self-realisation through unimpeded freedom of action, the individual citizen's ethical status as a separate and distinct moral being, whose identity is not subsumed within that of the civic order to which he belongs, is also confirmed.

But the principle of duty cannot be observed by individual citizens incapable of it. In Montaigne's words (*Essays*, Bk. I, Chap. VII, p. 41), 'man's dutie' can only be 'grounded and established' in what it is in his 'power' to do; 'we cannot be tied beyond our strength and meanes' (ibid.) Excluded from observance of the principle of duty are all those citizens not yet capable of acting the citizen's part – such as minors – or who are, or have become, constitutionally or in other like ways unable to do so. Children, the sick and the aged, for example, are not so much subject to duty as the objects of it on the part of others.

223. All such exclusions from observance of the principle of the individual's co-responsibility for the well-being of the civic order

to which he belongs cannot, however, take anything from the principle itself, nor from its application, in the form of a general rule, to *all members of the civic order, whatever their status or condition.* A sovereign civic order, acting within its own discretion [sect. 218], may choose to exempt certain categories of citizen, such as those of few means and many social handicaps, from fulfilment of their duties to the civic order, or reduce the scope of their duties, or exempt such citizens from sanction. Nevertheless, the civic order remains obligated, in the interests of all, to preserve and maintain the civic bond, to permit and encourage all citizens to act the citizen's part, to arrest the process of civic disaggregation and where necessary to enforce the principle of duty by sanction, without regard to the individual's status or condition.

224. As certain special categories of citizen may be exempted by the civic order from observance of the principle of duty, so other categories of citizen may, under law, have special or additional civic duties expected of or imposed upon them, which are not expected to be borne by others, as I discuss further in Chapters Ten and Eleven. Such special or additional duties, especially duties to the civic order as a whole, may – provided that it is according to law, is practical, and in the interest of the well-being of the civic order as a whole – be determined by the means of the individual citizen. Likewise, exceptional civic duties and civic penalties may be imposed, under law, upon individual citizens as sanctions for acts of omission or commission which have caused exceptional harm to the well-being of the civic order as a whole.

But here, too, such exceptions – or seeming exceptions – to the general rule of the equitable application to all of the principle of duty [sects. 184–5] cannot derogate from such rule, which is the rule governing the application and enforcement of the principle of duty.

225. It is in the matter of the citizen's duty to maintain the civic order through the payment of national and local taxes that the means of the citizen become the sole criterion of his obligation. 'The subjects of every state', declared Adam Smith (*The Wealth of Nations*, Bk. V, Chap. 2, Part II (1)), 'ought to contribute towards the support of the government' – or, as I should say, the civic order

– 'as nearly as possible in proportion to their respective abilities'; that is, in proportion to their means.

The criterion of means, as I further discuss in Chapter Eleven, may also be the most ethical and most equitable, if not always the most practical, criterion for assessing the just measure of financial sanction for the citizen's non-observance, by refusal or neglect or other cause, of certain duties dictated to him by the principle of duty.

226. Apart from such particular exemptions and special exceptions from the citizen's otherwise common liability to observe in equal measure the principle of duty, the general rule to which I have referred [sect. 223] is fundamental to the principle of duty itself, being dictated by equity, reason, and practical necessity together. In particular, those who for the time being hold office in the democratic civic order, or who are otherwise responsible for the making, administration and enforcement of the law, are bound by – and cannot be exempt from, even at the discretion of the civic order – the principle of duty. As Rousseau expressed it (*Social Contract*, Bk. III, Chap. 16), 'no one has a right to require another to do what he does not do himself'.

227. In a democratic civic order, the extent and limit of the individual's duty are determined by a democratically representative and accountable legislative body, acting on behalf of the civic order, and are administered and enforced under the rule of law. (In Chapter Eleven, I consider how the administration and enforcement of the principle of duty may be improved.) But it is also an ethical presumption of the civic order, a presumption increasingly disappointed under the rule of dutiless right, that the individual citizen, while acting in his own practical interests and according to his own understanding of the common ethical direction of the civic order, will behave in such a way as not to harm his own well-being, the well-being of his fellows, or that of the civic order as a whole, whatever the law may provide.

This presumption of a general obligation so to act is derived from the civic bond itself [sect. 5], which dictates that the well-being of the civic order is a precondition of the well-being of the individual. Hence, the civic order, although setting limits upon the citizen's duty in accord with the principles I have discussed [sects. 217–22], cannot exempt the citizen from the general ethical obligation not to harm himself, his fellows, or the civic order to which he belongs. Where the civic order, as by inadvertence, neglect, or, in the corrupted liberal order, from the priority given to dutiless right, does permit such harm, it is in breach of the civic order's own fundamental duty of self-protection.

228. In conditions of accelerating civic disaggregation such as threaten the existence of the civic order itself, the general obligation of the citizen not to harm the well-being of the civic order to which he belongs, and the particular duties which such citizen owes under the law of a given civic order, take ethical and practical precedence over the rules as to 'limits and exceptions' [sect. 218]. *In extremis*, the 'limits to the authority of society over the individual', as Mill described them (*On Liberty*, pp. 134–67), are required to be relaxed by the civic order under its duty of self-protection. Such obligation is subject to the proviso only that no duty can be absolute or blind [sect. 219], nor such as to reduce the citizen to an idolater of power [sect. 217] or rightless slave [sect. 98].

Otherwise, in conditions when the civic order, a body which embraces and is superior to all other associations of citizens within its boundaries [sect. 4], is itself in peril, it has both a right and a duty – to the citizens as a whole – to insist upon a rigorous observance of the principle of duty, both as it applies to itself and to its instrument the state, and as it applies to the citizens themselves.

Such right, duty, and rigour are not only compatible with the liberal ideal but, in conditions of severe civic crisis, necessary to its defence. Even in conditions in which the civic order is not under threat, Mill can be found to allow at the very outset of *On Liberty* (p. 24), as I have shown [sect. 24], that there are 'many positive acts for the benefit of others' which 'anyone may rightfully be compelled to perform'; that the citizen may be required to bear a 'fair share' in 'any other joint work [sic] necessary to the interest of the society of which he enjoys the protection' (ibid.); and that 'things which . . . it is obviously a man's duty to do, he may rightfully be made responsible to society for not doing' (ibid.).

This conception of the scope of positive individual responsibility, wider than the corrupted liberal ideal now allows or understands, is also that which is dictated by the principle of duty, in particular under conditions which flout the civic bond and threaten the existence of the civic order.

229. The principle of duty, finally, remains in essence a principle of moral expectation – the expectation that the citizen will respect the civic bond and voluntarily accept co-responsibility for the condition of the civic order – and of anticipatory moral disapproval if he does not. Moreover, where there is in the civic order a 'free choice' of means by which the civic order may be preserved, it will always be preferable that the civic bond be voluntarily sustained by the members of the civic order. Thus, the principle of duty, being in essence an ethical principle as well as the sovereign principle of the civic order, dictates a moral preference for expectation over invitation, invitation over inducement, and inducement over compulsion, in securing the observance of the citizen's particular duties. Likewise, being in essence a principle of moral expectation, the principle of duty, as it applies to the duties of the citizen, dictates a presumption in favour of treating a-civic or anti-social acts as ethical transgressions which invite reproach, rather than as breaches of law which invite sanction.

Similarly, where in any free civic order particular duties are required of the citizen by law, and notwithstanding the wide scope given by Mill for the imposition of positive civic responsibilities upon the individual, the principle of duty continues to dictate the avoidance of the oppression of such individual. As in the majority of the injunctions of the Decalogue, so in the prescriptions of the principle of duty, it is less oppressive of the citizen that duty be conceived of, and enjoined, in negative form.

Therefore, just as the Mosaic law gives ethical priority to the negative injunction that men should 'not kill' over a positive prescription that men should create or protect life [**sect. 144**], so, too, in the civic order *prohibition* of the anti-civic, or that which is destructive of the well-being of such civic order, in general has ethical priority over positive, and potentially more oppressive, *prescriptions* of civic duty.

230. Nevertheless, despite all such ethical and practical scruples, limits, exemptions, and exceptions in the application and enforcement of the principle of duty, the principle of duty is the sovereign principle of the civic order. It is, therefore, the right and duty of the civic order to apply and enforce such principle freely and according to its discretion. Moreover, in the systems of law of numerous free civic orders, including in English common law and statute, there is to be found a wide range of positive civic duties, some in force and others fallen into desuetude, which are upheld by a variety of legal sanctions. These provisions furnish the ground for a renewed system of enforceable civic duty, as I further show in Chapters Ten and Eleven.

NINE

The Particular Duties
of the Civic Order

Duties of self-protection – the question of reciprocity –
general duty of protection of citizens – such duty cannot be delegated –
duties to the future – duties to the civic bond – the distinction between
citizen and stranger – duty to the citizen's self-esteem –
old socialism and the state – the need for superintendence and
coordination – discretion of the civic order – public and private provision
– duties to the integrity of the individual – sovereignty of the civic order
– preventing the citizen's estrangement – duty of prudent management –
duty to provide an impartial system of law – the principle of
non-discrimination – duty of scrutiny of officials – protection of
fundamental civic freedoms – duty of education of citizen-body.

231. The civic order is an ordered community which exists for the safety and common good of its members, whose well-being in turn depends upon the preservation of such civic order. It therefore has as its first and overriding obligation to its citizens, dictated by the principle of duty, that of *self-protection in the interests of all*. In the form of the nation, the sovereign civic order also has the duty to preserve and maintain its sovereignty, its territorial integrity and its capacity to pursue its ends to the maximum degree of its own choice and discretion.

The duty of self-protection in the interests of all has ethical and logical precedence over all other obligations to its citizens whatever. It includes the duty of the civic order to defend itself from assault from without or within; to prevent and arrest tendencies in the civic order towards the transformation of its citizens into strangers, and thus towards its own disaggregation; therefore, to deny the claims of dutiless right; and to uphold and enforce the principle of duty – including, where practical and necessary, by disqualifying the citizen from certain of his privileges, benefits, and rights – as the sovereign ethical principle of the civic order.

The duty of self-protection further includes the duty to meet, as far as it is reasonably able and without causing harm to the well-being of the civic order as a whole, the material and other requirements of those citizens whose lack of them, through no fault of their own, makes it difficult or impossible for them to act the citizen's part; the duty to educate the citizen-members of the civic order as to their duties and rights, and in other ways to provide to each individual the means of acquiring sufficient knowledge to act the citizen's part; the duty to protect, improve, and transmit to the care of the following generation of citizens the legacy of past civic effort which it has itself inherited; the duty to respect the natural environment of the civic order, since 'the tree of the field is man's life' (*Deuteronomy*, XX, 19); and otherwise, as a moral order, to protect and promote the integrity, dignity, and self-respect of the citizen and the exercise by him of his rights, to treat fairly and humanely resident non-citizens, and to avoid all measures, oppressive and other, whose tendency is to transform the citizen into a subject.

232. These *duties of self-protection* of the civic order are, in a democratic civic order, the duties of the sovereign body of citizens as a whole, acting through its representatives and governed ethically by the principle of duty. Where officials of the state, armed forces, law, or government – the instruments, all, of the civic order – are empowered by a democratic civic order to implement and execute the duties of such civic order on its behalf, the duties nevertheless remain those of the sovereign citizen-body to its members. They are duties which cannot be autonomously assumed by the instruments of a democratic civic order, acting on their own behalf.

233. The particular duties of the civic order to the citizen, and the particular duties of the citizen to the civic order – which I discuss in Chapter Ten – are not duties which either the civic order or the citizen may balance in a practical or ethical calculus one against the other. That is, each duty, or set of duties, is independently owed, whether to the citizen or to the civic order, even if the principle of duty, the sovereign principle of the civic order, commands them all, and they have a common end in the well-being of the civic order as a whole.

The ethical and practical ground of the duties owed by the civic order to the citizen is that, by their observance, the citizen's existence *qua* citizen is made possible and secure, that knowledge of the citizen's (ethically and logically prior) duties to himself, his fellows, and the civic order is acquired by him, and that such duties are fulfilled. But each duty, and set of duties, remain ethically and practically imperative in their own right, and each is independently dictated by the principle of duty.

234. By fulfilling its particular duties to the citizen, the civic order preserves itself and the civic bond, gives meaning and value to citizenship, increases the opportunities available to the citizen to play the citizen's part – as it is its particular obligation in a democratic order to do – and acts to prevent or arrest the process of civic disaggregation.

Conversely, for the civic order to turn a blind eye to citizen dutilessness, for example, is an anti-civic breach of its duty to the citizen-body; to act with excessive secrecy, or to provide the citizen (whether of nation, region, or city) with inadequate information as to the acts and intentions of the civic order or its instruments, is to prevent the citizen from acting the citizen's part; to set one group of citizens against another, whether wilfully or by inadvertence, or to make (or permit to be made) one group of citizens scapegoats for the ills of the civic order, or similarly to permit, or fail to prevent, the resolution by violence of conflicts between groups of citizens of differing interests or persuasions, is to act in breach of the civic order's *duty of self-protection* in the interests of all.

In practice, these examples of failures and breaches of the principle of duty, as they apply to the civic order's duties to the citizen-body of self-protection [sect. 231], are generally failures and breaches on the part of particular individuals, such as state or legal officials, acting on behalf of the civic order. But such individuals are no more, and no less, than citizens too. In discharging their functions, the members of executive bodies of the civic order are, as Rousseau expresses it (*Social Contract*, Bk. III, Chap. 18), 'only fulfilling their duties as citizens'. As such, they remain subject to the principle of duty and to such sanctions as the sovereign civic order, in its discretion, may choose for its enforcement, in respect of their omissions and failures.

235. The duties of the sovereign civic order to its citizen-members are the modern correlative of the duties owed in past times by sovereign monarchs, and sworn by them under solemn oath before the people. The widespread disappearance of sovereign monarchy does not absolve its successor forms of sovereign regime – *and least of all that which rules the democratic civic order* – from similar, and in some instances, the same obligations to the citizen-body.

Thus, it remains the duty of the democratic civic order not only to protect itself and its integrity, as an association of citizens which embraces and is superior to all others within its bounds, but so to act that its citizens live securely and – through a combination of good government and the exertions of the citizen himself – 'live well', in Aristotle's words.

But, in the first instance and under any form of rule whatever, the citizen has need of *physical* protection. It is thus (as it has always been) the duty of the sovereign civic order, and of its various instruments, to provide him with a refuge, security from the violence of others, and what Montesquieu in *The Spirit of the Laws* (Bk. XI, Chap. 6) called 'tranquillity of mind, arising from the assurance each has of his own safety'. Such condition Montesquieu made into a premise of, and even synonymous with, the political liberty of the subject, a political liberty found only where 'the government is so constituted that one man need not be afraid of another' (ibid.).

This primary duty of the civic order to provide the citizen with physical security must be exercised by the sovereign civic order itself and by its instruments the state and the law. It cannot be surrendered to individual citizens, or groups of citizens, acting in their own behalf and taking the law into their own hands, nor, by the same or similar ethical token, be delegated to private individuals acting in their own interest and to their own profit.

Likewise, the physical security of the citizen must be further reinforced by the civic order through an impartial administration of justice – which equally cannot be delegated to private individuals acting for their own interest and profit – before whose tribunals each citizen may have expectation of equitable treatment without regard to his condition, and to whose tribunals he may have right of access without regard to his means.

236. The duties of the self-protection of the civic order, and of the protection by the civic order of its citizen-members, also imply the protection both of the natural environment of the civic order and of the legacy of such past civic effort as is conducive to the present well-being and sense of security of the citizen-body.

These, and the other duties of citizen protection and civic self-protection already mentioned [sects. 231, 233, 235], which are complemented by the individual's own duties to the civic order – as I further show in Chapter Ten – have the common purpose not only of maintaining the present existence of such civic order, but of securing, as far as is possible, its future survival. The duty of self-protection of the civic order is a duty to the future as well as to the present and past; an obligation to those unborn whose well-being is imperilled by failure to observe the principle of duty now.

In particular, the rule in the corrupted liberal orders of the politics of dutiless right, demand-satisfaction, and self-realisation through unimpeded freedom of action threatens the natural world with its egotism, rapacity, and greed; causing harm not only to fellow-citizens of the same civic order but to citizens of other civic orders also, as well as promising harm to future generations. Thus, each civic order and its individual citizens have a custodial responsibility, dictated by the principle of duty, so to manage – and, where necessary and practical, to conserve – their material and other resources that both the present and future well-being of such civic order, and of other civic orders, may be maintained.

237. The duty of the civic order to protect its citizens does not have a physical or material sense alone. It signifies, too, the protection and maintenance of the practical value, legitimacy and moral worth of the civic bond, and of voluntary acts of co-responsibility on the part of individual citizens for the well-being

of the civic order, on the one hand, and the penalisation of a-civic and anti-civic social acts committed by members of the civic order, on the other. Likewise, it implies the civic protection of the practical value and moral worth of the individual will to gainful and productive work, and the civic penalisation of the wilful refusal or rejection of such work. To protect the citizen, and thus to protect the civic order, is also to educate the citizen to his duties and rights as a member of the civic order, to strengthen his sense of the civic bond, and by all possible and practical means to restore to the life of the civic order the citizen-turned-stranger.

Hence, it is the duty of the civic order to protect, give legitimacy to, or restore all those principles and institutions which sustain the moral integrity, self-respect, and civic identity of the individual, and which serve to inhibit the processes of civic estrangement, dissolution of individual identity, and civic disaggregation.

Thus, the protection and sustaining of the family bond by all reasonable measures is a duty of the civic order. Such measures may include educational instruction and training, fiscal incentive, nursery provision, the use of increasing sanctions against failure to discharge parental responsibility, the making of divorce more difficult or disadvantageous – as, for example, during the first ten years of marriage or where there are young dependent children – and the sufficient provision to those in need of it of subsidised housing-for-rent, adequate for self-respecting family life.

'The laws which, in many countries on the Continent, forbid marriage unless the parties can show that they have the means of supporting a family', declared Mill (*On Liberty*, p. 194), 'do not exceed the legitimate powers of the state; and whether such laws be expedient or not . . . they are not violations of liberty'. He recoiled – a recoil which the corrupted liberal order has come to forbid – from the 'lives of wretchedness and depravity [in] the offspring' (ibid., p. 195) of such exercise of free choice, objecting also, in abrasive terms, to the 'manifold evils' visited upon all 'sufficiently within reach' as to be 'affected by their [sc. the parents'] actions' (ibid.); that is, 'evils' visited upon fellow-members of the civic order.

Or, as Gerrard Winstanley put it (*The Law of Freedom in a*

Platform, p. 387), addressing himself two centuries earlier to the same civic issue, 'when a man hath learned his trade, and the time of his seven years' apprenticeship is expired, he shall have his freedom to become master of a family'. To be 'of age and of rational carriage' was, for Winstanley, a precondition of marriage, so that 'the peace of the commonwealth be observed' (ibid., p. 389); but, Winstanley added (ibid., p. 388), 'if a man lie with a maid and beget a child, he shall marry her'.

In the corrupted liberal order, and in conjoined conditions of accelerating family breakdown and civic disaggregation, continuity with the ethical and practical thought of the past – not least, with liberal thought – on this subject, as on many others, is ever more difficult to sustain. But the duty of self-protection of the civic order, and of the protection of the citizen by the civic order, including protection from himself, continues to dictate that all deteriorations in the state of relations between citizens be (as far as is practicable) prevented, in the interests of preserving the civic bond and of avoiding harm to the well-being of the civic order as a whole.

To this end, it is the duty of the civic order to seek to protect and sustain, to the extent that it can, the familial and marital bonds. For they are a constituent part of that web of moral and social relations in the civic order upon which the well-being both of the individual and the civic order depends [sect. 1].

238. The duty of self-protection of the civic order, and of the protection of the citizen by the civic order, also dictate the maintenance of, and the giving of further substance to, the distinction between the citizen and the stranger, including the citizen-turned-stranger who rejects his co-responsibility for the well-being of the civic order to which he belongs.

Without such distinction, as I have argued [sects. 95–99], citizenship, the civic bond, and even the civic order itself lose, in part or in whole, their ethical status and practical meaning. Moreover, only with the confirmation and strengthening of such distinction can certain burdens of practical expectation and ethical obligation – hitherto directed to, and imposed upon, the civic order and state by some citizens – begin to be transferred from the state to the civic order, and from the civic order to the individual.

For only the citizen who knows himself to be such, including by distinguishing himself from the non-citizen and the citizen-turned-stranger, is fully capable of that *civic self-esteem* which is required to assume individual co-responsibility, however modest, for the well-being of the civic order. Acts of omission or commission on the part of the civic order itself which prevent, subvert, or deny such civic self-esteem also harm the possibility of restoring to the citizen, who knows himself to be so, those ethical and practical obligations which have been assumed by the corrupted liberal order and its instrument the state.

Therefore, it is the duty of the civic order – in protection both of itself and of the interests of the citizen – to nurture and support, where appropriate by grant and subsidy, all those social institutions, including voluntarist institutions of self-help and mutual aid, which most conduce to the free self-development and self-regard of the individual. Among such institutions are those which supply the means of education, including civic education, self-education, and adult education, as well as, for example, institutions of cultural and artistic provision, of technical instruction, of sports training, of health education, and of domestic training, so that the free-standing skills and abilities of the individual may be discovered and enhanced, and his self-esteem as a citizen encouraged.

Such facilities and resources are, and must once more be understood to be, the prizes, benefits, and privileges of membership of the civic order; diminished access to which may, in certain circumstances, be made a sanction of the principle of duty.

239. Under the rule of old socialism in its communist form, the state, no longer the instrument of the civic order but its master, was vested with extensive (and always expanding) powers and responsibilities on behalf of the individual, often to the detriment of his self-development and self-regard. In the communist state, the sovereignty of the civic order was usurped, the civic bond displaced by the bond between individual and party, citizenship made ethically and practically subordinate to party-belonging, and the principle of duty transformed from the sovereign ethical

principle of the civic order into the sovereign ethical principle of the party-state.

Wherever old socialism exerted its influence or sway, including in the corrupted liberal orders, citizens tended to become subjects, including welfare-subjects. In other respects, too, the management (and manipulation) by the state, however benign, of the economic and social well-being of such subjects had little practical or ethical regard for the civic consequences of such action, whether in the communist states or the corrupted liberal orders formerly under socialist sway. Thus, the individual's duties to himself and his fellows, and his co-responsibility for the well-being of the civic order, were increasingly transferred to the state and its officials; the principle of duty was rendered absurd in the eyes of many, and forgotten by others; and the civic rights of the individual in the corrupted liberal order were made over into dutiless rights to self-realisation and demand-satisfaction under the aegis of the managerial state.

240. However, in the modern civic order, whatever the form of its rule or politico-economic system, there can be no 'minimum' or mere 'night-watchman' state, as long as the well-being of the civic order is to be maintained, its citizens recalled from their condition as strangers, and the process of civic disaggregation halted. The very self-development and self-regard of the individual requires, as I have shown [sect. 238], substantial support, ethical and practical, from the civic order and its instrument the state.

It might be true in principle, as Adam Smith insists (*The Wealth of Nations*, Bk. IV, Chap. 9), that 'no human wisdom or knowledge, could ever be sufficient . . . [for] the duty of superintending the industry of private people, and of directing it towards the employments most suitable to the interest of the society'. At the same time, however, as Kant argues (*Lectures on Ethics*, p. 145), 'God' has not only 'placed us on the stage of this world, provided us with all the materials for our welfare and with freedom to use them as we please', but 'everything depends on how men divide these benefits among themselves.'

Such 'division of benefits', if it is to be both ethical and practical, requires a substantial measure of 'superintendence' by the civic order and its various instruments, in the interests of the citizen-body as a whole. Similarly, the ethical injunction that, for example, 'thou shalt not oppress an hired servant that is poor and needy, whether he be of thy brethren or of thy strangers that are in thy land within thy gate' (*Deuteronomy*, XXIV, 14) requires, for its practical enforcement, supervision by the civic order. Moreover, the manifold duties of self-protection of the civic order and of protection of the citizen by the civic order [sects. 231, 233, 235] – so that the ethical and practical purposes of the civic order may be fulfilled – demand a substantial degree of coordinated civic effort, and of effort on the part of the instruments of the civic order, if they are to be discharged. To this effort, the co-responsibility of the individual citizen is also directed.

But the principle of duty further dictates to the civic order that it does what it can – provided that due regard is had to the likely civic and anti-civic consequences of its actions – to assist the citizen to 'live well'. The civic order's duties are not confined to the satisfying, through concerted civic action, of the citizen's fundamental needs for, say, clean water, breathable air, sources of domestic energy, and safety from violence, but also of the citizen's reasonable requirements for public means of transportation and communication, public health and educational services, and an impartial administration of law.

241. Such particular duties owed by the civic order to the citizen are governed by the general ethic of the principle of duty, that of *humanitas* [sect. 69] and of the civic bond, as well as by the compulsions of reason and practical necessity. Together, they direct the civic order as a body to serve the common interests of its citizen-members as best it can and as its resources permit.

However, neither duties nor rights are (or can be) absolute, whether they appertain to the citizen or the civic order. In addition, since some of the duties of the civic order have ethical or practical priority over others, not all of the duties, actual or presumed, of the civic order can or will be fulfilled, or will be fulfilled only according to circumstance. Thus, a civic order may provide food or shelter, or both, to its citizens only *in extremis*; or, in other circumstances and exercising its discretion, it may provide, and consider itself under an ethical obligation to provide, housing, for example, on a wide scale. Again, certain provisions to meet citizen-need, as that for sexual pleasure, the civic order will not make at all – save for soldiers in time of war – finding such provision ethically objectionable. Or, in other circumstances, it will overcome such type of ethical scruple – as in the provision to citizens by the civic order of prophylaxis against sexually-transmitted disease – and extend the range, temporarily or permanently, of what is considered to be the duty of the civic order to its citizens' well-being.

Yet even if the civic order's duties, like the citizen's duties, cannot be absolute, and even if many are contingent upon circumstance, upon resources, and upon the exercise of discretion, those which have to do with the protection of the civic order's existence, with the maintenance of the civic bond, and with the arresting of the process of civic disaggregation stand at the heart of the principle of duty, the sovereign ethical principle of the civic order. Upon its observance the safety of the citizens and of the civic order alike depend.

242. In exercising its responsibility for the well-being of the civic order as a whole, the civic order may properly arrogate to itself, and to its instrument the state, the exclusive provision of any of the citizen's requirements, especially those which it regards as fundamental to such citizen's physical well-being. It may, likewise, properly refuse to individual citizens, on ethical or practical grounds, the right to own the means of making such provision, or the right otherwise to make such provision on their own accounts or for their own profit.

Thus, the civic order may hold it to be ethically offensive, or impractical, that individual citizens, or groups of citizens, should own for themselves, and profit from such ownership of, natural resources or forces which are indispensable to life, resources which other citizens cannot acquire or produce for themselves, and to which they cannot otherwise gain access without inordinate effort, cost, or other inconvenience.

Similarly, where certain means and services of benefit to the entire citizen-body can only be conveniently and efficiently made available by the civic order, or its instrument the state, to the citizen-body as a whole – and cannot practically or ethically be left to individual citizens, or associations of citizens, to provide for themselves from their own means and resources – the civic order, through its instrument the state, may consider it to be its duty to provide them. Likewise, where impartiality, or a condition of independence from individual interest, is regarded to be essential to the legitimacy and moral authority of a particular civic institution or service, the civic order may properly consider it necessary to exclude individual interest from it.

Again, where powerful or monopoly individual interest, insufficiently accountable to the civic order, puts at risk continuity of citizen-access to services and supplies necessary to the well-being of the civic order as a whole – and which the citizen cannot readily or at all make good for himself from his own means and resources – the civic order, through its instrument the state, may properly consider it necessary to prevent individual interest acquiring such power.

Or, where certain means and services are essential to the self-development of the citizen but are beyond the scope and resources of voluntary association and individual effort to provide, the civic order may properly choose to provide them. Finally, where the standard or quality of provision to the citizen-members of goods and services directed to their needs, whether fundamental or not, can only be safeguarded by the disinterested supervision and administration of such provision, the civic order may also properly choose to supervise and administer it, in the interests of the citizen-body as a whole.

243. One of the chief ethical purposes of the civic order, dictated by the principle of duty both as it applies to the citizen's duty to himself and the civic order's duty to him, is, as I have already pointed out [sects. 86, 98, 235], the protection both of the physical security and the self-regard of the citizen as a moral being. There is, therefore, a general and overarching duty vested in the civic order to do nothing which harms such safety and self-regard by acts, whether of omission or commission, which debase or degrade the physical and moral integrity of the individual, as by acts of cruelty and physical punishment, or acts which reduce the citizen to a slave or subject.

By the same ethical token, the principle of duty dictates the avoidance or amelioration by the civic order of conditions of life and work which deprive the individual citizen of dignity and self-regard; which permit to powerful citizens the exercise of dutiless rights of exploitation of the weak; and which impede any inadequately protected citizen, or group of citizens, from resort to the means of collective self-defence against the depredations of others. Failure on the part of the civic order to amend such conditions and circumstances damages the civic bond and harms the well-being of the civic order as a whole.

244. The fulfilment by the civic order of its duties to protect the citizen-body – whether such duties be carried out under the strong ethical and practical compulsion of the principle of duty, or in free exercise of its discretion – is an expression of the sovereign power of the civic order as nation [**sects. 83–5**]. It is a sovereign power which may be measured by the capacity of such civic order, acting through its instruments of state and law, to protect itself and its citizen-members by means and methods of its own choosing.

245. Such sovereign power vested in the civic order cannot be delegated or transferred when the physical and moral protection of its citizens, and the legal adjudication of disputes between them, are at issue. The duties and responsibilities of the sovereign civic order in these regards can be transferred neither to individual citizens acting in their own interests or for their own profit, nor to supranational bodies, direct membership of which is unavailable to individual citizens of the civic order in question, or membership of which by such civic order does not give rise to citizenship rights.

Rather, the sovereign civic order possesses, by virtue of its sovereignty, inalienable and 'necessary responsibilities', as Aristotle describes them (*Politics*, VI, viii, 1322b), chief among which is the responsibility of protecting their security and well-being. Thus, the armed defence of the civic order and the enforcement of law alike belong to the sovereignty of the civic order; its armed forces can no more be consigned into the hands of individual citizens acting in their own interests and for their own profit than can the court system, the police force, or the prison service. To defend the civic order from external aggression, to protect the citizen from his fellows, and to administer an impartial system of justice are one.

The practical and ethical ground for prohibiting the transfer, to individual citizens or supranational bodies, of the 'necessary responsibilities' to which the exercise of sovereignty gives rise is the defence and maintenance of the civic bond. Already under multiple forms of assault in the corrupted liberal orders at the hands of citizens-turned-strangers, it cannot, for reasons of practical necessity in conditions of civic disaggregation, be permitted to be further assaulted *by acts of the civic order itself*.

Moreover, if the civic order neglects, refuses, or surrenders responsibilities dictated to it by the principle of duty, the individual citizen, as well as the citizen-turned-stranger, may the more readily think himself absolved from his duties too.

246. The duty of the sovereign civic order to retain in its hands, and not to consign, delegate, or sub-contract to individual citizens' interest and profit, the making, efficient administration, and enforcement of law is in its turn directed to the maintenance of the rule of law, and to the preservation of respect for such rule of law [sect. 132].

Without efficient and impartial enforcement of law by a sovereign civic order, and when respect for the law and those who make and enforce it is lost, recourse by citizens to their own means – including violent means – of self-defence of their interests in the civic order becomes an increasing danger, particularly in conditions of civic disaggregation under the rule of dutiless right in the corrupted liberal orders. 'Having the protection of the commonwealth, he [sc. the 'private man'] needeth not the defence of private force', declares Hobbes (*Leviathan*, Chap. XXII). Without such protection, impartially administered for civic ends by the civic order itself, the individual citizen may not only fetch increasingly for his own protection, but may become obligated to do so by the principle of duty, as it applies to his duties to himself.

247. Just as there is a general duty vested in the civic order to do nothing which harms the citizen's safety or debases his self-regard [sect. 243], so the civic order has a general obligation to do all that is feasible, within its resources, to prevent the avoidable estrangement of the citizen from the civic order by reason of his indigence, sickness, unemployment, or other social or personal handicap.

The purpose of provision against such estrangement from the civic order – a condition in which the citizen, through no fault of his own, is unable to play the citizen's part – is, and must remain, civic. That is, it is both an expression of, and intended to sustain, the civic bond. (Conversely, as I further discuss in Chapter Eleven, the sovereign civic order may, in its discretion, and having the general well-being of the civic order in mind, also deny a greater or lesser part of such provision, for a greater or lesser time, to those citizens who wilfully refuse the citizen's part although able to perform it, or who commit serious anti-civic acts which harm the well-being of the civic order to which they belong.)

It is the principle of duty, as it applies to the *protection of the citizen* by the civic order, which dictates the obligation to prevent the reduction of the citizen – as the result of the civic order's own defect of policy, default, or neglect – to a condition in which he is willing but unable to play the citizen's part. To protect the citizen's capacity to contribute to the well-being of the civic order is to protect the civic order itself, in the interests of all.

248. In addition to such general duty to protect the citizen's safety, self-regard, and capacity to play the citizen's part, the civic order and its instrument the state are under a general ethical obligation to ensure that no citizen, or non-citizen, is (for whatever reason) left without basic means of support, nor finds himself (for whatever reason) in the condition which the Greeks described as that of the 'unhonoured vagrant', unless such condition is freely chosen. Under the general duty of protection, the civic order must also do whatever is practical and within its means to save and protect the oppressed [sect. 166] who are not citizens of such civic order, whether they be non-citizen residents, seekers after asylum, or citizens of another civic order which requests such assistance of it.

249. Flowing from the *general duty of protection*, the civic order and its instrument the state are under an ethical obligation to conduct and manage the practical affairs of the civic order prudently and in the interests of the well-being of such civic order as a whole. The

duty of prudent management is a duty of acting with integrity –
that is, through honest representatives and state officials – and with
openness of information, as well as in rejection of extremes of
particular interest. Such interest may, for example, express itself in
dutiless demands for a 'free market', for rights of exploitation of
the economically vulnerable or of the threatened resources of
nature, or make other forms of claim, including old socialist claims,
to dutiless right, demand-satisfaction, and self-realisation through
unimpeded freedom of action.

A duty in the civic order of prudent management of its economy
likewise implies the curbing of deficit; moderation in taxation and
public expenditure; discouragement of individual debt – 'care ought
to be taken', says Cicero (*Offices*, II, xxiv), 'to keep people from
running so much into debt as may bring any damage or inconvenience to the public'; and avoidance of the creation, whether as
an act of policy or from mismanagement, of avoidable large-scale
unemployment. The duty of prudent management also implies the
just apportionment of all those forms of spending by the civic
order, but only as resources permit, which are required for the self-
protection of the civic order and the protection of the citizen by the
civic order.

It is a further duty of prudent management of the civic order to
deny, in the interests of the civic order as a whole, the principle of
universality of entitlement to public provision regardless of need
for it; and likewise to deny related false claims to absolute 'social
right', such as the 'right to work', the 'right to benefit', the 'right
to opportunity' and so forth. ('Make yourself into honey', declares
Sancho Panza in *Don Quixote*, 'and the flies will eat you.') For there
are no such absolute 'social rights' in ethical principle, nor can such
asserted 'rights' be made absolute in practice. Claims of absolute
right in these respects are, instead, claims to qualified right or
contingent privilege and benefit, all of which are dependent upon
the resources and discretion of the sovereign civic order. In the
exercise of this discretion, the civic order may also make the
satisfying of such claims dependent upon the fulfilment of the
citizen's own duties to the civic order.

250. Indeed, it is the duty of the civic order, in the interests of the

citizen-body itself, to attempt to meet by public provision only need which exists, to direct such provision to those citizens – and no others – who have, and can show, such need, and to give priority to those whose need the civic order, in its discretion, considers to be the greatest. Moreover, it is a general ethical and practical presumption of the fulfilment of such duty to the citizen on the part of the civic order that, unless the need which is met by it is itself permanent, the provision made by the civic order is temporary only; that is, is made for the duration of the need.

'Succour', declared Montesquieu (*The Spirit of the Laws*, Bk. XXIII, Chap. 29), 'should be applied to particular accidents . . . Transient assistances are much better than perpetual foundations.' Even where such 'perpetual foundations' are ethically and practically required of the civic order, they remain contingent upon the means and resources of the civic order, and upon the perpetuation of the civic order itself.

251. It is the ethical duty of the civic order, acting in preservation of the civic bond through the instrument of the law, to act as impartially as can be in the adjudication of justiciable disputes between citizens, and in the imposition upon them of the penalties and awards of the law. Hence, the civic order has an obligation, dictated by the principle of duty, to give the citizen who comes before its courts a hearing which is fair, not determined by means, by social or racial origin, by sex, or by colour, and otherwise conducted in accord with the principles of natural justice.

It is also the duty of the civic order, as I argue further in Chapter Eleven, to establish Courts of Obligation, which will uphold and enforce, under the rule of law and including by a just system of sanctions of penalty and reward, the principle of duty, both as it applies to the citizen's duties and to the duties of the civic order.

252. Just as the principle of impartiality without regard to condition, origin, sex, or colour must be the governing principle of the procedures of law, so is it the ethical duty of the civic order and of its instrument the state to practise or permit discrimination *neither in favour of nor against* individual citizens on grounds of social or racial origin, sex, or colour, in administrative matters of choice and decision: as in choices and decisions concerning employment,

promotion, educational opportunity, training, and other access to
public provision. Such principle of impartiality also dictates that
women, for example, owe to the civic order the same duties of co-
responsibility for its condition and well-being as men, possess the
same rights, benefits, and privileges as men, are entitled to the
same remuneration for the same work or the same responsibility as
men, and have the same entitlement of access to institutions, offices,
powers, and places as men.

Likewise, wherever the criteria for the possession of rights,
benefits, and privileges, or for access to institutions, offices, powers,
and places include that of desert, or merit [**sects. 57, 146**], the
criterion of desert or merit must be impartially applied without
regard to social or racial origin, sex, or class; as Plato asserts
(*Republic*, V, 455d, 456a), 'none of the occupations involved in the
government of a city is peculiar to one sex or the other . . . Some
women have the capacity for wardenship [sc. political responsi-
bility] and others have not.'

253. In the interests of the citizen-body as a whole, the principle
of impartiality, qualified by the criterion of merit, applies with
particular ethical and practical force to the government of the civic
order, and to the choice and appointment of officers of state. It is
thus a continuous duty of the sovereign civic order, especially in its
democratic form, to subject those citizens who at any time occupy
leading positions of decision, judgment, and trust in the civic order
– whether politicians, judges, state administrators, or others, and
whether elected or appointed – to regular and rigorous scrutiny,
election, revision of appointment, or other examination of their
merit and fitness for the positions which they hold. The fulfilment
of such duty by the civic order is an expression of the sovereignty
of the civic order; it is also dictated by practical necessity, civic
sense, and the duty of protection of the civic order itself.

Moreover, the enforcement of the principle of duty, as it applies
to the citizen's obligations to the civic order, is made ethically the
more difficult the less the efficiency, ability, honesty, and other
merit of those who at any time, represent, legislate for, adjudicate
upon, or administer the interests of the citizen-body as a whole.

Where the civic order fails in its duty in this respect, the immediate (although not the furthest) consequence has long been plain. 'On my arrival in the United States', De Tocqueville declares (*Democracy in America*, pp. 179–80), 'I was surprised to find so much distinguished talent among the subjects, and so little among the heads of the government . . . At the present day [sc. in the early 1830s], the most talented men in the United States are very rarely placed at the head of affairs'; he is, further, 'amazed at the persons invested with public authority' (ibid., p. 183).

Such 'surprise' and 'amazement' continue to transfix citizens of today's corrupted liberal orders; their astonishment and alarm the greater, the more rapid the process of civic disaggregation. Yet the inadequacy, and even entire unfitness for office, of many who hold such office in the corrupted liberal orders is the outcome itself of the failure to uphold the principle of duty, as it applies both to the civic order's duty of self-protection and protection of the citizen, and the citizen's co-responsibility for the condition of the civic order; expressed, here, in the particular duty of regular and vigorous scrutiny of the merits of those who seek and hold office in such civic order. In Solon's Athens and in the Italian city-republics, the magistrate was obliged, on leaving office, to give an account of his stewardship to an assembly of the people, with liability to sanction – including, variously, prohibition from further office, restitution of gain, and loss of civic rights – in the event of discovered default.

In the corrupted liberal orders, under the pressures of the weakening of the civic bond and of accelerating civic disaggregation, the principle of duty dictates to the civic order as a whole and to the individual citizen that the representatives, officials, and other public servants of the civic order, elected and non-elected alike, be similarly subject to open and regular civic audit, in order that accounts may be given of their custodianship of public position; and that a Court of Obligation, as I shall discuss later, be made the court of adjudication of citizen appeals for the removal – where there is a *prima facie* case for it – of such representatives, officials, and public servants, or for the imposition of other civic sanction upon them.

In the case of elected representatives and elected public officials, the 'sanction of the ballot-box' has proved insufficient in many corrupted liberal orders as a means to promote and reward political honour and merit. In the case of appointed officials, other appointed public servants, and elected representatives and officials in the *most corrupted* of the liberal orders, neglect and abuse of office, peculation, fraud of the citizen, and the flouting of the principle of impartiality [sect. 252] require new measures of oversight and sanction if the civic bond is to be preserved, the principle of duty respected, and the citizen-turned-stranger restored to the civic order.

254. It is also the related duty of the civic order, and of its instruments the state and the system of law, to protect the citizen by protecting his fundamental civic freedoms of belief and speech, of association, organisation and assembly, and of movement. Without such freedoms, or in conditions of their severe restriction, the life of the civic order becomes a 'mere semblance of life' in Rosa Luxemburg's words (*Die Russische Revolution*, 1922, Frankfurt-am-Main, 1963, p. 75); citizenship loses its meaning and substance; the civic bond cannot be expressed; and the powers of officials are so strengthened as to make even easier the usurpation of the sovereignty of the civic order. Freedom of speech is not only the 'right to tell people what they do not want to hear', as Orwell put it, but the only means to maintain that discourse between citizens without which the civic bond itself is mute. Freedom of association, likewise, is a precondition of the civic order itself, being the means by which general and particular interests are expressed and the civic order is fashioned, modified and renewed by its members, acting in their common interest [sect. 4]. As for freedom of movement, it is the criterion, above all others, by which the citizen is distinguished from the slave.

Yet not even such freedoms, however fundamental, are or can be absolute, being contingent on the existence of the civic order itself. Moreover, in the corrupted liberal orders and under the rule of dutiless right, abuse of such freedoms, in the name of self-realisation through unimpeded freedom of action and the satisfaction of demand, has wrought damage to the civic bond, promoted and legitimated contempt for and refusal of the principle of duty, and harmed the civic order itself.

In earlier times, when the liberal ideal had not been thus corrupted, it might have been said of the freedom of the press, for instance, as was said by De Tocqueville (*Democracy in America*, p. 164), that 'in order to enjoy the inestimable benefits which the liberty of the press ensures, it is necessary to submit to the inevitable ills which it engenders'. But no such calculus can be made when the 'inevitable ills' of the exercise of such liberty have become part of the losing gamble of freedom, and when the assumption of reason is falsified on a grand scale, hastening the civic order to disaggregation.

Thus, when the excessive power of particular interest in the control and dissemination of information is able, in free pursuit of such interest, to impose upon the sovereign civic order systematic falsehood, or values which degrade the citizen who receives such information, the civic order, under its duty of self-protection and protection of the citizen, is obligated to prevent such abuse, including, where it becomes necessary, by censorship of the media of information. 'No one would even choose to allow falsehood about matters of deepest moment to get into the depth of his being', declares Plato (*Republic*, II, 382b); 'the last thing a man would want would be to harbour a lie in the soul' (ibid.). In the matter of violence, Plato enjoins in like fashion that 'we cannot permit young people to hear stories that may lead them to take the most horrible crimes for granted' (ibid., 378a). Against the 'lie in the soul', and the continuous exposure of the young to images of violence – whether as 'information' or 'entertainment' – the civic order is required by the principle of duty to take action, in preservation of the dignity and self-regard of the citizen and in fulfilment of its duty to educate the citizen to his citizen's part.

In the same way, it is the duty of the civic order to deny all other claims to dutiless right, demand-satisfaction, and self-realisation through unimpeded freedom of action – generally made in the corrupted liberal orders in the name of liberty itself – where such claims, if allowed, would harm the interests of the citizen-body as a whole.

255. Finally, in the particular duty of the civic order to provide its citizens with an educational system which is efficient, adequately funded, and of sufficient quality to produce trained, informed, ethically instructed, and participant members of the civic order, lies the secret of the civic bond. To arouse in, and draw from, each individual those capacities and virtues which make possible self-fulfilment on the one hand, and the voluntary assumption of co-responsibility for the well-being of the civic order on the other, is at the same time to teach such individual to play the citizen's part.

The individual who is not so taught becomes the more readily a stranger to civic sense and civic purpose; the fewer so taught, the weaker the civic bond and the swifter the process of civic disaggregation; the larger the default of the civic order in providing such system of education, the greater its breach of the principle of duty as it applies to the civic order's obligations of self-protection in the interests of the citizen-body as a whole. Such breach is greatest wherever respect for education is discouraged and undermined by the values and practices of the civic order itself, as in the case of many of the corrupted liberal orders.

256. It is within the discretion of each sovereign civic order to determine by what pedagogical principles, for what length of time, in what matters, in what types of school, under the guidance of what manner of teachers and subject to what tests of ability and attainment (in both teachers and taught) the citizen will be provided with the education which, as a citizen, he requires.

Moreover, in a plural civic order where, in addition to varieties of ability, effort, and intellectual interest found in the teachers and students of the education system, there are to be found in the citizen-body itself diverse faiths, origins, cultural traditions, and levels of expectation as to the quality and content of education – and thus a multiplicity of educational demands made of the civic order – common civic rules must nevertheless be established and maintained in all the educational institutions of such civic order, however the educational system be structured.

Thus, whether schools, for instance, be organised at a determinate stage according to the criteria of ability, specialised interest, faith, or sex of the pupils, or without regard to such criteria, it is the duty of the civic order, in the interests of the preservation of the civic bond and the provision of a civic education to all its citizens, to ensure that all such schools adhere to common standards, inculcate the same civic principles, and help to sustain a common ethical direction in the civic order.

257. In describing how 'necessity, convenience and inclination' in the first place brought man 'into society' from his (mythical) 'state of Nature', Locke declares (*Two Treatises of Government*, Bk. II, para. 77) that God 'fitted him with understanding and language to continue and enjoy it'. That is, 'understanding and language' are the means, for Locke, by which the individual's life in the civic order, a life shared with others, may be sustained.

Otherwise put, the possession of civic sense and a vocabulary of civic discourse – making possible the exchanges, communications, civilities (a just word), and necessary participations of the democratic civic order – give life to the civic bond. Conversely, as in the corrupted liberal orders, the less civic sense and civic skill in the citizen, the less sovereign is the civic order [**sects. 83–5**], and, in a vicious circle hard to break, the less able become the civic order and its officials themselves to make good such defects of education, failure compounding failure under conditions of accelerating civic disaggregation. Such failure is, above all, a failure to observe the principle of duty, as it applies to the self-protection of the civic order and the protection of the citizen-body as a whole.

258. In some corrupted liberal orders, the citizen-turned-stranger, and in particular the universal plebeian, is now often both victim and protagonist of a widening disrespect for learning and training, and of contempt – even violent contempt – for teachers. ('Nobody', declares Xenophon [*Memorabilia of Socrates*, Bk. 1, Chap. 2, sect. 39], 'ever received any education from a man he did not care for.') Increasing rates of illiteracy and semi-literacy, truanting, drop-out, and physical harm committed against schools and teachers are the stigmata of the failure of the civic order to observe its educational duties to the citizen, and of the citizen's failure to observe related duties [**sect. 170**] to himself and to the civic order as a whole.

In particular, as I have argued, the civic order is under an ethical and practical obligation to render its members fit to be citizens

among citizens by suitable education and training; a 'state education' which is not directed to the formation of citizens and the
inculcation in them of (*inter alia*) a civic ethic is thus a formal
contradiction in terms.

259. In a democratic civic order, the duty of the civic order in the
matter of the education of the citizen is all the greater, since a
democratic system depends the more for its strength upon an
informed and participant citizen-body [**sect. 170**]; or, as De
Tocqueville expressed it (*Democracy in America*, p. **192**), 'a democratic government . . . always presupposes the existence of a high
degree of culture and enlightenment in society'. Instead, the
corrupted liberal orders in general continue to pretend to, or insist
upon, their democratic well-being while failing to educate increasing numbers of their citizens to play the citizen's part. Here, there
is the form – and sometimes, now, not even the form – of a
participant and educated democracy, but increasingly little of its
substance; the semblance of democratic citizenship, but in a world
of increasing numbers of mutually hostile citizens-turned-strangers;
and the seeming rule of the democratically informed *homme moyen*,
but in corrupted liberal orders governed by dutiless right and,
hence, subordinated increasingly to the ethically uneducated
interests of the universal plebeian.

260. Almost every individual, whoever or whatever he may be,
possesses a latent capacity to act the citizen's part [**sect. 80**], a
capacity which it is a main purpose of education to evoke. The
responsibility, dictated by the principle of duty, for doing so, while
shared by such individual's familiars and part-discharged by the
individual's fulfilment of his duties to himself, rests in its largest
part upon the civic order to fulfil. As Aristotle declared (*Politics*,
VIII, i, 1337a), 'the responsibility for education must be a public
one . . . In matters that concern the public, training for them must
be the public's concern.'

Moreover, however important the moral and other education
provided by an individual's familiars, and acquired throughout life
by the process of self-education, the civic order cannot evade its
responsibility, dictated by the principle of duty, to ensure the
general education of the citizen-body. It is not essential that the

civic order, through its instrument the state, should conduct education itself in state or public institutions, and by means of employees of the state. But it also cannot delegate its responsibility to individuals acting in their own interest and for their own profit, if such delegation imports an abandonment of its duty of oversight of the training of individuals to act their citizen's parts.

Thus, it is not acceptable, either ethically or in practice, that any individual, 'looking after his own children, and teaching them privately whatever private curriculum he thinks they ought to study', as Aristotle has it (ibid.), should be immune or exempt, once a child's infancy is past, from supervision by the civic order. No more acceptable is it that private institutions of education should be permitted by a sovereign civic order to educate their pupils entirely as they see fit, or in matters of their own choosing, or for ethical and practical purposes determined wholly by them.

For the ultimate responsibility for education is a civic not a private one. The individual who is uneducated to play the citizen's part detracts from the well-being of the civic order as a whole, while failures of education 'redound to the harm of the republic', in Campanella's judgment (*La Città del Sole*, pp. 127–8). In particular, the citizen-turned-stranger, who at worst may be unknowing even of the existence of the civic order, is both agent of the latter's disaggregation and a standing reproach to the civic order's failure to observe its duty.

261. The individual whom the civic order has failed to educate to his citizen's part is not only a stranger to the civic order but must remain a mere *subject* of it; just as a sovereign civic order which has failed adequately to educate and train the majority of its members must eventually lose its sovereignty and become subject to another, better educated and trained than itself. In the corrupted liberal orders, the uneducated citizen, or *subject*, additionally lives under the rule of dutiless right and demand-satisfaction, a rule over which he can exercise no independent civic judgment, and which instead holds him in its thrall.

Such condition of subjection to the corrupted values of the civic order is the antithesis of that condition in which a citizen has been taught, and knows, 'how far he may make use of his freedom', in

Locke's words (*Two Treatises of Civil Government*, Bk. II, para. 59) [**sects. 94, 134**], without at the same time undermining the well-being of others. In the former condition, the individual has citizenship in name, but not in substance; asserts his right without awareness of his duty; equates his liberty with claims to the unimpeded satisfaction of his demands; and has lost the means of self-government and self-correction, to the potential or actual harm of the civic order as a whole.

The amendment of such condition of subjection is the task of the civic order; and better, ethically and practically, that it should be amended by education than by the imposition of sanction, a potential further subjection. However, under the rule of dutiless right, in conditions of civic disaggregation and of growing contempt for education itself, education of the citizen to play the citizen's part requires of the corrupted liberal order a civic effort which is in danger of becoming increasingly beyond its grasp. What Hobbes called the 'inconvenience' (*Leviathan*, Chap. XIX) which arises 'when people are not well instructed in their duty' is not easily remedied by instruction alone; the more violent risks posed to the civic order by the individual who neither knows, nor cares, 'how far he may make use of his freedom' are such as to be met only by sanction.

Nevertheless, education remains the 'best safeguard', as Plato put it, both of the individual citizen's interests and of the well-being of the civic order as a whole, examples of cultivated wickedness in a nation or individual notwithstanding; and civic rule by imposition of sanction, however necessary to the fulfilment of the civic order's own obligations it may become, remains its moral poor-relation.

262. The civic order is a moral as well as a political construct, in which a civic morality requires to be both practised and taught. 'An education which only aims at money-making', declared Plato in the *Laws* (I, 644), 'or at the cultivation of physical strength, or at some kind of cleverness without regard to justice or reason, is vulgar and illiberal, and is not worthy to be called education at all.' The ethic of the civic bond requires that education be perceived and treated in the civic order as a means not merely to the self-development of the individual beneficiary of it but to the enhancement of the common interests of all. To educate is to carry out a civic and a social act; to be educated is to become a citizen and a social being. Hence, among the principal ethical and practical purposes of such civic education is to provide individuals with, in Hobbes' words (*Leviathan*, Chap. XXIII), 'knowledge of what is just and unjust, thereby to render them more apt to live . . . in peace amongst themselves'.

The civic order cannot be a civic order without this knowledge, and can possess no common ethical direction, whatever such direction may be; the citizen can be no true citizen; and the civic bond can only with difficulty cohere. Yet in most corrupted liberal orders, the very proposition that there exists such 'knowledge of what is just and unjust' is increasingly subject to disregard and contempt, notwithstanding that such disregard and contempt are further cause, as well as consequence, of the process of civic disaggregation and the transformation of citizens into strangers.

But, as Spinoza teaches us, the mutual relations of citizens in the civic order are not, and cannot be, self-sustaining; the civic bond and civic order require both ethical and practical support; the citizen cannot be a citizen merely by resort to his own devices. In particular, the individual must be educated to a life of just action and mutuality; must be educated, that is, to his citizen's part.

263. In the corrupted liberal orders, however, education, in its substance and in the disciplines demanded to acquire it, comes increasingly into direct ethical and even emotional conflict with the early-acquired habituation of the individual to the rule of dutiless right and of claims to swift demand-satisfaction. Moreover, education, in such conditions, is seen not as the means of amendment of those conditions, or of protection and escape from their corrupted values, but of better access to their enjoyment.

Likewise, it comes to be considered in the corrupted liberal orders that the 'right to study', for instance, has ethical priority over the duty to do so, a duty which in practice may even be denied or flouted entirely. Or, the process of education in the corrupted liberal orders is increasingly obliged to satisfy emotional, not intellectual, demands – themselves the product of the rule of

dutiless right and demand-satisfaction – that instruction be a form
of diversion, fun, or entertainment. Aristotle thought otherwise. 'It
is clear', he declares (*Politics*, VIII, v, 1339a) 'that we are not to
educate the young with a view to their amusement. Learning brings
pain' – at least, to some degree – 'and while children are learning
they are not playing'; 'whether the child likes or dislikes learning',
similarly declared Plato (*Laws*, VII, 810), he 'must be required to
come to school'.

Such notions, in the ethical demeanour towards education which
they suggest, now fly in the face of ruling pedagogical principle in
the corrupted liberal orders, despite the scale of citizen-estrange-
ment and the speed of their disaggregation. That it is 'in infancy
more than at any other time that character is formed by habit', as
Plato argued in the *Laws* (VII, 792); that 'lawless play makes lawless
children, and such children will never grow up good . . . citizens',
as he argued in the *Republic* (IV, 424e); that the best kind of stories
to be told them are those which lead them to 'live on friendly terms
with each other in later life' (ibid., III, 386a) – all similarly offend,
both in their manner and their matter, the pedagogical principles
most commonly found in corrupted liberal orders.

Yet they might be seen not to offend the liberal ideal, were such
ideal still known and understood. 'Is it not almost a self-evident
axiom', asks Mill (*On Liberty*, pp. 188–9), 'that the State should
require and compel the education up to a certain standard of every
human being who is born its citizen?' Such axiom, in the corrupted
liberal orders, is 'self-evident' no longer, being hedged around with
a variety of ethical and practical qualifications, qualifications which
have helped to weaken the civic bond and to promote the quickening disaggregation of the civic order.

264. Nevertheless, it remains a particular duty of the civic order to
secure such education of every citizen as Mill by implication
demands. It is also the duty of the civic order to promote and
reward individual educational merit, effort, and achievement, without regard, as I have already stated [sect. **252**], to the means,
condition, origin, or sex of the individual. Conversely, it is the duty
of the civic order, as part of its obligation of education of the
citizen-body, *not* to reward, on false principles of equity and justice,

those whose own lack of merit or effort has prevented such achievement. Moreover, wherever adequate educational provision by the civic order is abused or misused by the individual, it is within the discretion of the civic order to employ whatever reasonable inducements and sanctions it sees fit in order to assist it to fulfil its own duty to such individual, as I further discuss in Chapter Eleven.

265. It is also the particular duty of every civic order to disseminate, including to school-children and even if only in elementary form, such specific civic knowledge as is required to maintain and strengthen the civic bond. This knowledge will, in most cases, be composed of information as to the citizens' duties and rights, the laws under which they live, the methods by which a sovereign civic order may change such laws, and the matters considered under such laws to be justiciable and wrong. Or, as Mazzini expressed the same principle (*The Duties of Man*, p. 89), 'every citizen ought to receive . . . moral teaching, including . . . a popular exposition of the principles which direct the legislation of the country'.

In the absence of such information, the citizen has the less knowledge of his civic self, and of the nature and bounds of his civic relations with others. By failing to provide such knowledge, the civic order is in breach of its duties of self-protection, protection of the individual from himself and his fellows, and thus the protection of the civic order as a whole.

266. The obligation to provide a civic education to the members of the civic order also includes the duty of furnishing to each new generation of citizens a sufficient knowledge of the civic order's past [sect. 168]. Its purpose is, above all, to give such citizens a sense of place and time, of respect (where it is warranted) for past civic effort, and of co-responsibility for the present and future condition of the civic order to which they belong. Such co-responsibility includes responsibility for the improvement, transformation and, *in extremis*, overthrow of such condition.

267. All these duties of the civic order of self-protection, protection of the civic bond, education of the citizen, and promotion of the interests of the civic order as a whole are dictated by the principle of duty. Failure by the civic order to observe such principle, including as the result of failure to enforce it in respect of the citizen's own duties, is to put at risk the civic order itself.

But such failure, in the democratic civic order where sovereignty resides in the citizen-body as a whole, is subject itself to the sanction of objection, and ultimately rebellion, on the part of the citizen-members themselves [**sect. 211**]. Yet in conditions of civic disaggregation in the corrupted liberal orders, where the rule of dutiless right renders increasing numbers of citizens strangers to one another, even objection and rebellion become gradually harder to assert and achieve.

This is the stasis of the corrupted free civic order, in which neither the civic order nor the free individual members of it are capable of radical self-amendment, but all are subject to one rule of dutiless right, a rule which holds them in thrall together. Against such conditions, and with whatever difficulty, the rediscovery and enforcement by the civic order of the particular duties of the citizen must be pitted, until the civic order is reconstituted in the interests of all.

TEN

The Particular Duties
of the Citizen

General duty of care towards the civic order –
particular duties summarised – the moral minimum – positive duty –
existing legal duties – the sustaining of familial relations – duty to the law
– duty to live peaceably and sociably – duty to help construct the
civic order – voluntary acts of public service – local civic affiliation –
inducement and sanction – transfer of duties to citizen – duties to self–
duty of self-education – duty to work – duties to the past and to place –
the practice of faith not a civic duty – duty of physical self-care –
against suicide – duty to respect the physical lives of others and the
natural world – duties to safeguard the future.

268. The individual citizen, whose well-being is the purpose of the
civic order, owes a general duty of care towards such civic order,
the ethical and practical condition of which determines the degree
of his safety and of his capacity to realise his purposes as a moral
being. For such citizen to fulfil the particular duties to which his
general duty gives rise, is to give expression to his civic sense and
co-responsibility for the condition of the civic order to which he
belongs; a responsibility which is not confined to power-holders
and officials of the civic order or of its instrument the state. Rather,
such duties belong to all citizens, their fulfilment being a means to
the retention of the sovereignty of the civic order, the prevention
of the usurpation of its sovereignty by the state or by supranational
bodies, and the observance in general of the principle of duty, the
sovereign principle of the civic order.

The general duty of care and of co-responsibility which the

individual citizen owes to the civic order is the duty of a free
citizen, not of a subject or slave; a duty preferably voluntarily
assumed but which may, in the discretion of the civic order, be
enforced by sanction in regard to the particular duties which it
dictates. In the fulfilment of such duties, the civic bond is sustained
and the civic order – as an association of citizens which embraces
and is superior to all other associations within its bounds – is
upheld by the particular acts of the citizen himself.

269. It is in such acts that the citizen declares himself to be a
citizen, distinguishes himself from the citizen-turned-stranger,
demonstrates practically and ethically that he is part of the web of
moral relations which composes the civic order, and acknowledges
the sources and ground of his own well-being. Whether in 'sweep-
ing before his own door' or in civic acts of larger scope, he acts the
citizen's part, enhancing his own self-regard while contributing to
the well-being of the civic order as a whole. Such acts, dictated to
the individual by the principle of duty, may be acts of fulfilment of
duty to self, to one's fellows, or to the civic order to which one
belongs; in some cases, all together.

In a free civic order composed of free citizens, such acts are also
(at best) free expressions of the individual citizen's personal ethical
responsibility for himself and his fellow-citizens; they are not
covenanted or contracted acts of civic exchange for the benefits,
privileges, and rights of the citizen, being free-standing and
ethically prior acts, autonomously dictated by the principle of duty
as the sovereign ethical principle of the civic order [**sects. 172,
189–94**].

270. The particular duties of the citizen include duties which relate
to the past, the present, and the future; duties to self, to one's
fellows, and to the civic order as a whole; duties which can be
enforced, and duties which cannot; duties which the civic order in
its discretion may choose to enforce, and duties which it may
equally choose to leave to the voluntary assumption by the individual of co-responsibility for the condition of the civic order. It is,
likewise, for each civic order to determine which of the citizen's
particular duties have practical priority – a priority which may
change according to circumstance, including, above all, according

to the degree of disaggregation in the civic order – as also to determine the nature of the sanctions by which, where appropriate, the enforcement of the citizen's duties will be secured.

271. In Plato's ideal republic, or civic order, the citizen was to have been so well educated and trained as a citizen, and so to have embodied in himself the principle of duty in general, that no enforcement against him of particular duty nor system of sanction would be required, nor any anti-civic act, wilful or inadvertent, be committed by him.

In the non-Platonic world, as in the world created by the corrupted liberal order under the rule of dutiless right, no such expectation can be entertained. Without enforceable duties – even if not all duties can be enforced – the process of civic disaggregation could not be arrested. Moreover, the principle of duty must remain an ethical abstraction as long as it is not translated into particular actions. 'He who would do good', proclaim the 'Living Creatures' in William Blake's 'Jerusalem' (1804, Chap. 3, 55–63) – rejecting 'generalizing Demonstrations of the Rational Power' – 'must do it in Minute Particulars: / General good is the plea of the scoundrel, hypocrite and flatterer.'

272. It is also in the particular performance of civic duty, whether it be the duty of the civic order to the citizen, or the citizen's duty to the civic order, that the principle of duty discloses its true moral and practical scope. It is not a principle of the moral minimum, or lowest degree of duty compatible with the maintenance of the civic bond.

Thus, the payment by the citizen to the civic order, and its instrument the state, of taxes for 'cash-value' services rendered to the citizen by the civic order is not, as I have pointed out [sect. 21], a sufficient civic relation. 'The state', likewise declared Burke (*Reflections on the Revolution in France*, 1790, London, 1968, p. 194), 'ought not to be considered as nothing better than a partnership agreement in a trade of pepper and coffee, calico or tobacco.' The civic order, or aggregate of citizens under common rule and possessed of a common ethical direction governed by the principle of duty, is more than the casual locus of the self-interest of the citizen-turned-stranger in a relation of mere agglomeration with others; in which relation, the criterion of the moral minimum gives the ethical rule.

273. The rejection of the principle of the moral minimum – the lowest degree of duty, compatible only with the barest subsistence of the civic bond – dictates the ethical rejection of the reduction to its narrowest practical limits of individual responsibility to self, to one's fellows, and to the civic order. Moreover, such rejection is fully compatible with the liberal ideal, as I have already shown [sects. 24, 228]. For, as Mill argued (*On Liberty*, p. 24), there are not only 'many positive acts for the benefit of others' which 'anyone may rightfully be compelled to perform', but also 'certain acts of individual beneficence, such as saving a fellow-creature's life', which, 'whenever it is obviously a man's duty to do, he may rightfully be made responsible to society for not doing' (ibid.). Or, in Mazzini's words (*The Duties of Man*, p. 35), 'your most important duties are positive. It is not enough *not to do*; you must *do* . . . It is not enough *not to harm*; you must *do good* to your brothers' (emphasis in original).

Such positive prescription of civic duty beyond that of the moral minimum, although subject to provisos which dictate preference for ethical voluntarism and the avoidance of the oppression of the individual [sect. 229], becomes more imperative the greater the degree of civic disaggregation, and the weaker the civic bond. Kant might argue (*Lectures on Ethics*, p. 61) that 'to leave undone something which no law can compel us to do . . . is no wrongdoing', but on such a principle – sustainable in law, but not in ethics – the civic bond cannot cohere. Hence, the dictates of the civic bond and of the principle of duty which serves to sustain it, being wider than the existing commands of law, may give new responsibilities to the citizen which, in conditions of civic disaggregation in the corrupted liberal orders, are required to be observed if the civic order is to be maintained.

Thus, even though the Decalogue's injunctions do not urge the individual positively to protect the safety of his neighbour [sect. 229], and the law (in general) makes it no crime not to come to his assistance, the civic order, being itself obligated by the principle of duty to sustain and strengthen the civic bond, may in its discretion impose and enforce by sanction exactly such duty of care and co-responsibility upon the members of the civic order. For the citizen who does not protect the safety of his neighbour turns from citizen to stranger; and if such omission is followed by no disadvantageous civic consequence or legal sanction, or even, at worst, earns no ethical disapproval from fellow-citizens, it is an immunity gained by a stranger in a world of strangers.

'Cursed be he', declares *Deuteronomy* (XXVII, 18), 'that maketh the blind to wander out of the way'; but cursed, too, the citizen who takes no step to bring the blind back to their paths.

274. Under the rules of most systems of law – which are not always the rules either of ethics or justice, nor always co-terminous with the obligations dictated by the principle of civic duty – positive legal duty is generally created by prior contractual undertaking or special personal relationship, as that between parent and child, and may also arise from the obligations of public office. In addition to such duties, already enforceable in most legal systems by sanction and all of which have to do (to a greater or lesser degree) with the maintenance of the civic bond, there is to be found in most civic orders a variety of other enforceable legal duties of a civic kind. However limited they may be in scope, or often fallen into disuse in practice, they too may furnish the basis and model for the wider enforcement of the principle of duty, and the wider entry of the law into the realm of civic obligation.

Such existing and enforceable legal duties of a civic kind generally include other duties than those of mere payment of taxes for civic services, of military duty, or of a duty (in some civic orders) to vote in elections. Thus, variously, under English statute and common law, a citizen can be forced – by means of legal sanction for failure or refusal – to serve as a special constable, to give active help to a policeman in apprehending an offender, to serve on a jury, to give evidence in legal proceedings and, whether in nominated or elected civic office, to serve in such office once chosen to it: obligations, under sanction, which admit of extension, within the discretion of the civic order, to other and related forms of civic obligation dictated by the principle of duty.

Duties already enforceable (but not always enforced) against the citizen by virtue of a special personal relationship, and neglect of which can be considered harmful to the civic order, include in England the obligation of the parent not only to register the birth of a child or to subject such child to vaccination, but to ensure such child's education; the Elementary Education Act of 1876, for example, makes it the duty of the parent to 'cause such child to receive elementary instruction in reading, writing and arithmetic', and 'if such parent fail to perform such duty, he shall be liable to such orders and penalties as are provided by this Act' (39 and 40 Vict., c. 79, s. 4).

The very notion that such latter type of duty, dictated by the liberal ideal itself, should be enforced by sanction has come under increasing contempt in the corrupted liberal orders, where it offends the rule of dutiless right. But the principle on which it rests, that of the principle of civic duty, cannot be disowned either ethically or in practice, and remains the sovereign principle of the civic order. Moreover, existing duties of payment, service, contractual obligation, and personal responsibility to the civic order for the well-being of familiars stand – however neglected, begrudged or ethically degraded – at the heart of moral and practical relations among citizens, and between such citizens and the civic order.

To insist upon and to enforce such duties is to sustain the civic bond; to fail to do so is to depend upon the moral minimum, and, in the corrupted liberal orders, to watch with arms folded as the citizen-body drowns.

275. Even in the citizen's most personal familial and domestic relations, let alone in those relations which directly and publicly involve the interests of the civic order, the law, in most legal systems, has found ethical and practical ground for attempting to enforce duty, including in marital relations. But the principle of duty, as it applies to the individual citizen's duties to himself, his familiars and to the civic order, also dictates, *without regard to any sanction of law*, that such individual's familial, domestic, and marital relations be sustained, as far as is practicable and provided that it is in the interests of the parties concerned. Moreover, as a general ethical principle, where formal relations are voluntarily entered into in the civic order with the full consent of the parties and are

sanctioned by law – in marriage, as in other contractual relations – the individual's duty of care and co-responsibility for the well-being of the civic order *prima facie* dictates that such relations be respected, as any voluntary civic engagement or undertaking should be respected, and as the preservation of the civic bond demands [sect. 237].

276. The existence of the relation, among other relations, between parent and parent, and between parents and child, is a given of the civic order, as it is of the order of human relations itself. The family, or institution of such relations between parent and parent, and parents and child, can no more be finally dissolved – although its form may, within limits, be changed, and some of its features and implications vary from civic order to civic order – than human relations in general, and sexual relations in particular, can be denied and their main characteristics and outcomes cancelled. The family, whether the individual member of it wishes it so or not, and whether (as parent or child) he regards his own family with favour or disfavour, is, like the community and civic order to which he belongs, the ground of the moral perceptions of such individual. Upon their content and quality the practical well-being of the individual-*qua*-citizen may also be considered to stand.

But more can be, and always has been, claimed for the family than this. It has been readily perceived, for instance, as the microcosm of the civic order itself, and of its ethical condition. To Cicero, the family was the 'seed-plot of the whole commonwealth' (*Offices*, I, xvii), a metaphor suggesting that successful familial nurture is the source of the civic order's well-being, and that, conversely, when the 'seed-plot' is once trampled underfoot the 'commonwealth' itself must perish. To Rousseau – who abandoned his own offspring to the orphanage – the 'earliest and the only natural societies' and the 'first models of political societies' were 'families' (*Social Contract*, Bk. I, Chap. 2). Indeed, the family is not only one of the oldest objects of ethical respect and practical duty in the human community, but has served the speculative philosopher from earliest times as a source of ideas upon the nature of the civic order.

Now, not only the family's stability but its ethical status have

been reduced. In the corrupted liberal orders, rising volumes of
divorce, of births out of wedlock, and of single parenting of children
have been accompanied by the transfer and dispersal of old familial
duties and functions to officials of the civic order and of its
instrument the state. But this breaking of the 'bond of nature' in
familial relations, to use Rousseau's term (ibid.), is also the breaking
of the civic bond; the accelerating process of family dispersal is a
microcosm, cause, and further consequence of civic disaggregation;
the abandonment of familial duty is a flouting of the principle of
duty itself. To respect the dictates of the 'bond of nature' therefore
remains a particular duty of the citizen, a duty which now requires
increasingly to be reinforced by sanction, as I further argue in
Chapter Eleven.

277. The duty of the citizen to respect and observe the law, subject
to proviso [sects. 132, 140, 217–22], complements the civic order's
duties of self-protection and protection of the citizen-body. It is
not duty for duty's sake, being a duty owed by each citizen to live
peaceably and sociably in the interests of the well-being of all. In a
democratic civic order, such duty is expressed in an obligation to
observe laws which are democratically made, impartially administered and enforced, and which are capable of being changed or
replaced by democratic means. But in any civic order whatever, it
is *prima facie* the citizen's obligation to observe and sustain the law,
provided that the making, content and administration of such law
are not governed by cruel, inhuman, and wicked intent which
causes harm to the well-being of some or all of the citizens
themselves. It is also the citizen's general duty to reject ethically,
and to resist in practice, recourse to physical violence, whether on
the part of fellow-citizens in their disputes with one another, or on
the part of the civic order in meting out inordinate punishment to
its citizens.

However, the duty of the citizen to live peaceably and sociably
with his fellow-citizens is decreasingly observed in the corrupted
liberal orders, where the rule of the politics and ethics of dutiless
right, self-realisation through unimpeded freedom of action and
dutiless demand-satisfaction has given always greater practical
licence and even (in some minds) ethical legitimacy to the use of

violence, including armed violence, in the pursuit of such presumed rights and claims. But the violent negation by the individual of his duty to live peaceably and sociably with his fellows, in the interests of the civic order as a whole, is also a product of the failure of the civic order to fulfil its duties of self-protection and of protection of the individual (including from himself) in the interests of all. At worst, as in the corrupted liberal orders under conditions of accelerating civic disaggregation, the habitually aggressive and destructive citizen-turned-stranger may become increasingly the archetype of the citizen himself.

To arrest such process of violent civic degeneration is the first duty of the civic order, being the duty whose fulfilment most comports to the safety and security of the individual and to the well-being of all. It is a duty which can now be met in the corrupted liberal orders only by a redoubtable effort of civic education, and by increased resort to sanction against the violent and destructive, including not only loss of liberty but deprivation of civic privileges, benefits and rights, as I discuss further in Chapter Eleven.

278. The duty to live peaceably and sociably with one's fellows, not being a duty of the moral minimum [sects. 272–3], is more than a negative obligation laid upon the citizen to act without violence in the civic order to which he belongs. It implies a duty to add to, rather than merely not to subtract from, the well-being of the civic order; not simply to maintain, but to help construct, such well-being.

It is on these grounds that the payment by the citizen of taxes for services [sects 24, 272] can be further seen to be an insufficient civic relation. Citizenship – or the readiness of the citizen to act his citizen's part – carries the presumption of a willingness and capacity actively to assist, and to participate in, the civic order; the walls of Athens in 478 BC, like the walls of thirteenth-century Pisa, were built with the help of the citizen-body. Nor is the presumption of such readiness offensive to the modern liberal ideal, as I have already shown. To bear a 'fair share' in 'joint work necessary to the interest of the society of which he enjoys the protection' was thought by Mill (*On Liberty*, p. 24) to be a 'positive act' to which the citizen 'may rightfully be compelled' [sects. 24, 228].

To participate actively in the civic order is, therefore, not merely to pay taxes to officials of the civic order and its instrument the state, nor to register a quinquennial vote, but metaphorically to build its walls. Hence, the citizen is ethically obligated by the principle of duty not simply to *find work in*, but – as occasion allows and his capacity permits – to *share the work of*, the civic order to which he belongs.

279. Such ethical obligation is best discharged, in the first instance, by the voluntary assumption and fulfilment by the individual citizen of his co-responsibility for the condition of the civic order. In such voluntary acts – acts of community and public service, carried out through membership of voluntary civic organisations – the civic bond is both acknowledged and sustained; conversely, the neglect of such acts, and of the organisations which give them ethical and practical direction, is symptom and further cause of the process of civic disaggregation itself. Thus, in the corrupted liberal orders, phantom forms of association, such as those which nightly gather (in tens of millions, but isolated unit by unit) to watch the electronic shadows playing upon their cave-walls, have displaced much of that voluntary giving by the free citizen of aid, counsel, and other service to his fellows upon which the well-being of the civic order to a large extent depends.

The ethical obligation of community and public service requires to be restored in the interests of the civic order as a whole. Moreover, such obligation to render assistance to the civic order, albeit best discharged voluntarily and in response to the dictates of civic sense, must be reinforced both by inducement and – in respect of certain forms of a-civic conduct – by the sanction of compelled assistance to the civic order, as I further discuss in Chapter Eleven. The unrequited desire on the part of many citizens to *render voluntary service to the community and civic order to which they belong* it is also the obligation of the civic order to encourage and to satisfy; including, where necessary, by reform of its laws, administrative institutions, practices, and methods.

280. To permit, in the interests of the civic order as a whole, the wider expression of the latent civic sense in the individual of his co-responsibility for the condition of the civic order demands: the

strengthening of *the sense of local civic affiliation* [sect. 82]; increased devolution of fiscal, administrative, and other forms of civic authority to locally and regionally elected civic bodies, provided only that such devolution is compatible with the maintenance of the national civic order as a whole; and wider access to local participation in the practical work of the civic order of the nation, region, or city, including through voluntary and part-time service in local administration, in policing, in social service, and in other local acts of guardianship, which, as in the case of jury service, strengthen the civic bond.

To local suffrage, local taxes, local civic participation, local civic responsibilities, and varieties of other local service of the civic order, must be added forms of (removable) local benefit and privilege, whose removal may also serve as sanction for a-civic and anti-social conduct. The governing principle of all such measures which enhance the value of civic affiliation – whether to nation, region, or city – is that the citizen of any civic order generally requires to express, by particular acts, the fact of his citizenship. Where he does not, he may be brought to such expression by invitation, inducement and, should the civic sense fail (to the harm of the civic order), by sanction.

281. In the particular duty of jury service, a duty and service which may be compelled by sanction in the ethical and practical interests of the civic order as a whole, there is expressed the co-responsibility of the individual citizen for the administration of justice in the civic order to which he belongs. The rationale for such duty, and for the sanction which is available to enforce it, partake of the same civic nature: that of permitting the expression of the civic sense, penalising its refusal, and, by so doing, securing the civic bond.

In order to arrest the process of civic disaggregation, the performance of all other particular duties of the citizen requires to be invested with a similar ethical status to that of jury service; and the refusal of such duties, whether or not subject to legal sanction, requires to attract a similar ethical censure.

282. Indeed, to protect and sustain the civic bond, in particular in conditions of civic disaggregation, the civic order, in fulfilment of its own duty to the citizen-body, must seek by all ethical and

practical means to secure the performance by the citizen of his duties to himself, his fellows and the civic order. Where voluntary expectation fails, and sanction is impractical or unfitting, *inducements* – to the performance of public service, for example – may reasonably be offered, *faute de mieux*, to the citizen by the civic order. Thus, the performance of certain forms of public service may be rewarded with particular privilege and honour; or, access to certain of the advantages and benefits of citizenship, such as access to higher education or other benefits of public provision, may be made dependent, as I further argue in Chapter Eleven, upon the performance of community or other public service.

283. Public service or community service, that is service of the civic order by the individual citizen, may, both ethically and in practice, be voluntary, involuntary or secured by the persuasive inducement of the civic order. Moreover, in conditions of civic disaggregation and provided that the civic order itself is not founded upon a principle of evil and oppression, the fact of the performance of such service is of greater moral and practical import than the grounds upon which such service is performed. 'As soon as men cease to consider public service as the principal duty of citizens', declares Rousseau (*Social Contract*, Bk. III, Chap. 15), '. . . we may pronounce the State to be on the very verge of ruin'; or, as I should say, when the principle of duty ceases to be the sovereign principle of the civic order, and dutiless right rules in its stead, the process of civic disaggregation is accelerated and can barely be halted.

To secure the citizen's fulfilment of duty to the civic order to which he belongs by acts of public or community service is a precondition (among others) of the arresting of such process, as well as a task of the civic social-ism of the future.

284. A further precondition of the gradual restoration of the civic order from disaggregation is that many of the practical duties which have to do with its guardianship and well-being – and which are at present carried out by paid public servants on its behalf, and, in respect of some duties, in entire moral absolution of the citizen-body – should be increasingly shared by the citizens themselves. Thus, in the provision of social care for the elderly and for children at risk, in nursery care, in medical and educational auxiliary service, in the maintenance of a night-watch and the guardianship of public buildings, in the protection of the environment and the upkeep of place, in safeguarding the quality of foodstuffs and other supplies to the civic order, and in related acts of local oversight and administration, the expression of the citizen's co-responsibility for the condition of the civic order must be increasingly permitted, encouraged by inducement, and enforced by sanction.

In this way, the practical burden, ethical duty and civic privilege of helping to maintain the civic order, now largely carried out by officials and public employees paid from the proceeds of central and local taxation, can be more widely disseminated throughout the citizen-body, enhancing the civic bond, increasing the civic sense, reducing the degree to which civic responsibility is transferred to others in the corrupted liberal order, and thus strengthening the civic order itself in the interests of the well-being of all.

285. But at the heart of the principle of duty, as it applies to the particular duties of the individual, is the duty to *self*, which transcends and is the *fons et origo* of all others. 'This law', declares Epictetus (*Discourses*, I, xxxix), 'hath God ordained, who says, "If you wish for good, receive it from yourself."' Of the 'several duties man owes to himself', duties which Kant describes as 'universal', the first is that of 'so ordering his life as to be fit for the performance of all moral duties' (*Lectures on Ethics*, p. 125). It is duty to self which dictates duty to others; duty to self which, properly under-stood, is the least selfish of all duties; duty to self which, fulfilled, is the source of self-esteem; and self-esteem which is a precondition and further consequence of the possession of civic sense, or sense of co-responsibility for the well-being of others.

'The fact that a person is living for nobody', Seneca warns (*Letters*, LV), 'does not automatically mean that he is living for himself', or not to the extent of perceiving the nature of his duties to himself. The licensed egotist of the corrupted liberal order is governed, rather, by a sense of dutiless right in himself and against others, not of duty to himself, self-preoccupied as he may otherwise be; or, if possessed of a sense of duty to self, only in regard to a 'duty' to exercise such dutiless right on his own behalf, whatever the consequences to himself, his fellows, and the civic order. To

Mill, the term 'duty to oneself' meant 'self-respect or self-development', but for which, so Mill asserted, the individual was not 'accountable to his fellow-creatures' (*On Liberty*, p. 141). However, there can be no such rule, since lack of 'self-respect or self-development' in the individual is likely to place a burden – including that derived from the propensity, in those without self-regard, to a-civic conduct – on the civic order as a whole. These are precisely the circumstances in which the 'evil consequences' of 'purely personal conduct' are likely to afflict not merely the individual in question but to 'fall on others' (ibid., pp. 142–3); and simultaneously to bring down Mill's distinction between 'the part of a person's life which concerns only himself, and that which concerns others' (ibid., p. 143).

If the individual 'spoils his life by mismanagement', Mill adds (ibid., p. 142), 'we shall not, for that reason, desire to spoil it still further'. But if a 'mismanaged' life, led without regard to the principle of duty to self – or to others – 'spoils the life' of fellow-members of the civic order, such civic order is under an obligation to act in its self-protection and in protection of the citizen-body as a whole.

286. The duty of self-protection and self-defence of the civic order cannot be fulfilled without fulfilment by the individual citizen of his duty to himself. Such duty, whose content I shall shortly describe, is a correlate of the individual's freedom of will as a moral being. Or, as Kant expresses it (*Lectures on Ethics*, p. 123) [**sect. 66**], 'all evil in the world springs from freedom . . . It is essential, therefore, that man should restrain by rules the free actions which relate to himself. These are the rules of his self-regarding duties.'

Such self-regarding duties are both ethical imperatives and practical necessities in the civic order. The sustaining of the civic bond demands the restraint by the citizen himself of his appetites, material and other; and, in the corrupted liberal orders, requires a related self-denial in regard to claims to dutiless right and to self-realisation through unimpeded freedom of action. The correlative of such self-denial of claims to dutiless right is not only the assumption by the individual citizen of co-responsibility for the condition of the civic order, but the return to the sphere of duty-to-self of many of the ethical and practical responsibilities transferred in the corrupted liberal order to others; a transfer which, by masking the truth of where duty lies, has further helped to perpetuate rule over the civic order by the politics and ethics of dutiless right.

287. Of the particular duties which the individual citizen owes to himself, that of educating himself, and of availing himself of the opportunities of education provided by the civic order, stand at the head. A citizen, as I have already pointed out [sects. 255–66], is an individual who possesses such knowledge of himself, of his fellows, and of the civic order to which he belongs as to be able to act the citizen's part; while to know more about his fellows and about the civic order – its history, customs, laws, and language – than does the stranger is one of the marks which distinguishes the one from the other.

To assume active co-responsibility for the condition of the civic order requires adequate knowledge, however modest, to do so. In this respect, as in others, education is, in Kant's words, 'the forming of the mind for the civil state' (*Lectures on Ethics*, p. 248). Hence, the acquisition by the individual citizen of education and training is a 'self-regarding duty' before it is a right; to study, within the limits of the individual's capacities, is thus a duty also; so, too, is it a duty to acquire sufficient knowledge to be a useful citizen, a duty upon the fulfilment of which the well-being of the civic order itself depends.

Even without regard to the interests of others, the gaining of knowledge and technical skill is a precondition of the individual's 'good life'. In a democratic civic order, in particular, the duties and rights of suffrage, of participation, and of co-responsibility require the elector, the participant, and the citizen-as-moral-being to be sufficiently informed [sect. 170]. 'As he enters upon manhood', Kant declares (*Lectures on Ethics*, p. 251), the individual – who, ideally, will already have acquired at home a 'conception of propriety' (ibid.) – 'must be taught his real duties, the dignity of humanity in his own person and respect for humanity in others.' Such knowledge is both self-knowledge and knowledge acquired from others; the duty of *providing* such knowledge is the duty of familiars in the first instance, and thereafter of the institutions of the civic order. But the duty of *obtaining* such knowledge remains the particular (and continuous) duty of the individual himself, provided only that such individual is of sufficient age and capacity to be aware of his obligation.

'Solomon adviseth a man to bind the ten commandments upon his ten fingers', Hobbes says of the Judaic rule (*Leviathan*, Chap. XXVI). 'And for the law which Moses gave to the people of Israel at the renewing of the covenant, he biddeth them to teach it their children, by discoursing of it both at home and upon the way; at going to bed and rising from bed; and to write it upon the posts and doors of their houses, and to assemble the people, man, woman and child, to hear it read' (ibid.); or, as Amiel puts it (*Ethics and Legality in Jewish Law*, p. 18), 'our laws are given over to the entire nation, who are obligated to learn them'.

Such obligation – to educate and to be educated – holds in any civic order whatever, upon whatever ethical principles it rests, and however it may be politically ruled. For no civic order can be preserved from disaggregation without possessing a common ethical direction; and no common ethical direction can be sustained without the ethical education of the citizen-body. In the modern, and especially the democratic, civic order the imperative of education is larger and wider still; the duty of the individual to seek and to acquire it, also.

288. This particular duty of the individual citizen as to education and training, self-regarding as may be, is not an end in itself, as I have shown, being directed both to the well-being of the individual and of the civic order to which he belongs. It is, further, specifically directed to the imparting and acquiring of sufficient knowledge and technical capacity for useful work, work which both meets the needs of the civic order and enhances the 'self-respect and self-development' of the individual who acquires it.

For, as I have already argued [**sect. 163**], there is a moral duty in the citizen, a duty which is owed to himself in the first instance, to work, and seek work wherever it may be found. To this end, the acquiring of skills and knowledge which meet the needs of the civic order forms part of, and is a means to fulfilling, the duty to work.

Such duty to work – a duty before it is a right, once more – is a duty not only to find but (as far as possible) to keep gainful employment; to work industriously and efficiently, provided that other conditions [sect. 243] are met; and, as a citizen, to work not only for the end of self-realisation but for the well-being of the civic order itself.

289. It is also a particular duty owed by the citizen to himself to show respect not only to his own elders but to the past of the civic order, where it is ethically worthy of such respect [sects. 168, 266]. 'Failure to respect the past', thought Burckhardt (*Weltgeschichtliche Betrachtungen*, Bern, 1941, p. 50), 'is barbarism', provided only that such past is not barbarous itself. Associated with such duty is the duty owed by the citizen of respect for place [sect. 93], a duty which demands – and thus permits the civic order to expect and to enforce – the assumption by the individual of responsibilities of custodianship and care for the natural environment and material patrimony of the civic order to which he belongs.

Such duties of respect, in regard to persons, the past, and place (where they are worthy of it), are duties of self-regard also, since their fulfilment is a ground and source of the individual citizen's own self-esteem.

290. It is not a particular duty which the individual owes to himself as citizen that he should possess and profess a faith in God [sect. 11], matters of personal religious faith being outside the scope of the principle of duty as it applies to the duties of the individual to himself, his fellows, and the civic order, and of the civic order's duties to its members. In some instances, the common ethical direction of the civic order may, to a greater or lesser extent, be determined by religious ethics. But the personal faith, or lack of faith, of the individual cannot be made the subject of duty as such, least of all enforceable civic duty, since private belief is unamenable practically to public scrutiny and control, and ethically improper to pursue.

Where, however, the practice of faith is harmful to the interests of the civic order as a whole – for its fanaticism, odium directed to non-believers, or for other reason – the civic order is bound by the duties of self-protection and of protection of the citizen-body to act against it; but it cannot impose either belief or non-belief upon the citizen as a matter of civic duty. Epictetus *(Discourses*, I, xvi, 3) thought somewhat differently. 'If I was a nightingale', he declares, 'I would act the part of a nightingale; if a swan, the part of a swan. But since I am a reasonable creature, it is my duty to praise God. This is my business. I do it.' But even if to 'praise God' is considered a duty by the pious, the duty to have and profess a particular faith – that is, to praise God in a particular fashion – cannot without oppression and the risk of the reduction of the citizen to a subject [sects. 217–22] be made a citizen-duty as such. To respect and honour the beliefs of fellow-citizens, provided such beliefs are worthy of respect and honour and conduce to the well-being of the civic order as a whole, is, however, both compatible with and (in many cases) necessary to the maintenance of the common ethical direction of a given civic order.

Indeed, the habit of piety – where innocent of odium towards non-believers or individuals of different faith – may reasonably be considered a civic virtue and a spur to civic virtue in others, insofar as such habit of piety is itself a habit of showing respect and honour to universal ethical principle, to the past, and to place. So, certainly, do faith and piety generally appear a civic virtue to believers themselves, and, even, as the entire ground of their well-being, a ground which they therefore fear to lose. 'If I forget thee, O Jerusalem', sings the Psalmist (Psalm CXXXVII), 'let my right hand forget her cunning. If I do not remember thee, let my tongue cleave to the roof of my mouth; if I prefer not Jerusalem above my chief joy.' Moreover, in conditions such as those found in the corrupted liberal orders, where 'religion has lost its empire over the souls of men', as De Tocqueville argued (*Democracy in America*, p. 308), sceptical objection to faith, provided that the practice of such faith is not harmful to the well-being of the civic order as a whole, is increasingly hard to justify and sustain. For wherever ethical principle, and even the very notion of ethical principle, have come to be subordinated to the amoral rule of dutiless right and demand-satisfaction, any ethical principle may in turn come to seem, and to be, preferable to the gradual disappearance of all ethical principle whatever.

Nevertheless, a civic or secular faith which 'attaches the hearts of citizens to the State', such as Rousseau sought (*Social Contract*, Bk. IV, Chap. 8), is no more to be desired; worship of 'the State' is the act not of the free citizen but of the subject or slave. On the one hand, in the words of Rousseau (ibid.), 'wherever theological intolerance is admitted [sc. to the civic order], it is impossible for it not to produce some civic effect . . . Those who dare to say: "Outside the Church there is no salvation" should be driven from the State.' On the other hand, an entire religion or faith oppressively made of civic duty and its performance must itself be destructive of the civic bond. Hence, it is preferable, both ethically and in practice, that only that which is Caesar's should be rendered unto Caesar, that it be rendered voluntarily, but, where appropriate and necessary, be enforced by sanction.

For the rest, for that which concerns the individual citizen's personal belief, 'no man shall be troubled for his judgment or practice in the things of his God', as Gerrard Winstanley expressed it (*Law of Freedom in a Platform*, p. 379), 'so he live quiet in the land'. That is, faith is a matter of private right, albeit not absolute, and not a matter of duty. 'If Jews still believe themselves bound to fulfil their religious duties', declared Bruno Bauer (*Die Judenfrage*, Brunswick, 1843, p. 65, cited in K. Marx, 'On The Jewish Question', *Collected Works*, London, 1975, vol. 3, p. 152), 'then this must be allowed them as a purely private matter'; 'an Englishman, as one to whom liberty is natural', said Voltaire (*Letters on the English*, 1731, London, 1889, Letter V, p. 36), 'may go to heaven his own way'. And so he should, provided only that his manner of going does no harm to the interests of the civic order as a whole.

291. Of the particular duties which the citizen owes to himself, that of physical self-care and self-preservation – the essence of self-regard – is, as far as such self-care is practicable, the plainest precondition of the health and well-being of the individual. 'God', declares Epictetus (*Discourses*, II, viii), 'hath delivered yourself to your care and says, "I had no one fitter to be trusted [sc. with yourself] than you: preserve this person for me." And will you not preserve him?' Observance of, and respect for, the duty of self-care and self-preservation is the practical expression both of the ethical

imperative which commands each person to live, and of the principle of duty as it applies to the citizen's obligation to assume – and, therefore, to be able to assume – active co-responsibility for the condition of the civic order to which he belongs.

The duty of physical self-care, as far as such self-care is practicable and possible, is a fundamental civic duty in other respects also. It represents the assumption by the individual, as a free moral being, of physical responsibility for himself in the first instance and as a first resort, rather than the transfer – in the first instance and as a first resort – of such responsibility to others, in particular to officials and servants of the civic order. Such duty of individual self-preservation is also the correlate, in microcosm, of the civic order's duty of self-preservation in general, to which the citizen contributes by fulfilling his duty to himself of self-care. It is, further, an expression of that duty of self-restraint of material appetite and demand [sect. 286], including of the demand for self-realisation through unimpeded freedom of action, which is required to sustain the civic bond. 'We should . . . have respect . . . to the preservation of our health and strength, in our victuals, clothes and other conveniences belonging to the body', says Cicero likewise (*Offices*, I, xxx). 'How base and unworthy a thing it is to dissolve in luxury', he adds, 'and not to keep within the bounds of reason and moderation.'

In corrupted liberal orders ruled by dutiless right and demand-satisfaction, self-applied limits of 'reason and moderation' in consumption are all the more dictated by the principle of duty, in the interests of the entire citizen-body. It is not abstract rule, but civic sense, which increasingly insists upon such self-command in conditions where the growing burden (and cost) of pain and sickness from excess, and from refusal of self-care, are transferred – by the citizen-turned-stranger – to the civic order as a whole. To live a healthy regime is an individual duty before it is a right, notwithstanding the duty of the civic order itself to provide to the citizen the basic conditions for a healthy existence [sects. 67, 76, 242]. Moreover, refusal of such individual duty of self-care is susceptible, within the discretion of the civic order, to sanction, including by loss of certain benefits of health provision furnished to the citizen by the civic order, as I argue further in Chapter Eleven.

Mill, in times before the liberal ideal had come to be so generally corrupted by the rule and ethic of dutiless right, held a different view. 'Each is the proper guardian of his own health, whether bodily, or mental and spiritual', he declares (*On Liberty*, p. 27), but only to derive from such autonomous moral responsibility a 'principle' of unconcern on the part of others: 'mankind are greater gainers by suffering each other to live as seems good to themselves', Mill asserts, 'than by compelling each to live as seems good to the rest' (ibid.). But the antithesis between moral autonomy on the one hand and compulsion on the other is too sharply drawn by Mill, or false; and the present condition of the corrupted liberal order, in which the gamble of liberty is being lost, dictates another ethic in the interest of the liberal ideal itself, that ethic which is dictated by the principle of duty.

Better, because ethically rooted in an understanding of the duty of self-preservation – and not merely of the duty to live 'as seems good' to oneself– is the moral stoicism of a Goethe, when he urges that 'all that we poor mortals have to do is endure and keep ourselves upright as well and as long as we can' (*Conversations with Eckermann*, p. 322). By such principle of 'endurance', absent from Mill's utilitarian logic, suicide is ethically forbidden. 'Suicide is an abomination', holds Kant (*Lectures on Ethics*, p. 120), 'because it implies the abuse of man's freedom of action: he uses his freedom to destroy himself. His freedom should be employed to enable him to live as a man . . . he may not use his freedom against himself'; not least because, as Kant put it in his 'Doctrine of Virtue' (*The Metaphysics of Morals*, p. 218), 'killing oneself can . . . be regarded as a violation of one's duty to other human beings'.

An Epictetus might remind us that 'the door' – to suicide – 'is always open' (*Discourses*, I, xxiv, 4); 'do not be more fearful than children', he enjoins, 'but, as they, when the play doth not please them, say "I will play no longer", so do you in the same case say "I will play no longer, and go"'. ('If you stay, do not complain', he adds.) However, the individual's duty of self-care and self-preservation not only forbids suicide but, being more than an ethically

passive principle of tragic endurance – noble as such Job-like
fortitude may be – demands the active expression of the individual's
moral and practical responsibility for his own well-being, upon
which the well-being of others also depends.

Such responsibility is a responsibility in the individual citizen
not merely to stay alive as long as possible, but so to live that the
individual's co-responsibility for the condition of the civic order
may be expressed and acted upon for as long as possible also.

292. To evince, and act upon, a sense of respect for the physical
lives of others, and other living creatures in general, is also the
particular duty of the individual, being a further fulfilment of the
individual's duty to his fellows and to the civic order as a whole.
Such respect for the physical lives of others, and of other living
creatures, is an expression of ethical self-identification with other
living beings; an identification which, deriving from a compassion-
ate sense of the common needs, frailty, and vulnerability of one's
fellows and of other living things, may also carry the individual to a
greater sense of the duty of care which he owes to himself.

To show such respect for the physical lives of others is a civic
act; just as to refuse such respect, or, worse, to do physical harm to
others, as by violence, stands at the height of the anti-civic. It is no
less a civic act to show respect for, and to protect, the natural
environment of the civic order [**sect. 167**], of which natural
environment the lives of sentient fellow-creatures of other species
constitute, ethically, the most important part. Respect for such lives
is also an act of self-respect, insofar as the nature of such lives
partakes of the nature of our own.

'If a bird's nest chance to be before thee', declares *Deuteronomy*
(XXII, 6–7), '. . . thou shalt not take the dam with the young', but
'let the dam go, and take the young to thee, that it may be well with
thee, and that thou mayest prolong thy days.'

By the same moral token, cruelty to animals is both a self-
affliction and an affliction of the civic order; 'violent and cruel
treatment of animals', asserts Kant, 'is . . . intimately opposed to
man's duty to himself' (*The Metaphysics of Morals*, p. 238). Indeed,
'Thou shalt not muzzle the ox when he treadeth the corn'
(*Deuteronomy*, XXV, 4) is an ethical injunction whose moral status

is little less than that of the prescriptions of the Decalogue itself, and is dictated both by the individual's duty to himself and to the civic order as a whole.

293. The duties of the individual citizen – and of the civic order also – are generally duties which, in the first instance, have regard to the present condition of the civic order. But they may have regard, too, to the past, as where respect for the past and its legacy is enjoined upon the present, and, more frequently, to the future, as where the well-being of future generations is a determinant of duties owed by the citizen and civic order today. Duties which have to do, for example, with the welfare of the family, with the quality of education, or with the safeguarding of the environment are future-directed as well as present obligations.

Thus, in the matter of the welfare of the family, to marry at an age of sufficient maturity to exercise responsibility for the well-being of the offspring of such marriage [sect. 237] implies a duty of care for the future of the civic order, which, if not exercised, may, in the discretion of the civic order, invite sanction, as I argue further in Chapter Eleven. Likewise future-directed is the duty of the citizen to sustain the marital relation into which he or she has voluntarily entered [sect. 275]: that is, to remain married and cohabitant – provided only that such relation is not seriously harmful to the well-being of the partners – as long as there are dependent minor children whose welfare will be put at risk by parental division. The principle of duty, insofar as it is future-directed, dictates the maintenance of the civic bond; and the maintenance of the civic bond in turn dictates a presumption in favour of sustaining, including by sanction, all voluntarily-entered relations between citizens, marital relations included, in the interests of the civic order as a whole.

On the same ground of future implication, the joint parental duty of care for children's physical and emotional welfare may dictate the imposition of sanction for neglect of such duty in the interests of the future condition of the civic order; just as future-directed duty enjoins disclosures to each other by future spouses and partners of their medical condition. But it is the duty of oversight of the moral and other education of children which stands at the head of the citizen-parent's future-directed obligations. 'It is one of the most sacred duties of parents . . . after summoning a human being into the world', declares Mill (*On Liberty*, p. 189), 'to give that being an education fitting him to perform his part well in life towards others and towards himself'; that is, to fulfil the present citizen's civic duty to educate, and to have educated, under whatever system of education, the future citizens of the civic order.

'The duty devolves upon each individual', Aristotle similarly argues, (*Ethics*, X, 1180a), 'to contribute to the cause of virtue with his own children . . . or, at least, to make this his aim and purpose: and this . . . he will be best able to do by making a legislator of himself.' So great was the importance attributed by Solon to the parental duty to educate, and to supervise the education of, the child that he made it a law of Athens that no man should be obliged to maintain his father if the latter had failed to teach him a skill or trade. Indeed, in all societies but those of the corrupted liberal orders, the assumption of co-responsibility by the citizen for the future condition of the civic order, and the ethical and legal obligations of parents in regard to their children's education and conduct, have been understood – by civic sense – to be conjoined.

Now, in conditions of accelerating civic disaggregation, the principle of duty dictates that, within the limits of reason and practicality, the moral and legal responsibility of the natural parents of a minor child for the welfare and the actions of such child should be both increased and enforced; an increase in responsibility which is in the present and future interests of the civic order as a whole.

294. In observance of a similar duty to safeguard the future well-being of the civic order, the individual citizen is under an ethical and practical obligation, dictated by the principle of duty and subject to sanction, to minimise such avoidable harm to the physical or material environment as may be caused by his own actions; in the words of Kant (*The Metaphysics of Morals*, p. 237), a 'propensity to wanton destruction of what is beautiful in inanimate nature (*spiritus destructionis*) is opposed to man's duty to himself'. It is an obligation in turn dependent for its fulfilment upon the citizen's prior duty to acquire sufficient information [sects. 92–3, 170] by which to guide judgment in such matters.

For the future condition of the environment of the civic order is a present responsibility not only of the civic order, and of its instrument the state, but a co-responsibility of the individual citizen himself [sect. 167]. Moreover, the duty of self-restraint of appetite and demand [sect. 291] also dictates self-control in the seeking of access to environments under threat, or places otherwise burdened by excessive attention and movement. In the absence of such self-restraint, it is the duty of the civic order, in self-protection and protection of the interests of the citizen-body as a whole, to ration such access, or, in extreme circumstances, to prevent it entirely.

295. Having given a general account of the principle of duty and of its grounds and nature [sects. 154–99], determined its limits [sects. 217–22], and specified the particular obligations of the civic order [sects. 268–94], I now Pass to questions of how such obligations may be sustained and enforced, and how their neglect or refusal may be penalised by sanction.

ELEVEN

The Sanctions of Duty

296. 'Consideration of the rule is useless', declared Kant (*Lectures on Ethics*, p. 3), 'unless people can be made willing to follow the rule.' So it is with the principle of duty, whose ethical sovereignty in the civic order depends upon its observance, whether voluntarily, by inducement, or under sanction. Moreover, the civic bond, the bond which exists between individuals as fellow-citizens, is not self-sustaining, requiring special measures for its protection and enhancement. Without sanction, or the threat and risk of sanction, a sense of civic right and wrong [**sect. 92**] – particularly in corrupted liberal orders ruled by the ethics and politics of dutiless right – is the harder to induce: a purely voluntarily-assumed sense (in some citizens) of co-responsibility for the condition of the civic order is an insufficient support for such civic order, especially in conditions of civic disaggregation.

Hence, such responsibility may, within the discretion of the civic order [sect. 273], be enforced by particular sanction; and such sanction may be applied to responsibility for acts both of commission and omission. That is, sanction may attach both to the 'many positive acts for the benefit of others', as Mill puts it (*On Liberty*, p. 24) [sect. 24], which 'anyone may rightfully be compelled to perform', and to 'things which whenever it is obviously a man's duty to do he may rightfully be made responsible to society for not doing' (ibid.). As to the latter, 'leaving undone what we are required to do is an action for which we can be held responsible', in the words of Kant (*Lectures on Ethics*, p. 60): 'legal omissions are actions and can give rise to responsibility' (ibid.).

Indeed, without the availability and appropriate use of sanction against a-civic and anti-civic acts – whether of commission or omission – it comes to be readily assumed in the corrupted liberal order, under the rule of dutiless right, that such acts, remaining uncensured, are either unjusticiable or, worse, justly exempt from blame. Likewise, without the availability and appropriate use of sanction, the restoration of civic sense to the citizen-turned-stranger, and especially the reimposition upon such stranger of omitted responsibilities for self which have been transferred to the corrupted civic order, must in general be a lost civic cause.

In addition, where selfish claims to dutiless demand-satisfaction and self-realisation through unimpeded freedom of action have taken hold of the morality of the individual, and even of the civic order as a whole, or where the citizen-turned-stranger is no more than a welfare-subject of the state, obligation by imposition may alone serve to restore the citizen to himself and permit the civic order to discharge its own duties of self-protection and protection of the citizen-body. Indeed, where the citizen-turned-stranger manifests by his actions, in particular by violent actions, an unconcern for all interests but his own (as he perceives them), it is both equitable and necessary that his claims to pursue such interests without fetter or responsibility should be tempered by the enforcement of the principle of duty.

Furthermore, if it is, as Locke argues (*Two Treatises of Civil Government*, Bk. II, para. 123), a rational impulse which brings individuals to associate with one another in the civic order for their mutual preservation, so much the less can the civic order permit irrational a-civic or anti-civic action to pass with impunity, when such action harms the well-being of the civic order as a whole. It is both the duty and the right of the civic order to correct such action, using (at its own discretion) the ethical and practical means at its disposal. In particular, where the citizen-body is sovereign in a democratic civic order, such sovereignty cannot be retained unless, *inter alia*, the strength of the civic bond is maintained by the acts of the citizens themselves; who, if they do not willingly show respect for such bond, must be brought to it by sanction.

Moreover, if in a free civic order a free citizen may be compelled – as he may – on pain of sanction, and notwithstanding his freedom, to pay taxes, to serve on a jury, or to give evidence in a court of justice, he may be compelled to other and related civic duties. And in the corrupted liberal orders where dutiless right rules and the pace of civic disaggregation quickens, the securing by the civic order of the performance of the citizen's duties – including by the extension of the scope and rigour of sanction – becomes increasingly a precondition of the civic order's fulfilment of its own duties. Thus, wherever the expectation of what may be achieved by ethical voluntarism increasingly fails, sanction, subject to the provisos discussed earlier [**sects. 217–22**], must increasingly take its place, *pari passu*.

297. The sanctions available to the civic order are various in type and purpose. Acts of refusal or neglect of the citizen's part may be subjected to consequent disadvantage, as by loss or curtailment for a greater or lesser time of citizen privileges, benefits, licences, and rights; or may be subject to other more conventional penalty, as by punishment by fine, attachment of earnings, or loss of liberty.

The fulfilment of civic obligation, and the exercise of co-responsibility for the condition of the civic order, may be otherwise made enforceable by becoming the precondition of access to certain forms of public provision, as where access to higher education is made dependent on the performance of community or other public service; abuse or misuse of, and other like harm done to, the resources of public provision (and its providers) may be visited by ethically-related loss of access to such provision, for a greater or lesser time; diminished access to the benefits, resources, and facilities of the civic order's national, or local, social and public institutions, and other places of public resort, may be made a sanction of anti-civic and anti-social conduct; or compelled service of the civic order, for a greater or lesser time, may, subject to proviso [sects. 217–22], be made a penalty of certain forms of such conduct.

The application of all these and other sanctions must rest within the discretion of the civic order. They should also be subject, as I argue later, to adjudication and supervision by local Courts of Obligation and their justices, and ultimately to the jurisdiction, as in matters of appeal, of a high Court of Obligation; the task of which courts and justices must be the upholding and enforcement of the principle of duty where ethical voluntarism fails. The ulterior ethical and practical purpose of sanction must be, in all cases, the enhancement of the notion of citizenship as a privilege, the strengthening of the civic bond, and the protection of the civic order.

298. The enforcement by sanction of the principle of duty, as it applies to the duties of the citizen, is a means both to the raising of the self-regard of the individual as a citizen and to the restoration of the meaning and substance of citizenship itself. Even where the imposition of civic duty involves the loss of civic benefit and right – and, *in extremis*, the loss of citizenship itself – its purpose remains that of re-establishing the worth of such citizenship in the citizen's own eyes. Citizenship, invested or reinvested with the citizen's understanding of its particular privileges and benefits, the removal and loss of which may be made a sanction for anti-civic conduct, may thus acquire or re-acquire both its ethical and its practical value. To be estranged from the civic order, or to be transformed from citizen to stranger – increasingly the norm in the corrupted liberal order – must instead become an ultimate penalty for refusal or serious neglect of, or other assault upon, the principle of duty. To act the citizen's part must once again be both the price and privilege of membership of the civic order; to cease to be a citizen, whether *de facto* or (by order of the Court of Obligation) *de jure*, must be a measurable loss, both ethically and in practice.

299. Local citizenship [**sect. 82**], that is membership of the local civic order of the region or city, must be similarly invested with removable benefit and privilege [**sect. 280**], and obligation be owed to such civic order, if citizenship in general is to have its value restored, and if the civic bond is to be strengthened. Like the benefits and privileges of *national* citizenship, the benefits and privileges of *local* citizenship may also be made dependent – whether for the possession of such benefits and privileges by newcomers, or for their continuance – upon peaceful residence for a quantum of years, or upon such other proofs of the civic sense of the individual as the civic order may determine.

In every circumstance, the purpose of such requirements must be the restoration in the citizen of knowledge of citizenship as the source of benefit and right, and thus restoration of the ethical and practical value of citizenship itself. In the case of non-citizens who seek citizenship in the civic order where they are settled – the prospect of which should, *prima facie*, be in general open to them – the same considerations apply: that non-citizen settlement, and the benefits of public and other provision which may attach to it, should be valued, and that citizenship should, even more, be perceived to be a prize.

300. There are nevertheless many aspects of the life of the citizen in a free civic order which, as I have argued [**sect. 198**], cannot be made the subject of obligation; for example, voluntary matters of worship, personal belief and opinion, and many equally voluntary matters of civic association and participation. At the same time, the presumption in the corrupted liberal order in favour of the rule of dutiless right and of the ethic of self-realisation through unimpeded freedom of action cannot be permitted to remain, as the process of civic disaggregation accelerates. Inducement and compulsion to duty, the imposition of preconditions in the acquisition of citizenship, the employment of sanction against a-civic and anti-civic conduct, and other means of arousing respect in the individual for the citizenship which he possesses all necessarily encroach upon the licence of dutiless right.

But all such encroachment should continue itself to be kept in check, as far as is possible and justified, by an ethical and practical preference in the civic order and its instruments, the state and law, for *invitation* to observance of the principle of duty over *inducement* to it, and *inducement* over *compulsion* to such observance, as I have already argued [sect. 229]. Compulsion by use of sanction is a last resort, being a form of subjection of the citizen; even where practically necessary in the interest of the well-being of the civic order as a whole, it remains an ethical poor-relation of other means [sect. 261], unless the existence of the civic order itself is imperilled.

Moreover, from the objection to servitude and bondage [sect. 217], no absolute duties which are untempered by right – including a right of appeal to the higher Court of Obligation – can be imposed upon the citizen. In addition, the principle of duty must be equitably enforced, without regard to the status of persons [sect. 184].

301. To secure the widespread observance of the principle of duty on the part of the citizens of a determinate civic order, it does not follow that a widespread imposition of duty by sanction is required; even in corrupted liberal orders, it may be anticipated that the very existence of sanctions, and a demonstrated readiness to use them, will be sufficient for the most part [sect. 197], and for most citizens. Indeed, the reassertion by the civic order of the principle of duty, including in corrupted liberal orders where moral exhaustion with claims to dutiless right and demand-satisfaction is already (in many citizens) profound, can be expected to have some effect upon the individual's ethical awareness and civic sense, even without the direct intervention of law and the use of sanction. The clear determination of the civic order to impose itself upon the asocial claims and conduct of the citizen-turned-stranger, and to enforce the principle of duty, must command the greater assent the greater the anxiety at the quickening process of civic disaggregation.

Moreover, notwithstanding already-discussed ethical provisos [sects. 132, 140, 217–22] and practical exemptions in regard to the imposition of the principle of duty – such as that the principle of duty cannot ethically be imposed by those who do not observe it themselves [sect. 226], or that it cannot in practice be observed by those citizens incapable, for whatever reason, of observing it [sect.

222] – the principle of duty remains the sovereign principle of the civic order. Its enforcement by sanction is a means by which, in Kant's words, 'people can be made willing to follow the rule' [sect. 296], wherever voluntary assumption of co-responsibility for the condition of the civic order, invitation, and inducement have failed.

302. There is no principle of contracted or covenanted reciprocity [sect. 269] between the duties of the citizen and the duties owed to him by the civic order; the duties of the citizen, as I have argued [sects. 10–13], are ethically and logically prior. This is so, despite the fact that the civic order has, for example, a general obligation not only to do all that is feasible, within its resources, to prevent the avoidable estrangement of the citizen from the civic order by reason of his indigence, sickness, unemployment, or other social and personal handicap, but also to protect the citizen's capacity to play the citizen's part [sect. 247].

Thus, even where the civic order and its instrument the state fail in some of their duties to the citizen, there is a general presumption that such citizen remains *prima facie* bound by the principle of duty, unless the already-discussed ethical provisos and practical exemptions exclude him from obligation. For without such *prima facie* obligation and the general fulfilment of the citizen's duties – duties owed to the civic order as such, rather than to any particular politico-economic system in the civic order, or to particular individuals who may at any time govern such civic order – the civic order could neither continue to be the source of the citizen's security and right (however flawed), nor in other respects provide the locus for the citizen's realisation of his ends.

That the citizen continues to be bound by the sovereign principle of the civic order, even where the civic order fails such citizen in respect of some of its duties to him, is, however, without prejudice to his right to seek to amend the conditions under which he lives; as well as to criticise, remove democratically, rebel against, and, in extreme circumstances, to overthrow by force a particular politico-economic system, or particular individuals who may command the civic order [sects. 132, 211]. But these rights are themselves subject to the proviso that they be exercised in defence of the integrity of the civic bond and the preservation from damage and harm of the civic order itself.

Nevertheless, the citizen's rights – in extreme conditions, civic duties also, dictated by the principle of duty – are the citizen's ultimate sanction against the failures of the civic order to which he belongs. But since he himself, as a citizen, remains always co-responsible for the condition of such civic order, since no right can be absolute, and since the citizen's duties to the civic order are ethically and logically prior to the duties of the civic order to him, there is an *a priori* ethical and practical presumption – which only the most serious defects in the government and conduct of the civic order can displace – that the citizen's duties to the civic order to which he belongs continue at all times to be owed to such civic order.

Moreover, one form of damage and harm committed to the civic bond, as by neglect or other default on the part of the civic order itself in relation to the citizen, cannot be permitted to be met with, or countered by, another form of damage and harm committed by the citizen, as in reprisal for the neglect of his particular interest in the civic order to which he belongs. For to permit such acts to be carried out with impunity would lend ethical justification to the destructive and self-destructive actions of the citizen-turned-stranger also; and neither in the one case nor the other are acts which harm the civic bond compatible with the principle of duty, whether in its application to the civic order's duty of self-protection, or to the citizen's duty of care towards the civic order.

303. Instead, it is within the discretion of a sovereign civic order to determine which of its ethical and practical duties to the citizen shall be justiciable and which not, and, acting through its instruments the law and new Courts of Obligation, to provide individual citizens with the means of gaining legal redress for neglect or default by the civic order in the performance of its duties to the citizen; in a democratic civic order, such determination is required to be arrived at by democratic decision. This legal redress may include the award of damages to citizen complainants, the issuing of writs against the civic order and its instruments to compel performance of duty to citizens, the issuing of injunctions to stop

or prevent certain forms of default of duty on the part of the civic order, and – also as a form of redress – the granting of exemptions to individuals, or classes of citizens, from duties which they would otherwise owe.

304. The civic bond, not being self-sustaining [sect. 296], requires for its maintenance and strengthening the taking of special measures, as by enforcement of the principle of duty by sanction. But just as not all duties can be enforced by, for example, making their breach unlawful – as when they are obligations susceptible only to moral encouragement or moral disapproval – so the making of their breach unlawful is not the only means, as I showed earlier [sect. 297], by which duties may be enforced, or their non-performance discouraged and deterred.

It is also the general duty of the civic order, and of its instruments the state and law, so to act that oppressive sanction may be the less needed as a means to induce or persuade the citizen to civic sense, respect for the civic bond, and the performance of civic duty. In individual cases, too, quite apart from those in which the civic order has acted in default of its own duty to the citizen, 'there are often good reasons for not holding him to his [sc. civic] responsibility', as Mill argues (*On Liberty*, p. 25), 'but these reasons must arise from the special expediencies of the case: either because it is a kind of case in which he is on the whole likely to act better when left to his own discretion . . . or because the attempt to exercise control would produce other evils greater than those which it would prevent'. Upon such cases of exception it is for Courts of Obligation ultimately to adjudicate, but without derogation from the principle of duty itself as the sovereign principle of the civic order.

Nor are sanctions of imposition and deprivation the only sanctions available to secure observance by the citizen of the principle of duty. 'They do not only fear [sc. frighten] their people from doing evil by punishments,' said Thomas More of his *Utopia* (Bk. II, Chap. 7), 'but also allure them to virtue with rewards of honour.' As Hobbes also argues (*Leviathan*, Chap. XXVIII), reward may justly be given to encourage the fulfilment of duty; for Aristotle (*Politics*, III, ix, 1281a), those who contributed most to the civic order, or *polis*, were 'entitled to a larger share in it . . . than those who are inferior in civic virtue'. A practical expression of such discriminatory reward in Athens was the payment made to those who served the city, such as councillors and jurors; indeed, not only were councillors, jurors, civic administrators, soldiers, and guards paid for their services, but 'benefactors' of the civic order might be maintained at the public expense.

In the modern civic order, those who serve it may receive 'rewards of honour' for their service, but such inducements are insufficient sanctions for the ordinary observance of the principle of duty, while encouragement of the civic sense by direct payment is incompatible with the ethic of duty. Instead, active demonstration of a sense of co-responsibility for the condition of the civic order – as through participant membership of voluntary social organisations whose purposes promote the well-being of such civic order – may be treated as a qualification for those seeking representative office, may attract tax advantages, may earn exemption from obligatory community service, and may be taken into account in individual cases in off-setting the penalties of anti-civic and anti-social conduct.

305. Sanctions, whether of reward or of deprivation, and whether used or merely at the disposal of the civic order, are not ends but means, to make the individual citizen willing – or, if not willing, ready – to carry out his duties to himself, his fellows and the civic order. Nor is this itself the final purpose of such sanction, which is the maintenance of the civic bond by all means, that of sanction among them; by which means the civic order may be assisted to cohere, and the sovereignty of such civic order be preserved.

Moreover, even where resort is had to sanctions of deprivation and compulsion, their purpose is not to demonstrate or reinforce the powers of the state – the instrument of the civic order – but to strengthen relations among citizens, and thus to sustain the civic order itself. Hence, where compulsory community or public service is employed as a sanction for anti-civic conduct, its purpose is to halt or reverse the process of civic disaggregation, and not to make of the citizen, or citizen-turned-stranger, a mere subject or captive of the civic order. To punish such citizen is also not to exact retribution from him, but to seek to induce or persuade him to play the citizen's part, or, failing this, to dissuade and prevent him from acting against the well-being of his fellows or of the civic order as a whole.

Those who do not respect, or assail and imperil, the civic bond must, however, expect to have the civic bond drawn more tightly around them, in their own interest and in the interests of the civic order; or, when other measures have failed, to have such civic bond severed in part, or entirely, for a greater or lesser time, and the benefits, privileges, or rights of their citizenship removed or curtailed. For those who damage the civic bond and the civic order which it upholds, particularly if such damage is committed repeatedly and wilfully, cease to be entitled to unqualified membership of the civic order; and, ultimately, cease to be entitled to it at all.

Indeed, to fail to deprive such individuals of some, or all, of the benefits of the citizenship which their actions declare them to hold in low regard is a dereliction of the civic order's own duties of self-protection and protection of the citizen-body. It is also an invitation to others – particularly in the corrupted liberal orders – similarly to despise their citizenship and the civic order to which they belong; yet others may observe the impunity of their fellows with alarm for their own security but also with increased doubt as to their own duty. Or, as Locke put it (*Two Treatises of Civil Government*, Bk. II, para. 94), 'when people perceive that any man. . . is out of the bounds of the civil society they are of . . . they are apt to think themselves in the state of Nature, in respect of him whom they find to be so'; that is, to think themselves in an a-civic world of dutiless right where, at the last, no citizen can be safe, nor his liberties and rights be assured.

Thus, the ends of civic sanction are to keep the citizen within the bounds of the civic order, and to restore the citizen-turned-stranger to it; a means to which is to deprive the individual of some of its benefits, for a greater or lesser time, so that respect may be induced for the civic order to which he belongs, and, failing which, to deprive him, for a greater or lesser time, of his citizenship and its benefits entirely.

306. Such sanction, commanded with greater urgency by the principle of duty the swifter the process of civic disaggregation, is

directed, as Locke also would have had it directed, to the individual who 'slights and breaks' the 'tie' (*Two Treatises of Civil Government*, Bk. II, para. 8), or civic bond, that bond which helps to secure citizens in their rights and to protect them from injury at the hands of their fellows. Such individual can not only be made, justly, to 'repent the doing of it' but be deterred – along with others who might be minded to follow – 'from doing like mischief' (ibid.).

In the corrupted liberal order, moreover, civic sanction by deprivation and compulsion is required to overcome the egoism of claims to dutiless right and the refusal of co-responsibility for the condition of the civic order. 'Though meekness and clemency be laudable virtues', says Cicero (*Offices*, I, xxv), 'yet no farther than as they leave room for a just severity, wherever the occasions of the public require it, without which a city can never be well governed.' The refusal of such severity is itself the mark of many corrupted liberal orders, as well as a further cause of their corruption. This was long ago understood by Goethe, who, referring to 'the difficulties an excess of liberalism presents' (*Conversations with Eckermann*, p. 514), declares that 'it will be found that one cannot succeed in the long run with over-great goodness, mildness and moral delicacy, while one has beneath a mixed and sometimes vicious world to manage'.

Now, the increasing viciousness in the corrupted liberal orders of some aspects of the conduct of citizens-turned-strangers, and in particular of the universal plebeian, makes 'mildness and moral delicacy', or Cicero's 'meekness and clemency', of ever-diminishing ethical and practical effect. Nevertheless, even in such conditions, observance by the citizen of the principle of duty must remain in the first instance, and in the free civic order, a matter of moral expectation, of invitation and inducement, and of voluntary action; but, in the second, where ethical voluntarism fails or is insufficient, must be increasingly subject to sanction.

'Those who are not to be repressed with words and philosophical discourses', as Cicero wryly puts it (*Offices*, III, xviii), require stronger means to 'vex' them to civic sense. Or, in Hobbes' account of the same notion (*Leviathan*, Chap. XIV), 'the bonds of words are too weak to bridle men's ambition, avarice, anger and other

passions, without the fear of some coercive form', or 'evil consequence', of their actions. That is, there must continue to be danger
for the individual, even (or especially) in corrupted liberal orders
which have sought to make an ethical – but self-destructive –
principle out of 'over-great goodness', in acting a-civically and anti-
socially to the injury of the civic order as a whole.

307. The greater the degree to which the civic order fulfils its
obligation to the citizen-body to *educate* the individual to his
citizen's part, the less the need, in principle, of recourse to sanction,
whether of reward or deprivation. At the same time, in particular
in corrupted liberal orders ruled by dutiless right and demand-
satisfaction, the rationalist's assumption of reason in others, upon
which the impulse both to teach and to learn rests, is increasingly
falsified in the event; even where the civic order's duty to educate
the citizen is, or seems to be, adequately fulfilled, expectation of its
civic effect is also increasingly disappointed. So, too, is the educated
rationalist's assumption – that educated reason is sufficient in itself
to dictate to the citizen the fulfilment of his duties – shown to be
an increasingly unrealistic assumption in the corrupted liberal
orders.

Hence, just as it would be unethical for the civic order to have
recourse only to sanctions of deprivation for the purpose of securing
observance of the principle of duty, so it would be impractical to
depend only on civic education for such observance. Moreover, the
civic order, being under its own obligation of self-protection, has a
particular responsibility to impose itself with determination upon
the citizen-turned-stranger who, otherwise sound in mind but
murderously violent in conduct, 'comes not to such a degree of
reason', in Locke's words (*Two Treatises of Civil Government*, Bk.
II, para. 60), as to live voluntarily and non-violently within the
ethical bounds of the civic order. It is the duty of the civic order to
ensure, above all, that such violent individual is 'never let loose to
the disposure of his own will' (ibid.), and to the harm of the well-
being of the civic order as a whole, as long as well-founded doubt
remains as to his danger to others.

Only the individual who knows – whether from civic sense or
bitter experience – 'how far he may make use of his freedom', and

acts accordingly, 'comes to have it' (ibid. para. 59) [sect. 94].
Conversely, the individual who does not know, or, knowing, does
not care what such limits to his freedom in the civic order might
be, may justly come to lose that freedom.

308. In addition, the ethical principle that an individual may not
use his freedom against himself to his own destruction [sect. 160]
forbids not only suicide but all action on the part of the citizen, or
groups of citizens, which threatens the existence of the civic order
itself. Such action it is the supreme duty of the civic order, being
obligated both to its own self-preservation and the preservation of
its citizens' well-being, to prevent. These obligations at the same
time, and upon the same ethical principle, forbid the self-destruc-
tion of the civic order; that is, the destructive use by the civic
order, in the form of the nation, of its own sovereign powers against
itself, and which it is the duty of the citizen-body as a whole to
prevent.

309. All civic measures of restraint, constraint, deprivation, and
compulsion in defence of the civic bond and of the civic order
which it upholds are, subject to proviso [sects. 140, 217–22],
compatible with the uncorrupted liberal ideal, such measures being
for the purpose of enforcing the principle of duty so that injury to
individual citizens, and to the citizen-body as a whole, may be
avoided. 'The only purpose for which power can be rightfully
exercised over any member of a civilised community against his
will', declares Mill (*On Liberty*, p. 22), 'is to prevent harm to
others.' But this is itself a wide rubric. Thus, says Mill (ibid.,
p. 169), 'for such actions as are prejudicial to the interests of others,
the individual is accountable and may be subjected either to social
or legal punishment, if society is of opinion that the one or the
other is requisite for its protection'.

Furthermore, in conditions of civic flux, breakdown, and disaggregation, fewer of the acts which Mill regarded as purely 'self-
regarding' – that is, acts which concern only the individual, and in
whose consequences the civic order can and should have no interest
– have effects only upon the actor. Under the rule of dutiless right,
the arc of those whose interests are affected (and to whom wrong
may be done) by such 'self-regarding' acts is constantly widening;

interest in securing that such acts are stopped by sanction is widening likewise.

Indeed, in corrupted liberal orders in which there is increasing recourse to personal violence in pursuit of demand-satisfaction and self-realisation through unimpeded freedom of action, it is precisely such 'self-regarding' acts which could be said to cause the most immediate harm to the well-being of the civic order as a whole. In such deteriorating conditions, the danger grows that the *terminus ad quem* will be one in which, as Aristotle put it (*Ethics*, X, 1180a), 'the mass of men are amenable to compulsion rather than to Reason, and to punishment rather than to a sense of honour'. Epictetus (*Discourses*, IV, x, 3) despaired in like fashion of his fellows: to appeal to their reason was to 'argue with a hog not to roll in the mire'. But even in the worst of times, and especially then, 'human nature must be trained', as Kant argued (*Lectures on Ethics*, p. 249), including by compulsion and the sanction of deprivation.

310. Compulsion and deprivation in defence of the civic order may take many forms, including the ordering of the citizen to do certain things so that those particular things are done, the ordering of the citizen to do certain things so that other civic purposes may be achieved, and the taking away of certain things from the citizen, including his liberty, but also his privileges, benefits, licences, and rights, and even citizenship itself.

It is ethically and practically preferable, as a general rule, that loss of citizen-rights and powers, privileges and benefits rather than custodial loss of freedom should be employed as a sanction of the principle of duty, provided only that the individual against whom the sanction is applied is not a physical danger to others. When the question is asked, 'What is it that the citizen possesses – apart from his life and liberty – which can, and in some circumstances ethically should, be at risk of being taken away by the civic order as a sanction of civic responsibility?' the clear answer is, 'The rights and powers, privileges and benefits possessed by the citizen, by virtue of his membership of the civic order.'

311. As I showed earlier [sects. 23, 133, 230], the kinds of sanction which I discuss here already exist in many civic orders, albeit often in embryonic form only, or as historic relics, or in hesitant and

inconsistent application. In their stead, however, ethically unimaginative and impractical custodial sanctions – and more barbarous punishments besides – are the judicial rule, including in civic orders whose disaggregation such sanctions have done nothing to check.

312. Rather, civic punishment must the better fit civic offence. Thus, abuse of right may justly lead to the curtailment and loss of right; abuse of privilege and licence, to curtailment and loss of such privilege and licence; abuse and misuse of public provision and benefit, to loss and curtailment of such provision and benefit; to the point at which extreme abuse of citizenship may justly be visited with the loss of such citizenship itself. Thus, for example, harm to public provision, as in vandalism of public buildings and services, or violence committed against public providers, may justly be met, apart from other penalty, with loss of the benefits – to a greater or lesser degree, and for a greater or lesser time, depending upon the offence – of such public provision. Likewise, as I have indicated, the loss of any privilege or licence whatever, including loss for a lifetime, may justly be the price of the abuse of such privilege or licence. Thus, for example, crimes of violence committed by the citizens of one civic order on the territory of another should incur, apart from other penalty, the risk of removal of the offender's passport, or licence to travel; as crimes committed on the roads may justly be visited with loss of the licence to drive, for a greater or lesser time.

Again, restriction upon access and movement is a just price of harm and damage done to place; confiscation of property and of ill-gotten gain, a just price of abuse of financial trust or deceitful exploitation of the financial weakness of others. For abuse of the trust of the civic order by the commission of further offences while on bail, redoubled penalty is a just price; curtailment and loss of the right to employ or to have custody over others is a just price of the exploitation or abuse of others; as loss of entitlement to right, benefit, licence, grant, and other civic provision is a just price in general, and for all citizens, of the refusal of the principle of civic duty, in the interests of the civic order as a whole.

313. In all such and other recourse to sanctions of deprivation,

whether involving loss of entitlements and privileges, limitation of rights, or curtailment of powers, the end is civic: to secure that the citizen, or citizen-turned-stranger, who, to the detriment of his fellows and the civic order, abuses or misuses the privileges, entitlements, benefits, powers, and rights which he possesses as citizen, returns to the civic order to which he belongs, and voluntarily assumes, and acts upon, his co-responsibility for its condition.

314. The curtailment or removal, for a greater or lesser time, of the citizen's *powers* is also an ethical and practical sanction against such citizen's abuse of his economic or other strength, where he possesses it, as well as of his claims to dutiless right. Thus, as I have already indicated [sect. 312], the abuse or misuse by the citizen, or group of citizens, of his or their economic power in the employment of others – as may be expressed in the wrongful treatment of a workforce – may be met, apart from other penalty, with the prohibition of such citizens, or their agents, from the employment of others; the abuse of children by their parents or carers, apart from other penalty, may be visited with related prohibition. Indeed, in all cases where the weak, vulnerable, or dependent are exploited by the strong, as by employers, trade unions, financial institutions, and other corporate bodies, as well as by individual citizens, the curtailment of the powers of the strong, for a greater or lesser time, is a legitimate civic sanction against them.

But, in other respects too, the power of the citizen may be limited and restrained by sanction in the interest of the civic order as a whole. Thus, the power to spend and consume – whether as expression of a claim to dutiless right, to satisfaction of demand, or to self-realisation through unimpeded freedom of action – may be limited or restrained where such spending and consumption are wasteful, or otherwise harmful to the civic order as a whole. To this end, selective sumptuary taxation, selective restrictions upon access to credit, and, where a just price also requires to be exacted for financial or other anti-civic crime, confiscation and attachment of earnings may be employed.

315. Deprivation, for a greater or lesser time, of the citizen's civic

honours and entitlements to office or position is also, in appropriate cases, a legitimate sanction of the principle of duty. Thus, a citizen of status who has been 'minded to mock or else violently to break the common laws of his country', as Thomas More put it (*Utopia*, Bk. II, Chap. 9), may be 'deprived of all honours, excluded from all offices, and reject from all common administrations in the weal public', or civic order. In Campanella's City of the Sun (*La Città del Sole*, pp. 80–1), 'prohibition of honours' was similarly employed. So, too, argued Hobbes (*Leviathan*, Chap. XXVIII), 'badges, titles, offices . . . may be taken away by the public authority that made them honourable'.

Other goods, greater or lesser according to estimation, such as, say, entitlement to practise a profession, to hold a position of trust or to teach children, may also be removed from citizens as sanctions in certain forms of failure to observe the principle of duty. In particular, those who commit violently anti-social acts against their fellows and the peace and well-being of the local civic order to which they belong may be denied related civic privileges and local entitlements [**sects. 280, 299**], including those of access to place, right of movement at night, and other civic privileges which the local civic order may, in its discretion, make a benefit of membership of such civic order.

316. Loss of possessions and other forms of financial confiscation may, in addition to the commoner fine, also be employed as sanctions of deprivation, especially for serious offences committed by the wealthy citizen-turned-stranger against the well-being of the citizen-body as a whole. All such financial sanctions, whether of fine or confiscation, should, where practical, be means-based: that is, be related to wealth and income – the capacity to pay – as is, or should be, the case in regard to the civic duty to pay taxes.

Distraint of goods and chattels, often a cruel sanction when unjustly employed, as it most frequently is, against the already poor, is ethically and practically better employed, where appropriate, in support of the principle of duty as it applies to the prosperous citizen's duties to his fellows, and to the civic order to which he belongs. Or, instead of the exaction of fines unrelated to the means of the wealthy, and the (for the most part) ethically even less efficacious resort to custodial sanction, more prosperous offenders against the principle of duty may be required to bear the cost, in whole or in part, of the provision of commodities and services to less advantaged fellow-members of the civic order; in the case of the most prosperous offenders, the cost, in whole or in part, of substantial public works which bring benefit to the civic order as a whole, as in health-care, education and cultural provision.

Likewise, in cases of tax evasion, extortion, fraud, and theft by the rich, a proportion of the latter's wealth may be compulsorily allocated by the Court of Obligation, after due process of law, to the social uses of the civic order; or, an individual, by the sanction of attachment, may have part of his wealth or earnings directed to charitable contribution. In all such cases, what Hobbes terms 'pecuniary punishment' (*Leviathan*, Chap. XXVIII) is exacted as a sanction not for its own sake, nor in vindictiveness, but to the end that the civic bond is strengthened, in the interests of the well-being of the citizen-body.

317. Loss and curtailment of the benefits of public provision may also be employed by the civic order as a sanction for the citizen's neglect, refusal, or other flouting of the principle of duty. Such benefits, which are provided on ethical grounds or for practical purposes from the resources of the citizen-body itself, may be taken away, suspended, reduced, or otherwise varied, also on ethical grounds or for practical purposes, within the discretion of the civic order which provides them.

Thus, the abuse, neglect, misuse, or (in some circumstances) refusal of certain benefits of public provision may reasonably lead, as I have suggested [**sect. 198**], to the denial of access to them for a greater or lesser time; to their curtailment; to the requirement of payment, or additional payment, for their provision; or to the curtailment and loss of other benefits of public provision. In the case of misuse, neglect, or abuse of educational, training, and health provision, for example – and especially where such abuse takes, in extreme cases, violent or vandalistic forms – reduction of access, withholding or reduction of grant, imposition of special charges, and loss or curtailment of other benefit may ensue.

Those who wilfully refuse to fulfil their duties to themselves, as in the matter of the self-care of health, may reasonably be required by the civic order and their fellows to pay for the consequent treatment they may need; those who are in receipt of educational grants from the civic order, and wilfully neglect their studies, may reasonably expect such grants to be reduced or withheld; those who are in need of, but reject or refuse, opportunity of training at the civic order's expense, or unreasonably refuse offers of work, may in turn reasonably expect denial or curtailment of their claims to unemployment benefit at the civic order's expense; and those who destroy or damage facilities for public provision, or physically harm the providers, may reasonably expect the denial to them of such and other public provision, and even, in the most serious cases, the loss, for a greater or lesser time, of their citizenship itself.

318. To lose, or to have curtailed for a greater or lesser time, the benefits and grants of public provision in circumstances of neglect and default of civic duty – a sanction to be determined under the rule of law by local Courts of Obligation – is an exaction of the civic order which also accords with the ethical principles of merit [sects. 57, 146] and of reward for effort.

Without such principles in the civic order, and their enforcement by the civic order, dutiless right, the 'right' to demand-satisfaction and the 'right' to self-realisation through unimpeded freedom of action must otherwise hold ethical and practical sway. 'It is in the interest of every man', declared Adam Smith (*The Wealth of Nations*, Bk. V, Chap. 1), 'to live as much at his ease as he can; and if his emoluments are to be precisely the same whether he does, or he does not, perform some very laborious duty, it is certainly his interest . . . to neglect it altogether.' If so, it is equally in his 'interest' to neglect duty to self and to the civic order when the latter's benefits, privileges, and rights may be obtained without merit, ethical entitlement, or effort.

In default of the voluntary assumption of such duties, sanction to secure their performance may, where appropriate, again include the loss or curtailment of certain benefits of public provision, or of entitlement to them. Such loss or curtailment is again in accord with liberal principle. Thus, argues Mill (*On Liberty*, p. 175), 'idleness, *except in a person receiving support from the public*, cannot without tyranny be made a subject of legal punishment' (my emphasis). Conversely, then, 'idleness' in a person 'receiving support from the public' *can*, 'without tyranny' – that is, without oppression and compatibly with the liberal ideal – be made so subject to 'punishment'; or, as I should say, be made subject to a sanction of deprivation in the interests of the civic order as a whole. Indeed, in all ages and societies, and whether with extensive public provision or not, sanction against 'idleness' has been sought; in the Florentine republic, as Burckhardt tells us (*The Civilization of the Renaissance in Italy*, p. 233), 'fathers left property to their children on condition that they should have some occupation', and in their wills 'begged governments . . . to fine their sons 1000 florins if they declined to practise a regular profession' (ibid. p. 69).

The benefits of public provision are not less amenable than the benefits of inheritance to being thus employed by the civic order so that the civic bond may be sustained, and in order to deter refusal by the citizen of the duties which he owes to himself and to the civic order to which he belongs.

319. All such sanctions, whether of deprivation or reward, are directed, as I have already argued, to the end of enforcing the individual citizen's co-responsibility for the condition of the civic order. Moreover, especially in conditions of civic disaggregation, such responsibility requires not merely to be enforced, but (where practical) extended, and the consequences of neglect and refusal of such responsibility made more serious for the individual.

Thus, the responsibility of parents for their own acts of commission and omission in respect of the care, welfare, education, crimes, and misdemeanours of their minor children requires to be extended, and sanctions for the neglect or refusal of such responsibility introduced, or increased, in the interests of the civic order as a whole. Nor, once more, are such measures offensive to liberal principle. For Mill himself proposed (*On Liberty*, p. 192) that the father who failed in his obligation to teach his child to read 'might be subjected to a moderate fine' unless he had 'some sufficient ground of excuse'.

In the corrupted liberal orders, the renewal and extension of such form of civic responsibility are dictated by the principle of duty, the sovereign ethical principle of the civic order. Thus, for the educational absenteeism of minor children, their acts of vandalism, violent acts, and other delinquency, parents may reasonably become liable to sanction, including the payment of damages for their minor children's crimes. Likewise, in application and extension of the principle of responsibility and co-responsibility for the condition of the civic order, even fellow-members of a local community may be made liable in damages for the material consequences of neighbourhood crime.

In particular, the violent or otherwise delinquent citizen-turned-stranger (and, if a minor, his parents or guardians also) may reasonably be made liable for the direct material compensation of his victim, or if the latter requests or wishes it, and it is otherwise appropriate, be directed to acts of service to him. On such civic principle, 'a sum of money', thought Hobbes (*Leviathan*, Chap. XXVIII), should be 'paid [sc. by the malefactor] to him that has been injured'; likewise (ibid., Chap. XXX), 'an offence against a private man cannot in equity be pardoned without the consent of him that is injured or [without] reasonable satisfaction'. In More's Utopia, too, 'they that in this land be attainted and convict of felony [sc. of theft], make restitution of that which they stole to the right owner . . . But if the thing be lost or made away, then the value of it is paid off the goods of such offenders' (Bk. I, Chap. 1).

But in all such instances of the imposition of responsibility and duty upon the citizen, only that which is practical as well as ethical may be sought. Moreover, all such imposition must be governed by the rule of law; no duty may be made absolute or without possibility of exception; and, in all cases, the end of such imposition must be the strengthening of the civic bond and the well-being of the civic order as a whole.

320. Civic obligation may be imposed on the citizen in response to acts of civic omission [**sect. 296**] which have caused harm to others, or in order to procure the commission of acts of benefit to others, by the requiring, under sanction, of specific performance of omitted or neglected duty, whether to self, familiars, fellows, or the civic order as a whole. Just as a citizen may be required in this way to ensure his child's attendance at school, so he may also be made responsible for the condition of his property and immediate environment, or, by extension of such form of ethical and practical responsibility, co-responsible for the safety of the neighbourhood in which he lives [sect. 319].

On the same principle, that of the principle of duty, a citizen, or citizen-turned-stranger, may be required to carry out acts of community, social, or public service not only as a penalty for certain forms of anti-social violence or other harm to the civic order, but also as a sanction for refusal to seek work, or as a means of acquiring, or re-acquiring, entitlement and access to certain forms of public provision. Thus, those forms of civic duty which, in any civic order, are considered disagreeable – and some are so disagreeable that they are not carried out at all – may be used as sanctions in the same way that the defraying of the costs of certain forms of public and community service may be imposed as a penalty upon those with the means to pay for them [sect. 224].

Moreover, setting an individual citizen, by way of sanction for asocial acts of commission or omission, to practically necessary social or community tasks which serve the well-being of the civic order as a whole is, in general, ethically preferable – save, for example, where the individual is a danger to others – to the purposeless and therefore amoral deprivation of such individual's physical freedom on the one hand, or the equally amoral surrender to the rule of dutiless right on the other.

321. The individual's general ethical duty to uphold and sustain, as far as is practicable and in the interests of the parties concerned, the 'bond of nature' [sect. 277] – that is, his familial and marital relations – together with a widened ethical and legal responsibility of parents for the care, welfare, education, and misdemeanours of their minor children [sect. 319], are duties and responsibilities dictated by the principle of duty, as it applies to the citizen's obligations to himself, his familiars, and the civic order as a whole, and in relation both to the present and future well-being of such civic order. They require, where appropriate and practical, increased reinforcement by sanction.

This is especially urgent in the corrupted liberal orders, as has already been argued [sect. 276], where rising volumes of divorce, of births out of wedlock and of single-parenting of minor children, together with the abandonment and transfer to others of old familial duties and functions, are both a cause and consequence of civic disaggregation.

Here, as a precondition for, and ground of, enlarging and enforcing the moral and legal responsibilities of parents for their children, it is necessary that, where there are dependent minor children, divorce should in general now become more difficult to obtain and more disadvantageous to the putative divorcing parties [sect. 237]. 'The next [sc. nearest] way to break love between man and wife', thought Thomas More (*Utopia*, Bk. II, Chap. 7), was 'to be in easy hope of new marriage.' Instead, there must once again be a general ethical presumption in favour of sustaining such relationships, as far as is practicable and in the interests of the parties concerned; as well as such tax and other benefits – and their loss, including of benefits of public provision – as may provide a further inducement to parents to remain together.

Similarly, as sanctions of disadvantage and inducement, increased tax benefits and penalties, as well as increased benefits of public provision and risks of loss of such provision, may be attached both to immature marriage and to unmarried or immature child-bearing, in particular where a single man fathers children with different mothers, or a single mother bears children to different fathers. In cases of wilful neglect or abandonment by a father of the duties, as of maintenance, which he owes to the mother of his child or children, and of neglect of his related duties to such child or children, as well as in cases of similar abandonment of duty to child or children by a mother, loss by the individual, for greater or lesser time, of civic benefits and privileges may follow, provided only that no harm is caused thereby to the well-being of the child or children. In the grossest cases of wilful abandonment and neglect of parental obligation, and in particular where children suffer cruelty and violence at the hands of their parents, such parents may reasonably risk the forfeiture of citizenship itself, in the interest of the well-being of the civic order as a whole.

322. Just as a citizen is made such, as, for example, by familial moral upbringing and civic education, or by the imposition of

conditions of birth, residence, and other qualification for the acquisition of citizenship, so a citizen may be *unmade*, as when he turns himself by his own acts from citizen to stranger, or, if the civic order wills it, formally loses his citizen-privileges, benefits, and rights, and thus citizenship itself, for a greater or lesser time. Even the loss of part of such civic privileges, benefits, and rights, as by the loss of certain benefits of public provision by way of sanction, constitutes the loss of part of what belongs to membership of the civic order, where such benefits attach to membership; and thus the loss, in part, of citizenship itself.

Indeed, the sovereignty of every civic order consists, *inter alia*, in its right and capacity to grant, withhold or withdraw citizenship, as well as to vary the nature of the benefits, privileges and rights which attach to such citizenship, on terms and in circumstances which the civic order may freely determine.

It may, if it chooses and sees fit, and provided that it seeks to impose no absolute duty nor to reduce the citizen to a subject, erect a ring-fence of legal and administrative obstructions to the citizen's claims to dutiless right, demand-satisfaction, and self-realisation through unimpeded freedom of action. It may, likewise, deny to and take away from the individual citizen whatever benefits, licences, privileges, and rights it may choose, as the sanction and price of such individual's a-civic or anti-social conduct. It may, also, as did past civic orders – for both worthy and wicked ends – make a citizen into less than a citizen, or into a stranger, or, at worst, into an outcast, for a greater or lesser time. Thus, Machiavelli speaks approvingly (*Discourses on Livy*, 1513–19, Bk. 1, sect. 8) of the judicial procedure of the *accusa*, by which a citizen, for his civic crimes and defaults, might be declared a figure 'hateful' to the civic order; proscription, outlawry, and exile from the civic order were among the severest sanctions of ancient and medieval jurisprudence, and felt to be so by the citizen himself. More modern political thought also retained, until recent times, the sense that the citizen who offended the civic order had, in so doing, placed himself beyond the civic pale.

Cicero perceived those who had done serious injury to their fellow-citizens as having 'thrust themselves out from partaking of any privileges, or from joining in common with the rest of the citizens for the public good' (*Offices*, III, vi); Locke considered such malefactors as 'out of the bounds of civil society' (*Two Treatises of Civil Government*, Bk. II, para. 94). In particular, for Locke, was this so of the violent: 'whoever uses force without right . . . puts himself into a state of war with those against whom he so uses it, and in that state all former ties are cancelled, all other rights cease' (ibid., para. 232). Likewise for Rousseau, the citizen guilty of serious crimes, especially of violence, 'by violating [sc. his country's] laws ceases to be a member of it, and in fact makes war upon it' (*Social Contract*, Bk. II, Chap. 5). 'He has broken the social treaty', declares Rousseau, 'and, consequently . . . is no longer a member of the State' (ibid.), even if, subsequently, he might be recalled to it by pardon.

Indeed, in most civic orders but the corrupted liberal order, civic sense and the principle of duty have generally dictated that citizenship and its benefits, provisions, privileges, and rights might be both gained and lost, whether in whole or in part; that, if lost, whether in whole or in part, such benefits and rights might be regained; and that the risk of loss of such benefits and rights, and the possibility of regaining them, constitute sanctions of deprivation and reward which serve the interests both of the individual citizen and of the civic order as a whole.

323. Underlying the principle that that which is possessed, including the benefits and rights of citizenship, may be lost, is the further principle, already adverted to [**sect. 97**], that, in Cicero's words, 'he who is no citizen should not have the privileges of those who are' (*Offices*, III, xi). To lose, for a greater or lesser time, the privileges of citizenship is, or ought to be, to lose the privileges which also distinguish the citizen from the stranger, and to become, in Rousseau's words (*Social Contract*, Bk. IV, Chap. 2), a 'foreigner among citizens'. Conversely, for an individual to be readmitted to the privileges, benefits, and rights of the citizen permits the sovereign civic order to choose the terms for such readmission, including by pledge of guarantors – as in the case of bail – regarding the future civic conduct of the individual in question.

324. Conditionally to deprive the individual citizen, as a sanction

of the principle of duty, of certain of the benefits, privileges, provisions, and rights of his citizenship – provided that such deprivation does not oppressively reduce him to a subject, nor demean his condition to one of unsustainable indigence – is, ethically, to match actions which are judged to have harmed the civic order with the disqualification, to a greater or lesser degree, of such individual's claims against the civic order.

Such disqualification, where it falls short of loss of citizenship itself, may make the individual citizen-turned-stranger a greater stranger still to the civic order to which he continues to belong. However, it must remain within the discretion of the civic order – and its instrument the law, including the law applied in the Courts of Obligation – to judge whether and when such effect upon the individual is outweighed by the greater civic ills which sanction seeks to arrest.

As has already been argued [**sects. 87, 296**], to strengthen the civic bond, since it is not self-sustaining, requires special means; in order to halt and reverse the quickening process of civic disaggregation, the principle of duty must be enforceable (and be enforced) by sanction, the sanction of loss of civic benefits and rights included; and by such means, as well as by others, the ethical and practical value of citizenship may be restored in the citizen's own eyes.

325. Of the possible forms of deprivation of civic benefits and rights, it is temporary deprivation of liberty, or freedom of movement, which, for all its general moral inefficacy, is the most commonly employed sanction of a-civic or anti-social conduct; in the most corrupted of the corrupt liberal orders, and especially among citizens-turned-strangers, it also carries a diminishing social stigma, or connotation of civic disgrace.

But, except where an individual is a danger to others, most forms of a-civic and anti-social refusal, neglect, or similar flouting of the principle of duty are ethically and logically best met by other forms of imposition and loss than that of temporary loss of liberty: including, as I have argued, by temporary loss of certain forms of public benefit, temporary imposition of community service or other special civic duty, temporary loss of other civic rights than that of physical liberty, and even temporary or permanent loss of citizen-ship itself.

A citizen's temporary loss of rights by sanction may, *and in some cases already does*, include loss of right to office, to vote, to occupy a position of public representation or trust, to conduct a company, to pursue a profession, to hold a passport or other licence, to have physical access to persons and places – including to places of resort and entertainment, places where the individual in question has committed a crime, and places outside the individual's own area of residence or home-town – and to freedom of movement at certain times, as during the night-hours. For repeated or wilful acts which cause particularly serious harm to the well-being of fellow-citizens and of the civic order as a whole, but where the individual is not considered a physical danger to others, such individual may, in addition to other penalties, but without losing his physical liberty, temporarily or permanently lose his citizenship entirely, and become a non-citizen resident of the civic order, subject to the disabilities of such status.

326. As I have already argued [sect. 133], *existing* laws which uphold the principle of duty and impose its particular obligations both upon the civic order and the individual citizen require to be observed; where they have fallen into desuetude, to be revived; and where inadequate in scope, to be extended. To achieve clarity in, and consistency among, the particular laws – in Britain, to be found both in common law and statute – which already make up the general body of law in relation to obligation in the civic order, a codification of such law may be required; and, in civic orders with written constitutions, amendment may be needed to establish the principle of duty as the sovereign principle of the civic order. Courts of Obligation also require to be created, lower courts in the local civic order to adjudicate upon local civic matters of duty, including the application of sanction, and a higher court, at the level of the national civic order, which will be part of the high court system of the land. The latter's function will be to adjudicate, including by way of reference and appeal from lower courts, upon issues which give rise to questions of principle or interpretation in respect of the law of duty, *whether such duty is that of the civic order to the citizen, or that of the citizen to the civic order.*

To the local Courts of Obligation, there will be appointed lay justices, or magistrates, of duty, with functions and powers similar to those of British justices of the peace. Indeed, there can be no assurance of *peace* in the civic order without prior observance of the principle of *duty*, both as it applies to the civic order's duties to the citizen, and the citizen's duties to himself, his familiars, his fellows, and the civic order as a whole. To the high Court of Obligation, there will be appointed judges of obligation, who will hear appeals (where the right of appeal is granted) from decisions of the local Courts of Obligation, cases of principle and interpretation, and cases otherwise placed outside the jurisdiction of the lower courts. On permission of the high Court of Obligation, there may be granted further right of appeal to higher courts, on issues of outstanding practical, ethical, and legal importance in the matter of the civic order's duties to the citizen, and the citizen's duties to others.

327. The purpose and function of such Courts of Obligation will be to uphold and enforce the principle of duty as it applies to the civic order's duties to the citizen and the citizen's duties to himself, his fellows, and the civic order as a whole, subject to the ethical and practical limits I have discussed [**sects. 132, 140, 217–22**].

As I have already argued [**sect. 303**], it is always within the discretion of the sovereign civic order to determine which of its ethical and practical duties to the citizen, and which of the citizen's duties, shall be justiciable, and which not; also to determine what forms of legal redress or remedy the citizen shall be given for the civic order's neglect or default in its own duties; and to determine what forms of sanction may be employed in order to secure performance of the citizen's obligations.

328. Among the remedies which Courts of Obligation, and more especially a high Court of Obligation, may provide to the citizen for the civic order's defaults of duty are *writs* to command specific performance by the civic order, and by its instrument the state, of its obligations to the citizen; *financial compensation* for such default or neglect; the *removal* of, or *imposition of sanction* upon, neglectful or defaulting officials of the civic order and its instrument the state; and *exemptions* of the citizen from the performance of certain of his own duties, for a greater or lesser time, or until the performance by the civic order of a particular duty to him.

Among the sanctions which Courts of Obligation may employ in order to secure performance by the citizen of his duties are *writs* to command specific performance by the citizen of omitted or neglected duty; *loss or curtailment* of the citizen's benefits, privileges, licences, and rights; *fines* and *attachment of earnings* where no other more appropriate civic sanction is available; the *imposition* of acts of social or public service; *confiscation* and *compulsory allocation* of part of a citizen's resources to social and charitable uses; and *reward* for the performance of duty.

In the event of refusal or failure, whether on the part of the civic order or of the citizen, to fulfil the terms of a *writ* commanding the performance of duty, such refusal or failure may reasonably be regarded as a *contempt* both of the law and of the principle of duty. Such contempt would invite further consequence, including, for the civic order, the risk of the payment of additional compensation to the aggrieved citizen, more extensive exemption of the citizen from the performance of his own duties – including, if a Court of Obligation so decided, duties to pay taxes – or where right and justice are wilfully and persistently refused to the citizen, the imprisonment of officials responsible for the neglect or refusal of duty, until the contempt is discharged.

Similarly, where the citizen refuses or fails to fulfil the terms of a writ commanding the performance of duty, the contempt of such writ would invite the risk of like consequences, including that of further loss or curtailment of benefits, privileges, and rights; and, where the doing of right and justice to the civic order is entirely and repeatedly refused by a citizen otherwise able to perform such duty, but only where no other sanction is thought fitting by or available to the court, a custodial sentence may be imposed until the contempt is discharged.

Such extension and enforcement of the doctrine of contempt is required, in particular, in the most corrupted liberal orders, where the rule of the politics and ethics of dutiless right, demand-satisfaction, and self-realisation through unimpeded freedom of action have undermined both the principle of duty and the rule of law. In the past, refusal by the citizen to give evidence in legal hearings, or the mere offering of insult to the dignities of the legal and parliamentary process, were considered punishable contempts. Now, in conditions of accelerating civic disaggregation, it is the duty of the civic order, in fulfilment of its obligations of self-protection and protection of the citizen-body as a whole, likewise to protect the principle of civic duty from more serious assault, insult, and neglect at the hands of members of the citizen-body, whether they are citizens-turned-strangers or officials of the civic order itself.

329. All the foregoing sanctions have in view the strengthening of the civic bond and the civic order which it upholds. To 'follow the rule' of the civic principle, or principle of duty, is at once to express the ideal of *humanitas*, to protect the source of right, to act justly, and to arrest the process of civic disaggregation. It is also to make possible a new civic social philosophy, or civic social-ism, to which I lastly turn.

TWELVE

Social-ism and the Civic Order

The new social-ism of the civic bond – tasks of civic social-ism –
obligations of the civic order summarised – nature of the principle of duty
restated – the social and the civic – resistance to the principle of duty –
possible consequences of weakening of the civic bond –
duty of the civic order *in extremis* – my own duty fulfilled.

330. The old socialism is dead; the new civic social-ism [**sects. 27–8**], neither of 'left' nor 'right' but transcending both and resting upon the principle of duty, is waiting to be born. The overthrow and fall of old socialism, with its dogmas, servitudes to class, party, and state, and – in its welfare socialist form – recoil from the principle of duty, especially as it applies to the citizen's obligations to himself, his familiars, and to the civic order in the form of nation, have opened the way to a new social-ism of the civic bond [**sect. 91**]. Under the rule of its ethical and practical principles, among which the principle of duty will be sovereign, civic sense will not be displaced by class sense, ethics will have precedence over economics, and the citizen, restored to pre-eminence, will be more than a mere 'comrade' or 'brother' [**sect. 22**]. Indeed, to return sovereignty to the civic order is the chief end of the restoration and enforcement of the principle of duty, in the name of the civic social-ism of the future.

331. The ethical and practical means for re-establishing the sovereignty of the civic order in the name of such civic social-ism, for defending and strengthening the civic bond, for returning the

citizen-turned-stranger to himself and to the civic order, and for arresting the accelerating process of civic disaggregation in the corrupted liberal orders, *include* the tempering and resisting of claims to dutiless right, demand-satisfaction, and self-realisation through unimpeded freedom of action; the resisting and reversing of the habit of transfer, to officials of the civic order and of its instrument the state, of the ethical and practical responsibilities of the citizen, or citizen-turned-stranger; the preventing of the transformation of the free citizen of the civic order into the protected subject of the state and its systems of public provision; and the re-establishing and enforcing of the principle of duty as the sovereign principle of the civic order, as it applies both to the duties of the civic order towards the citizen and the duties of the citizen towards himself, others, and the civic order as a whole.

332. In safeguarding and enlarging that which remains democratic in the corrupted liberal orders [sect. 170]; in incorporating the principle of desert or merit in the government and management of the civic order [sect. 146]; in removing protections from, providing obstacles to, and reducing the legitimacy of claims to dutiless right and demand-satisfaction, whether such demands are for dutiless rights to public provision, to consumption, or to the economic exploitation of others in a 'free market' [sect. 114]; in securing the civic order's fulfilment of its ethical and practical responsibilities for the well-being of the individual citizen and of the citizen-body as a whole [sects. 231–67]; in securing the citizen's fulfilment of his duties to himself, his familiars, his fellow-citizens and the civic order as a whole, including by acts of public or community service [sects. 268–95]; and in seeking to defend and strengthen the civic bond, both the civic order and the civic social-ism of the future find their due purposes and tasks.

333. In protecting the citizen from violence; in providing an impartial administration of justice; in educating the citizen to his citizen's part; in otherwise nurturing all those public institutions which are most conducive to the enhancement of the individual citizen's self-development and self-regard; in helping the citizen to sustain the 'bond of nature' and a self-respecting family life; in protecting the citizen from inadequate, undignified, unhealthy, or

otherwise exploitative conditions of work; and in preventing, as far as it can or should, all such avoidable deteriorations and deprivations in the material and other conditions of the civic order, and in the circumstances of its citizens' lives, as threaten both the well-being of the civic order as a whole and the capacity of individual citizens to fulfil their duties to themselves, their fellows, and the civic order to which they belong, the sovereign civic order finds its obligations to its citizen-members.

334. The principle of duty, as it applies both to the duties of the civic order and of the individual citizen, rests upon, and is an expression of, the civic bond. It imports an ethical readiness to act socially with others, on behalf of all. Such readiness (or civic sense), a readiness to act for the common good by observance of the principle of duty, is the ethical principle of the civic social-ism of the future. Moreover, observance of the principle of duty, whether by the individual citizen or the civic order as a whole, is an ethical and practical mark of civic progress, not a mark of 'reaction'. In particular, individual co-responsibility for the condition of the civic order is not only as necessary to a 'progressive' order as is individual right, but is ethically and logically prior to it, and, in the form of enforceable citizen obligation, is a foil to the a-civic and anti-social claims of dutiless right.

Further, an organised civic politics, the politics of the civic social-ism of the future, is directed, ethically and practically, to the defence of the civic order not only as the source or ground of individual right but as the ordered community or aggregate of citizens, living under a common rule, which is possessed – however plural its composition – of common interests and a common ethical direction. To such civic order duty is singly owed, but social in its end, because its end is civic; and *social-ist* the principle upon which such duty rests.

335. The civic social-ist principle of citizen duty, being that of duty owed not to dogma, class, party, or state but self, familiars, fellow-citizens, the civic bond, and the civic order, is also a principle of individual and social well-being – that is, εὐδαιμονία (*eudai-monia*) or happiness – not of oppression or subjection, which are incompatible with the good life.

336. Such civic social-ism, albeit directed towards the happiness and well-being of the individual and of the civic order to which he or she belongs, yet founded upon the principle of duty and transcending narrow doctrines of right, must encounter resistance. It must encounter reflex intellectual resistance on behalf of the sophistries of conventional 'academic' thought; it must encounter old socialist, or 'left', vested interest – *post-mortem* – in self-serving and wish-fulfilling falsehood, both in theory and in practice; and it must encounter objection, especially in the corrupted liberal orders, to the principle of duty as a principle of 'reaction' or oppression.

All represent obstacles to new thought as such, as well as to the revival of old thought which questions or subverts their own. Nevertheless, the intellectual and political interests which such true reaction sustains will continue to defend themselves from challenge. A destructive scepticism directed at the orthodoxies of both 'left' and 'right' – bad knowledge which not only obstructs, but drives out, good – will make its way only with the gradual physical passing of such orthodoxies' defenders, and the increasing intolerability of the ethical and practical consequences of civic disaggregation.

337. Where the civic bond becomes weakened and tenuous, especially in declining material conditions which it is beyond the means of the civic order to arrest, a combination of material deprivation and habituation in the citizen-turned-stranger to claims of dutiless right, demand-satisfaction, and self-realisation through unimpeded freedom of action may threaten not only the well-being, but the very existence, of the civic order. In the corrupted liberal orders where such consequences are most advanced, and in the absence of a civic social-ism founded upon the principle of duty, it is not impossible that citizens, acting in defence of the civic order, might one day be driven not to seek concord [sect. 208] but to take up arms against the citizen-turned-stranger, the unconscionable claimant of dutiless right, and the increasingly violent universal plebeian. Or, where a civic order has failed on a substantial scale both to temper the rule of dutiless right and to satisfy the demands to which it gives rise, and has failed to arrest the quickening process of civic disaggregation, it is also conceivable that, *in extremis*, an inchoate mass of frustrated citizens-turned-strangers, pursuing their dutiless claims, might seek violently to overthrow the civic order, and to establish more securely the rule over the civic order of the a-civic and anti-social interests of the universal plebeian.

Before such conditions can be reached, it may become the duty of the civic order, a duty of self-protection in the interests of the citizen-body as a whole, to impose special penalties, controls and deprivations upon the exercise of claims to dutiless right, from whatever source and interest they derive: whether such claims be to dutiless rights of exploitation, of public provision, of self-realisation through unimpeded freedom of action, or other expressions of claims to unimpeded and dutiless right. Moreover, in circumstances where increasingly general resort to violence, and especially *armed violence*, is had by citizens-turned-strangers pursuing such dutiless claims and demands, including the most a-civic and amoral of demands for self-realisation, the civic order's duties of self-protection and protection of the well-being of the citizen-body dictate the urgent and comprehensive disarming of such citizen-body, as well as whatever other emergency juridical and social measures are required to defend the civic order as a whole.

338. But even where such conditions are not reached, the ethics and politics of dutiless right, demand-satisfaction, and self-realisation through unimpeded freedom of action have been a costly moral failure in the corrupted liberal orders. In them, the dream of the 'good life', of peaceful and orderly cohabitation, of individual self-development and self-regard, and of self-government in a sovereign civic order has turned to nightmare or ashes, or merely been forgotten and lost from civic sense and sight.

So, too, has been increasingly hidden from view the sense of the civic order as a 'commonwealth' [sect. 27], for whose condition and well-being the individual citizen is co-responsible and to which he owes determinate duties, duties which are ethically prior to claims of right. In order once more to reveal to the citizens themselves the nature of the 'commonwealth', or civic order, to which they belong, a knowledge of the ethical principles upon which such civic order is founded, and a civic politics by which such principles may be given effect, are required.

In fulfilment of my own ethical and practical duty, I have in this essay sought to define and to describe the *sovereign principle* among such ethical principles, the principle of duty; upon whose observance and enforcement depend the civic bond, and the well-being of the civic order to which the citizen belongs.

REFERENCES

Reference is made in the text to a number of works – not in all cases regarded as the principal works of the authors – from which I have derived intellectual stimulus or moral instruction, or both, upon the matters discussed in this essay. Here I list only one edition of each work; but, in the case of translations, I have often employed several versions, or made my own.

Amiel, M. A. *Ethics and Legality in Jewish Law*, tr. M. and B. Slae, Jerusalem, 1992
– *Unto My People (El-Ami)*, tr. L. Rabinowitz, London, 1931
Aristotle *The Nicomachean Ethics*, tr. D. P. Chase, London, n.d.
– *The Politics*, tr. T. A. Sinclair, Harmondsworth, 1962
Bobbio, N. *The Future of Democracy*, tr. R. Griffin, Oxford, 1987
Bradley, F. H. *Ethical Studies*, Oxford, 1927
Burckhardt, J. *The Civilization of the Renaissance in Italy*, tr. S. G. C. Middlemore, Harmondsworth, 1990
Burke, E. *Reflections on the Revolution in France* (1790), London, 1968
– *Thoughts on the Cause of the Present Discontents* (1770), London, 1902
Campanella, T. *La Città del Sole*, ed. G. Scarpelli, Rome, 1993
Cicero *Offices, Essays and Letters*, tr. T. Cockman (1690), London, 1909
Engels, F. *The Condition of the Working-Class in England in* 1844, London, 1892
Epictetus *Moral Discourses* (incl. the *Enchiridion* and *Fragments*), tr. E. Carter, London, 1910
Goethe, J. W. *Conversations with Eckermann and Soret*, tr. J. Oxenford, London, 1883
Green, T. H. *Lectures on the Principles of Political Obligation* (incl. *Prolegomena to Ethics*), ed. P. Harris and J. Morrow, Cambridge, 1986
Hegel, F. W. *Philosophy of Right*, tr. T. M. Knox, Oxford, 1942
Herodotus *The History*, tr. G. Rawlinson, 2 vols., London, 1910
Hobbes, T. *Leviathan* (1651), London, 1914
Jonas, H. *Il Principio Responsabilità* (1979), tr. P. Rinaudo, Turin, 1990
Kant, I. *Lectures on Ethics* (incl. *Universal Practical Philosophy and Ethics*), tr. L. Infield, New York, 1963
– *The Metaphysics of Morals* (incl. *The Doctrine of Virtue*), tr. M. Gregor, Cambridge, 1991

Locke, J. *Two Treatises of Civil Government* (1690), London, 1924

Machiavelli, N. *The Discourses* (1513–19), tr. L. J. Walker, Harmondsworth, 1974

Marx, K. *Capital* (1867), Moscow and London, 1954

Mazzini, G. *The Duties of Man and Other Essays*, tr. E. Noyes, London, 1907

Mill, J. S. *On Liberty*, London, 1859

Montaigne, M. de *Essays* (1580–95), tr. J. Florio (1603), 3 vols., London, 1910

Montesquieu, C. de *The Spirit of the Laws* (1748), tr. A. M. Cohler, B. C. Miller and H. S. Stone, Cambridge, 1989

More, T. *Utopia* (1516), tr. R. Robinson, London, n.d.

Plato *Laws*, tr. A. E. Taylor, London, 1934

– *Protagoras*, tr. J. Wright, London, 1910

– *The Republic*, tr. P. Shorey, 2 vols., London, 1946

Rousseau, J. J. *The Social Contract*, tr. C. Frankel, New York, 1947

Seneca *Letters from a Stoic (Epistulae Morales ad Lucilium)*, tr. R. Campbell, Harmondsworth, 1969

Smith, A. *An Inquiry into the Nature and Causes of the Wealth of Nations* (1776), 2 vols., London, 1910

Spinoza, B. *Tractatus Politicus* (1677), tr. R. H. M. Elwes, London, 1883

Thucydides *The History of the Peloponnesian War*, tr. R. Crawley, London, 1910

Tocqueville, A. de *Democracy in America*, 2nd ed., New York, 1838

Vico, G. *La Scienza Nuova* (1744), Milan, 1963

Voltaire, J. F. M. de A. *Letters on the English* (1731), London, 1889

Winstanley, G. *The Law of Freedom and Other Writings*, Harmondsworth, 1973

Xenophon *Memorabilia of Socrates*, tr. J. S. Watson (1848), London, 1910

INDEX